Lieutenant Sonia Vagliano

Lieutenant Sonia Vagliano

A Memoir of the World War II Refugee Crisis

Sonia Vagliano Eloy

Edited and translated by Martha Noel Evans

UNIVERSITY PRESS OF KENTUCKY

Originally published in French as *Les Demoiselles de Gaulle,
1943–1945*. Paris: Plon, 1982.
Copyright © 2022 by The University Press of Kentucky

Scholarly publisher for the Commonwealth,
serving Bellarmine University, Berea College, Centre
College of Kentucky, Eastern Kentucky University,
The Filson Historical Society, Georgetown College,
Kentucky Historical Society, Kentucky State University,
Morehead State University, Murray State University,
Northern Kentucky University, Spalding University,
Transylvania University, University of Kentucky,
University of Louisville, and Western
Kentucky University.

All rights reserved.

Editorial and Sales Offices: The University Press of Kentucky
663 South Limestone Street, Lexington, Kentucky 40508-4008
www.kentuckypress.com

Unless otherwise noted, photographs are from the collection
of Sonia Vagliano Eloy.

Library of Congress Cataloging-in-Publication Data

Names: Vagliano-Eloy, Sonia, author. | Evans, Martha Noel, 1939– editor.
Title: Lieutenant Sonia Vagliano : a memoir of the World War II refugee
  crisis / Sonia Vagliano Eloy; edited and translated by Martha Noel Evans
Other titles: Demoiselles De Gaulle, 1943–1945. English.
Description: Lexington, Kentucky : The University Press of Kentucky, [2022] |
  "Originally published in French as Les Demoiselles de Gaulle,
  1943–1945. Paris: Plon, 1982." | Includes bibliographical references.
Identifiers: LCCN 2021039348 | ISBN 9780813182490 (hardcover) | ISBN
  9780813182506 (pdf) | ISBN 9780813182513 (epub)
Subjects: LCSH: Vagliano-Eloy, Sonia. | World War, 1939–1945—Personal
  narratives, French. | France combattante. Mission militaire de liaison
  administrative | France combattante—Biography. | Women
  soldiers—France—Biography. | World War, 1939–1945—Refugees.
Classification: LCC D811.V26 A3713 2022 | DDC 940.54/8144—dc23

This book is printed on acid-free paper meeting
the requirements of the American National Standard
for Permanence in Paper for Printed Library Materials.

Manufactured in the United States of America.

 Member of the Association of
University Presses

*To the memory of Sonia Vagliano Eloy
and her sister-in-law Sara Vagliano*

Contents

Introduction ix
A Note on the Translation xxiii

Part One: Crossing the Atlantic. London.

Crossing the Atlantic 3
London 9

Part Two: Normandy. France.

We Return to France 41
Bayeux 44
Our First Camp: Fontenay-sur-Mer 49
Cavigny near Saint-Lô 60
Mortain-Falaise 95

Part Three: Paris. Belgium.

Le Mans–Paris 109
Northern France 119
Belgium 126

Part Four: Germany. Buchenwald.

Brand 169
Brauweiler 177
Wetzlar 182
Buchenwald 185
Epilogue: In Germany after VE Day 219

Appendix 1. Acronyms 225
Appendix 2. People 227
Acknowledgments 239
Bibliography 241

Introduction

In 1943, when Sonia Vagliano, who had just turned twenty-one, volunteered for de Gaulle's Free French Army (Forces Françaises Libres, FFL), she could not have known that she was signing up to live in squalor, to care for thousands of refugees and displaced persons in the worst possible conditions, to defuse land mines, to be kidnapped, shot at, torpedoed, and bombed. And finally, there was no way she could have predicted that she would end up spending five weeks surrounded by the mind-boggling evidence of Nazi cruelty and sadism at the notorious Buchenwald concentration camp.

Numberless World War II memoirs have been written by combatants, prisoners, and members of resistance groups, but there are very few by those who worked to care for and repatriate the millions of refugees and displaced persons (DPs) created by the scourge of war in Europe. Vagliano's rare, engrossing, and informative description of the work performed by a group of idealistic, determined, and courageous young people confronted by the hideous realities of war comprises a valuable personal contribution to this aspect of the campaign in Western Europe. Indeed, her memoir is doubly precious since it provides the only detailed description we have of the interim period at Buchenwald between the liberation of the camp in April 1945, and the release of the camp to the Russians in July. Her memoir, by turns grave and irreverent, always informative, gives us a priceless view of the teams of young French women attached to American and British Army units tasked with establishing transit camps for refugees, DPs, and POWs in Western Europe after D-Day. Dedicated and persistent in the midst of unbelievably difficult conditions, Vagliano and her colleagues thus played an essential role in this unprecedented Allied effort.

Sonia Vagliano was the middle child of a wealthy Greek shipping and banking family on her father's side and, on her mother's side, of an influential New York family, the Gallatin-Allens. The paternal Greek family had made its way from Thessalonia to Venice, and finally to Paris by way of Marseille, changing its name en route from Ballianos to Vagliano. Born in 1922 in Paris, Sonia lived with her family in a large town house filled with fine furniture and art at number 8, rue Général Appert in the fashionable Sixteenth Arrondissement. The family had important friends, including the Rothschilds, and married into the aristocracy (her older sister married a vicomte). They were champion golfers.

Early in the occupation of Paris, following the family tradition of patriotic activism—her mother, Barbara Allen Vagliano, was a decorated ambulance driver in World War I, and her father, André Marino Vagliano, was a member of a Resistance committee that arranged for hiding Jewish children in the French countryside—the eighteen-year-old Vagliano responded to a call for a student demonstration against the Nazi occupation of Paris. On Armistice Day, November 11, 1940, she joined thousands of other students at the Tomb of the Unknown Soldier under the Arc de Triomphe. Since this kind of public gathering was strictly forbidden, the police soon arrived. Some two hundred students were arrested, Vagliano among them. She was registered as an offender and required to report every week to the German police authorities.

His daughter targeted by the German police and his wife, an American citizen, officially an enemy alien, André Vagliano became worried about the safety of his family. He and his wife finally decided that Vagliano and her mother should flee to the United States. In 1941, they were lucky to board one of the last ships leaving Lisbon for New York.

Motivated by her abhorrence of the German occupiers and her admiration for General de Gaulle, Vagliano attempted to volunteer for the FFL immediately upon her arrival in the United States. Rejected because at age eighteen she was too young, she instead enrolled in Smith College, where her unconventional spirit continued to assert itself. Rather than sticking to her political science major, she learned first aid, technical drawing, how to repair cars and to fly an airplane. She later credited her experience at Smith with teaching her "the

American way," that is, a can-do attitude including the ability to discard details and get straight to the point.

By a strange coincidence, at the very same time that Vagliano was attempting to join the FFL, her cousin, Hélène Vagliano, thirteen years older than Sonia, signed up with the Resistance effort in southern France. Operating near her home in Cannes and bilingual in French and English like her cousin, Hélène became what they called a "letter-box." Supplied with a radio, she exchanged messages with the Allies in London, sending information about local German military movements. Arrested by the Nazis at the end of July 1944, Hélène spent two weeks in various prisons, was tortured, and was finally executed with twenty-two other agents in a public garden in Nice on August 15, 1944.

Dedicated like her cousin to supporting the French in their resistance to the Nazis, Sonia Vagliano tried again to sign up for the FFL. Her effort this time was hampered by the fact that the US State Department had issued a regulation preventing women under the age of twenty-five from getting an exit visa from the United States to go to a country at war. She finally used subterfuge to obtain special authorization. Volunteering as a secretary at the headquarters of the FFL in New York City, she slipped her approval document into a pile of papers to be signed by her boss, Alexandre de Manziarly. Without realizing what he was doing, he signed the authorization. With papers in hand, Sonia Vagliano was off to London on a mission to save her country.

After a perilous crossing of the Atlantic in which one-half of her convoy was lost to German torpedoes, Vagliano arrived safely in London. Her welcome was not as warm as she had expected. Red tape and indifference on the part of administrative staff, and the cruelty of the officer in charge, collided with the young volunteer's idealism. Not to be deterred, she confronted these obstacles with grit, tenacity, and, at times, a wicked sense of humor that characterized her behavior then and throughout her service.

Vagliano was one of four thousand women who, by the end of the war, had become members of the FFL. They were meant to be temporary recruits, signed on for the duration of the war plus three or six months. The presence among male soldiers of thousands of single women between the ages of eighteen and forty caused the top brass to shift in their seats. Their concerns were overcome, however, by the need to free up men for battle by having a female corps to take on the traditional women's jobs doing secretarial work, taking care of maintenance and social issues, and attending to the sick, wounded, and displaced. Prior to World War II, there had never officially been women in the French military, although they participated as volunteer nurses and ambulance drivers in previous conflicts. Passed in 1938, the Paul-Boncour Law, which stated that during wartime "any person of an age to fight" could be admitted to the French military, opened the door to the admission of women to the armed services. Sexual and gender tensions ensued, of course, and romances blossomed, but taking these diversions in their stride, most women, like Vagliano, were able to keep focused on their jobs. At the outset, the training of the French women's forces was based on that of the already extant women's section of the British infantry, the Auxiliary Territorial Service (ATS). Later and during the next eight months, Vagliano's various training courses included men and women.

During basic training with the ATS, while Vagliano and her female colleagues were being run around in the glacial mud of the English countryside in their shorts and polo shirts, the Allied command was undertaking the gigantic task of planning for the liberation of Western Europe, including the eventual occupation of Germany. One facet of the plan called for the creation of a Civil Affairs arm of the United States Army called the G5. Their job was to follow the liberating army to deal with nonmilitary problems that were bound to arise in local governance, administration, and provisioning. The G5 was to maintain public order and to oversee the health needs of the locals. Their remit also included controlling the movement of civilian populations to keep them out of the way of the military. In addition, the farsighted G5 planning commission formed a Monuments, Fine Arts, and Archives unit later popularly known as the "Monument Men."

Five hundred G5 officers were subsequently attached to US and British army units deployed in Italy, southern France, and Normandy. After D-Day, it immediately became clear that the thousands of refugees and DPs in Normandy called for increased action by the G5. The Civil Affairs units were therefore ordered to set up transit camps behind the front lines for housing refugees and providing for their quick transfer either back to their own homes or to camps in the rear.

Responding to the need for French speakers in the G5, General de Gaulle mandated the formation of a liaison officers' corps in October 1943, just at the time that Vagliano entered military training. The Mission Militaire de Liaison Administrative (MMLA) was to be supplemented by a women's unit overseen by Captain Claude de Rothschild.

Vagliano had originally hoped to be put to work as a spy, but, encouraged by Captain Rothschild, she applied for a spot in the MMLA. After completing the six-week training course with flying colors, she emerged as an officer with the grade of lieutenant. As an MMLA officer, Vagliano had found her military home for the rest of the war.

Vagliano and sixty of her comrades were the first MMLA members to be shipped to France just two weeks after D-Day. The women's groups were organized into teams of four, specializing in setting up the forward transit camps. Throughout her service for the next two years, the camps were set up in already existing structures: schools, castles, convents, even former German Army barracks, whatever was available. At the outset in Normandy, the refugee and DP population was relatively limited—there were from one to two thousand people in the camps set up by the American First Army G5 unit Vagliano was attached to. The MMLA teams built ovens, obtained and served food, cleaned out and set up sleeping quarters, supervised the refugees, and looked after their health. The team also organized their return to their homes when that was possible.

The image of Vagliano that emerges from her memoir is that of a brave, dedicated, smart, tenacious, even feisty young woman who got into lots of trouble by fudging on the rules but who eventually won the respect of her peers and commanding officers. At the beginning of her service, she was part of a four-member team. By the end of the war, at age twenty-three, she was responsible for overseeing the work of her own and thirty other teams for the entire American zone in Germany.

With the advance of the war, the refugee and DP situation became steadily more critical. In a dramatic shift of policy due in large part to the pressure brought by Rothschild and Vagliano on the French command, the MMLA teams received permission to follow their US Army units outside of France. In Belgium, the number of people needing shelter and protection increased exponentially while the supply of food and equipment dwindled. The conditions in the camps became even more grave during the Battle of the Bulge in the winter of 1944–1945. When the G5 was ordered to leave the camp at Verviers temporarily, they left the twenty-two-year-old Vagliano in charge of thousands of DPs. Caught between the lines, the camp was shelled and strafed in a horrific friendly fire episode. Vagliano describes the desperate conditions:

> The nearest water supply is now three kilometers away. The gas and electricity are off again, and we are out of coal for the stoves.... Our vehicles are frozen and won't start. We have no more straw and no more blankets. Our stocks of food are alarmingly low. Refugees and victims from the city keep arriving. We deal with the problems as best we can and actually succeed in getting food supplies. But against the cold, there is nothing we can do.

The food supply she mentions came from the unique scrounging expeditions she organized, loading up frozen cattle left in the fields.

The strain on the MMLA officers in these conditions could be overwhelming. One of her fellow MMLA officers in Belgium committed suicide by shooting himself in the heart. He left a note stating that the weight of his responsibilities had overcome him.

Later in Germany, as the Germans retreated early in the spring of 1945, there was a tidal wave of millions of released POWs and slave laborers. Now in the camps that Vagliano was responsible for they were receiving up to twenty thousand people a day without a designated food supply or official medical doctors. Although she never complains, Vagliano and her teams had to endure the same hardships as the DPs. They slept on camp beds in hastily organized quarters, most often without heat or hot water or, indeed, running water at all.

Plus they got little sleep, often working into the night. In the course of her service, Vagliano contracted pneumonia, scabies (several times), colds, and influenza, and she was hospitalized with blood poisoning.

But the worst was Buchenwald.

Twelve days after the liberation of the concentration camp in April 1945, Vagliano was the first woman officer to enter the camp. What she and her American commanding officers found was beyond everyone's worst imagining. There were twenty-one thousand starving and desperately sick internees still there, including a thousand children. The commandant's house was furnished with lampshades made of human skin. Dead bodies were stacked up in the Little Camp outside the crematorium. The stench was nauseating.

Vagliano and her MMLA team spent five weeks at Buchenwald. They immediately helped with transferring the prisoners from the barracks, where they were literally piled up on one another, to clean accommodations in the former SS barracks. Then they turned to their main assignment, which was to arrange for and oversee the repatriation of the internees to their home countries (at least twenty nationalities were represented). Among the internees were the well-known French politicians Georges Mandel and Édouard Daladier, the industrialist Marcel Michelin, and two young men who would become famous: Elie Wiesel and Bruno Bettelheim.

With her insider's view, Vagliano documents the grim experiences of their five weeks at the camp: sorting out the living from the dead, the discovery of a group of wild children, the tours of the camp by VIPs that soon turned into a grisly but routine "horror show," the political pressure on the staff to repatriate certain internees ahead of others, and, finally, the tricksters and con men who tried to take advantage of the chaos and desperation that marked the period.

By the time the camp was transferred to the Russians as planned on July 4, it was nearly empty. Vagliano had completed her task.

After VE Day, the Allied G5 units were dispersed. Vagliano and her MMLA teams were then assigned to the United Nations Relief and Rehabilitation Administration (UNRRA). Her last task was to aid in the exchange of American and Soviet POWs and DPs. The conditions of the exchange, which had been set by the Malta agreement in February 1945, stipulated that Soviet nationals would be returned to the Soviet Union whether they wanted to return or not. Knowing that they faced execution or rendition to the Gulag, many Russian POWs desperately sought asylum in the West, a request that had to be denied. Vagliano thus witnessed what she called "the gruesome exchange of prisoners," watching families being split up and soldiers crying and having to be physically torn away from the vehicles that had transported them to the exchange point. These experiences formed for Vagliano a bitter end to a mission that had begun fired by idealism.

While Vagliano never comments explicitly on these issues, the status of women and the effects of social class in the military are omnipresent in her memoir. Vagliano's astute observations document the ambivalence that colored the treatment of women. She never reports any actual occurrences of sexual harassment but rather notes and experiences herself the nearly daily examples of condescension, inherent prejudice, and oversights that colored the women volunteers' lives. Some instances could be classified as trivial—the fact that Captain Rothschild had to set up her office in a refitted bathroom or that the women officers had to use uniforms handed down by the ATS or that the women's units were given diminutive nicknames like the Rochambelles, the Merlinettes, or, in Vagliano's case Les Demoiselles de Gaulle. Other examples of the different treatment of women were quite simply lives-threatening: while male officers in the MMLA were assigned drivers, the all-women teams often were not. This meant that the women had to make numerous sorties driving alone in combat zones, a situation that troubled even her American army commander (who called her "Missy" instead of Lieutenant) since it often put the women in dire peril.

Occasionally Vagliano's own behavior made the gender politics worse, like the time she temporarily housed her MMLA teams in a brothel in Verviers, Belgium. Word went out that the American First Army had shipped in French whores for the soldiers. The line was already around the block when Vagliano's commander got wind of what she had done. She got summoned to HQ for a dressing down, not so much because her team were taken for prostitutes but rather because her action had made her commander the laughingstock of his fellow officers.

On the other side of the coin, although the women were often looked down upon by macho soldiers, they also benefited from the gallantry of their male colleagues. Lost, her truck out of gas, stuck in ice and mud, Vagliano was unfailingly helped by GIs who would not pass by a woman in distress without offering aid. This protectiveness toward women took a dramatic and finally tragic turn when the commander of the MMLA, Colonel Claude Chandon, was shot and killed while trying to protect two of Vagliano's female colleagues from the German soldier who had captured them.

While gender politics often worked to the disadvantage of the women in the Volontaires Françaises (VF), class issues could work to their benefit. The class stratifications and attitudes vividly marked in French society at the time tended to color the organization of military hierarchy and functions as well. Although there were many members from the working and middle class in the VF, the women's units attracted a large number from the upper classes, including the upper bourgeoisie and aristocracy. Vagliano's commanding officer was the Baroness Rothschild. The Rochambeau unit was led by the Princess of Bourbon-Parma and the Princess of Breteuil.

Vagliano's first experience of class politics upon her arrival in London worked to her great detriment. The savage class resentment of the commander at the VF barracks in London took the form of continued persecution of Vagliano and the imposition of living conditions so brutal that she eventually came down with a serious case of pneumonia.

But generally, her privileged upbringing served Vagliano well in confronting the bureaucratic snarls of army life. There was no conscious sense of privilege or superiority on her part, but if there was a problem, she automatically felt entitled to go to the top to get it solved. Bypassing the chain of command often got her into trouble, but she got things done. As a result, she became a kind of unofficial liaison to the high command, dispatched to Paris to solve problems going from the practical, for example, the supply of uniforms, to the political, such as the question of whether the MMLA teams would be permitted to follow their army units outside the boundaries of France. Her assumption that she was the equal of the top brass eased her way into the offices of generals and government ministers. She often arrived for negotiations with cases of champagne and wine, a social nicety that would only occur to (and be affordable for) a member of the upper class. Things mostly went her way.

At odds with her rank of lieutenant, Vagliano's unstated but recognizable upper-class social status smoothed her welcome not only officially but socially as well. While in London, she drank tea with General Bradley and had drinks with General Patton, both of whom accepted her as a social equal in spite of her relatively low military rank. Later in the war, she ran into General Bradley at a party. The general asked the lieutenant to dance and then obligingly provided her with a special pass that helped her avoid being charged with going AWOL, which she had in fact done.

It is interesting to note that the massive contribution of women in the French military and Resistance during World War II did not occasion an equally far-reaching shift in the status of women in French society. After the war, when women were finally given the vote in municipal elections, it was done as much to counterbalance the numbers of voting Communists as it was to acknowledge the equal standing of women.

As one writer puts it, after the war, there was a kind of rush in France "to recover the virility of the nation" that had been compromised by the humiliating loss to the Germans in the Phony War. As a result, there was a dramatic return to traditional values and lifestyles even among the majority of women who, like Vagliano, had faced danger and hardship serving in distinctly nontraditional roles. Like so many others, Vagliano returned to the life she had known before the war. Married to Philippe Eloy, a doctor she had met toward the end of the war in Germany, Sonia Vagliano Eloy had two children and led the traditional life of the upper bourgeoisie, with an elegant apartment in Paris and a country home in Normandy, where she died in 2002.

Although women military and Resistance fighters tended to be recognized and honored less often and less publicly than their male counterparts, Vagliano Eloy was awarded the Bronze Star and the Croix de Guerre for her superior war service. She was made an officer of the Légion d'Honneur. One enduring aspect of the war years was her admiration for and dedication to General de Gaulle, whom she regarded as the savior of France. She worked at the Institut Charles de Gaulle in Paris for many years and was instrumental in organizing a demonstration in support of him during the troubles of 1968.

Like so many veterans and especially like those who had witnessed the horrors of the concentration camps, Vagliano Eloy did not speak of her experiences in the military even to those close to her. After over thirty years of silence, however, she did what few of her gender and class did—she sat down to write this memoir. One can only speculate about what motivated her after all those years to awaken the memories that had lain dormant for so long: approaching age, the desire to understand and integrate her young self into her identity, or perhaps the hope of explaining to her children what she had witnessed. Others seemed to be subject to the same impulse as numerous memoirs were published at this time: in France, *Bye Bye, Geneviève* (Paris: Laffont, 1981); in Holland, *The Upstairs Room* (New York: Crowell, 1972); in the United States, *At Dawn We Slept: The Untold Story of Pearl Harbor* (New York: McGraw Hill, 1981). Even Hitler's architect Albert Speer reflected on his life in *Spandau Tagebücher* (Frankfurt: Propylaen, 1975). In addition, the feminist movement of the 1970s stoked interest in revealing the previously unexamined aspects of women's personal lives, and a spate of life writing ensued. Whatever the mix of motives, Vagliano gathered together the diary she had kept during the war (characteristically) in violation of military code, letters she had written home, and archival documents and sat down to write—in English! Deciding against a traditional past-tense account that would call for reflection and commentary, she opted for a present-tense narrative that would engage the reader in a more immediate way in the trials and triumphs of this unprecedented war effort by young French women. Hoping not only to capture the interest of the American public but also to inspire a director to create a TV series based on her adventures, she sent a prospectus to twenty-five different American publishers. The answer twenty-five times was no.

In the face of these refusals, Vagliano Eloy demonstrated the same tenacity and determination she had shown during the war. She sat down and rewrote the entire manuscript in French. Focused on observation and careful description of her surroundings and professional experiences, Vagliano provided an original down-to-earth, sometimes humorous, sometimes grisly, and always informative eyewitness account of a young woman's encounter with one of the determining moments of modern history. It was quickly picked up by the editor Plon in Paris and published in 1982 to rave reviews with the title *Les Demoiselles de Gaulle* (De Gaulle's Girls). It won the prestigious Prix Saint Simon for the best memoir of the year. A contemporary newspaper, *L'Action républicaine*, noted that hers was the first account of the women who had participated in military actions but had been forgotten by the historians. What was true in 1982 is still true today.

Several years ago, while talking about her husband's family, my good friend Sara Vagliano handed me the World War II memoir written by her sister-in-law, Sonia Vagliano Eloy. I was blown away by *Les Demoiselles de Gaulle* and, sensing that others would share my reaction, I asked Sara if the book had been translated into English. Upon her answer in the negative, the project was born. As a result, now almost forty years after the French publication and almost eighty years after the events, Vagliano Eloy's dream of having her memoir published in the United States is at last coming true. We are now able to read this precious account of an intelligent and observant individual caught up in the major events of the war in Europe: the invasion of Normandy, the liberation of Paris, the Battle of the Bulge, the defeat of Germany, and the liberation of the concentration camps. In addition to the grand events, she shares with us unforgettable personal memories in her voyage from Normandy to Buchenwald: the exuberant prostitutes eager to set up shop in the refugee camp; the heroically stubborn resident of Saint-Lô who refused to leave her destroyed city; the nasty

French militia member who attempted to kidnap her; her teetotaling, ex-pastor commander filling up on whiskey after his first visit to Buchenwald; getting stuck on a pontoon bridge across the Rhine with the entire American army piling up behind her; holding the hand of a dying child in Buchenwald.

A human-interest story like Vagliano Eloy's memoir is always compelling, as is the drive to understand the past. But in an irony of history, other features of the memoir are still sadly relevant. The presence of women in the military is still mired in prejudice, unfair treatment, and outright harassment. The role of an unrecognized sense of privilege in social injustice has now burst into open view and taken to the streets. And, finally, Vagliano Eloy's insider description of what it takes to care for, feed, and resettle throngs of refugees, DPs, and POWs in the midst of a hot war has once more become tragically relevant as the world struggles to deal with millions of people displaced from their homes by the chaos of a new kind of war.

A Note on the Translation

After reading the original French publication of *Les demoiselles de Gaulle*, I was surprised to learn that Vagliano Eloy had first written large portions of the manuscript in English and had hoped to have it published in the United States. Her efforts were, unfortunately, fruitless. She then wrote the entire memoir in French. At the outset of this translation project, I had the opportunity to review some of the original English manuscript and considered adopting those portions word for word. After consideration, however, and with the concurrence of the author's heirs, I decided to start the current translation from scratch and checked back with Vagliano Eloy's original English only occasionally to clarify or make sure I was on the right track.

If you compare the original French text with the translation, you will find that very few changes have been made—a few cuts to streamline the presentation of technical or organizational details. Apparently, Vagliano Eloy considered writing a traditional past-tense narrative but very quickly realized that an account in the present tense was more lively and engaging, and I have, of course, followed her lead.

There is one vocabulary issue that needs to be addressed, and that is the use of the terms "refugee" and DP (displaced person). At the time of the Second World War, the usage was somewhat different from the conventions that have developed more recently. Then, "refugee" did not refer to someone who had fled their country to seek asylum elsewhere but rather to someone who had been forced to flee home as a result of armed conflict and had remained in their own country. Thus, the refugees Vagliano Eloy is dealing with are mostly locals eager to get back to their homes as quickly as possible.

The term IDP (internally displaced person) in current terminology was not used during the war or at the time Vagliano Eloy was writing. Then, a DP designated an individual who was forced from their native country as a result of war or who was removed as a prisoner or slave laborer. The majority of DPs also wished to return home as quickly as possible. The Russians, however, were a notable exception to this pattern and often sought asylum to avoid being sent back to certain deportation to Siberia or even execution.

I have added a short introduction to each major section in the book to provide background information and a short résumé of the events that are narrated. I hoped to form a context for the narrative and also to preclude the need for footnotes.

There are two appendices. The first is a list of the many acronyms used in the text. The second comprises short bios of many people who appear in the text. An asterisk following the first use of a person's name in the text indicates that there is a biographical entry for that person in the appendix. Unfortunately, the bios identify only a small number of the people mentioned. Vagliano Eloy very often refers to someone only by their last name. The lack of a first name often made it difficult to determine the identity of the person. Lamentably, this was true for Major, later Colonel, Lewis who was her commanding officer and with whom she had a complex but ultimately respectful and positive relationship. If any reader has information about the identity of Major Lewis, I would be delighted to learn about it.

Finally, the bibliography is not meant to be comprehensive but rather a starting point for further research.

Part 1
Crossing the Atlantic. London.

Sonia Vagliano opens her war memoirs with the sea voyage from New York to Liverpool in September 1943. During the three-week trip, Vagliano recalls the origins of her desire to serve with the Free French and the subterfuge she finally used to obtain formal orders to go to London. After losing one-half of its ships, the convoy finally arrived in England.

Upon her arrival in London, the idealistic young woman received an unexpectedly indifferent welcome, including many obstacles posed by the bureaucratic mindset of some of her new colleagues. Rescued from a fainting episode by Eve Curie, the daughter of Pierre and Marie, Vagliano awakened in the Moncorvo barracks of the French women volunteers and was greeted by a surly officer who, mistaking her for a spoiled, rich American, set about making her life miserable. At this time, Vagliano met Hélène Terré, who was to become the first commander of AFAT (Auxiliaires Féminines de l'Armée de Terre), and Claude de Rothschild, who was to become the head of the women's section of the MMLA (Mission Militaire de Liaison Administrative).

For the next five months, Vagliano underwent a tough, sometimes brutal, training regimen. Her detailed account of this period provides precious details about the training program, the physical conditions of the trainees' lives, and the occasional confusion and prejudice plaguing the new women's program. Her training began at Guildford, where the French volunteers trained with members of the British ATS (Auxiliary Territorial Service), the equivalent of the American WACs. Following this rigorous military training, Vagliano was accepted into the recently formed liaison corps and began classes as one of the minority of women in the group. Received into the corps after passing oral and written exams, Vagliano won her lieutenant's stripes in February 1944, the same month that the Germans reinstated their blitz bombing of London.

In March and April 1944, the members of the women's section of the MMLA underwent special training in hospitals and community centers, and then spent two weeks at a Ford factory learning how to operate and maintain British Army vehicles. Finally, at the end of April, the female MMLA officers were sent for a week to a camp in Camberley, Surrey, where they underwent further military training alongside their male counterparts. After a week at Camberley, Vagliano and her MMLA colleagues were the first women to be sent to the Civil Affairs Staff College in Wimbledon, where they enjoyed (comparatively) luxurious living conditions and, as a special addendum to the regular courses, learned how to construct an open-air kitchen, a skill that would serve them well during their tour of duty on the Continent.

Much to their surprise and to the envy of their male colleagues, Vagliano and sixty other members of the women's MMLA were the first to be ordered to France after D-Day; their job—to set up transit camps for refugees in Normandy.

Crossing the Atlantic

September 1943

The little red light sways back and forth. Our ship has just launched another depth charge and it moans, creaks, shivers, and rears up like a wild beast. The New Zealand freighter that I boarded in New York is part of a convoy of eighty ships out of Halifax. Four British escorts assigned to protect us surround the flotilla like guard dogs around a flock of sheep.

A volunteer in the Free French Army, I left New York at the end of August 1943, sailing for England. We've been at sea for two weeks and we're somewhere in the middle of the North Atlantic, still a dozen days from Liverpool, our destination. This is the most perilous part of the journey. Our distance from the coastline means that we will be without air cover for a week.

Our convoy has already been sighted by German submarines. They attack us every night. When the alarm rings, the passengers are supposed to go to the mess hall, which is dimly lit by a red lantern set on one of the tables. The ship's captain, who comes from one of the Channel Islands, bursts into the cabin that I share with two English women, shouting in French, "Into the hold, little Frenchie!" This amuses him greatly, but not me, because this giant old seadog scares me. We have been ordered to sleep in warm clothes and to wear our bulky "Mae West" lifejackets at all times. As soon as the sub or depth-charge alert sounds, we go down to the mess hall carrying our "torpedo bags," packed with necessities. We don't speak or move all night, waiting for dawn to come.

The other passengers, about a dozen in all, worked formerly in Bermuda, where they were mail censors. Quiet and disciplined even when there is no alert, these gentlemen place themselves at the table so that I can have the seat nearest the door leading to the bridge stairs. Sometimes I startle when there is a particularly violent explosion and, even in the darkness, I can feel the silent disapproval of these censors.

During these interminable nights, I struggle against the same irrational panic I felt in Paris when our parents made us go down into the cellar during the alerts in the Phony War in the winter of 1939–40. And to escape the present, I summon my memories of other places and other times....

I see Number 8 rue Général Appert, our beautiful house in Paris. I climb the stairs, stroll through the rooms, greet my favorite paintings, and affectionately stroke the familiar furniture and objects. When I finish the tour, I think about my loved ones. What luck to have a family like mine! We are a real clan and, even though we've been scattered by war, we are united by a common resolution to prevail. Not a day passes that we don't think of each other with an affection mixed with concern. At the end of the summer of 1940, my grandmother was the first to announce that de Gaulle was the hope of France. She has stayed in the house with my father Andreas Vagliano,* who, with his accustomed calm, helps everyone he can: friends, members of the Resistance, English aviators who have escaped from the Germans. My sister Dorothée Segard* called Lally, married and with children, is also in Paris. She is the one I miss the most. In the black hold of this drunken boat, I can imagine her scolding me, "What a dimwit you are to have launched on this old tub when you could have taken a plane!" And she's right.

My mother, Barbara Vagliano,* is exceptional. My sister, my young brother Alex, and I adore her. Even though she often seems to be as young as we are, she is nevertheless unyielding on her principles and is really quite strict. From the beginning, she has encouraged me in my desire to join the Free French Army. American by birth, she is free of the bourgeois prejudices of her French milieu. She volunteered as an ambulance driver in the First World War and received the Croix de Guerre from Marshall Pétain in person.

Since November 11, 1940, the day I joined a student demonstration in Paris, I have tried unsuccessfully to get to London to take part in the struggle. Everything began for me at the end of that bleak June when I saw the first victorious German soldiers occupy Niort, the sunny little city where the disasters of the Phony War had led us. Back in Paris on July 1, the shock was even worse: the occupiers were everywhere. In the otherwise deserted city, only the iron-gray vehicles of Hitler's army circulated, while his battalions goose-stepped at the Arc de Triomphe, the Place de la Concorde, on the great boulevards, and others roamed the streets singing. Our city was covered with yellow, black, and white Gothic-lettered banners. Paris was German.

A privileged child, it was the first time in my life that I had been in Paris in August, and I spent many hours criss-crossing the capital on foot. Full of rage, I would hold my breath each time I passed one of "them," as if I could avoid breathing the same air as they. The Parisians were quiet and submissive. I had the impression that, at the end of several weeks of occupation, the French had realized with relief that the Germans were not ogres who ate little children. From that moment on, only physical survival mattered.

You could hear people saying that Pétain was right. The hero of Verdun had taken France under his protective wing. We should rely on him and thus atone for the faults leading to the current disaster. This attitude shocked me, and I still don't understand it. In June, when we had "withdrawn" to Niort (as the expression had it), I had heard bits of sentences on the radio totally garbled by static. It was a month later that I learned that what I had heard was the voice of General de Gaulle, and that this French general had joined our English allies in the fight against the Germans.

My first thought was that his name was too good to be true and must have been made up! Some friends and I wrote out and carbon-copied the few speeches we were able to get on the radio and, more often, translations of news on the BBC. We put these in envelopes and dropped them in random mailboxes. An enthusiastic photographer, I also took photos of Paris under the German boot, especially of the occupiers' posters and banners. Even though these activities were definitely small-scale, they made us feel less useless, all the more so because they were *verboten*.

Christmas day, 1940: yielding to family pressure, I agreed to leave for the United States with my mother. My father was persuaded that America would enter the war soon and that my mother, who is a US citizen, would be interned in France if she stayed. Also, since being identified as a participant in the November 11 demonstration, I had been required to report once a week to the local police station. Even though I found this recognition of my protest in a strange way flattering, it greatly worried my parents. So, at the end of January, my mother and I left on the last train of Americans to be repatriated. We were to go to New York via Lisbon.

I thought that when I was in the US, it would be easy for me to join the Free French Army and go to England where the women's section was based. But it didn't work out that way. My applications went nowhere. I enrolled in an American university, but as soon as vacation came, I went in person to the New York delegation of the Free French Army and signed on as a volunteer worker. To bolster my chances of being accepted as a regular, I even learned to fly. But that effort didn't last long since, when the US entered the war after Pearl Harbor, foreigners were no longer allowed to pilot planes. I took lessons in industrial design, first aid, and car mechanics, but the months passed and my letters to the Free French headquarters at Carlton Gardens in London remained unanswered. I began to resent General de Gaulle himself, since in his speeches of June 18 and 20, 1940, he invited everyone to join him in the struggle. Everyone, it seemed, except French women! Everyone discouraged me and advised me to find work in the US that would further the war effort, but I remained convinced that all French citizens, me included, could and should join de Gaulle in the battle for France. The administrative obstacles were very discouraging: it was impossible to travel to England without orders for an official mission; Great Britain refused entry to all "non-essential" persons; and the US refused exit visas to women under twenty-five who wanted to go to countries at war.

I decided to lay siege to the Free French Army delegation in New York. At last in 1942, I succeeded in signing up—but my papers got lost. In the spring of 1943, I volunteered as a secretary at the Fifth Avenue headquarters of the Free French Army. Finally in August of 1943, my orders arrived. I was to leave with four others, including my friend Geneviève Tissot, for Algeria. But yet again, for reasons I can only now guess (my boss Alexandre de Manziarly,* known as Sacha, wanted to keep me as his secretary!), my name was erased from the list. It was a bitter disappointment, but I wasn't finished with them. In my work as a volunteer at the delegation office, I created my own orders for London and put the papers in a big pile to be signed by Captain Manziarly. In a hurry on his way to a radio appearance, he signed the papers without looking at them. Two weeks later, I was on my way from New York to London.

While I am reconstructing my memories of the past, the long crossing continues. The ocean has become relatively calm. The Liberty Ship, which accompanied us, has been sunk. One of the officers that I play ping pong with tells me that our convoy has lost a dozen ships.

Having become accustomed to life on board, I have begun to worry about the arrival in England with all its uncertainties. I spend the mornings typing and making an inventory of the cargo for the captain—who no longer frightens me. In fact, I dine with him every day at his table. He is delighted to be able to speak French, but I have difficulty understanding his Channel Island dialect. In the afternoons, I read and spend time on the bridge with the officers. Since we have arrived close enough to shore to be protected by the English air force, the night attacks have stopped, and life on board has taken on a slow, even monotonous, rhythm—until the day we see the English coast in the distance.

We debark at Liverpool at night in the middle of an air raid. DCA (Department of Civil Aviation) searchlights sweep the sky and occasionally catch an airplane in their shafts of light. The rumble of the bombardment becomes louder, almost deafening, as we reach shore.

The passengers disembark with their baggage. It is raining; the dock is deserted. After a few formalities, I find myself hitched to a cart piled high with the seemingly numberless suitcases of the elderly English woman whose cabin I had shared and whom I didn't have the heart to abandon. We arrive at last at a gloomy, cold hotel where we spend the night before catching the first train to London.

London

September 1943

Finally arriving at Euston Station, I discover that after twenty-four days at sea I'm staggering like a drunk. I find a telephone booth but have trouble figuring out how it works and get completely unnerved as I watch my pennies rejected one after the other. After getting two wrong numbers, I breathe a sigh of relief when I hear a French voice on the other end of the line. I have finally reached FFL headquarters at Carlton Gardens. I introduce myself. The voice becomes irritable: "You've got the wrong number. Call the French Volunteers."

"I don't have the number. Can you give it to me?"

"If you are a French Volunteer, you should have the number."

"But I don't have it, sir. I just got in from New York."

"Ah, you're American. I'm not authorized to give out any addresses or telephone numbers. But you can't get through to the FV today anyway."

After this remark, which upsets me not a little, he hangs up.

Unsteadily, I leave the telephone booth and bump into a very English mustachioed gentleman wearing a bowler hat and carrying an umbrella. He mutters something under his breath about telephones and chatty women. Giving me a very severe look, he declares, "There's a war on!" I apologize humbly, gather up my suitcase and my portable typewriter, and go to look for a taxi.

I give the driver the address of the French Volunteers and, on the way, observe the streets of a city at war. After New York, everything seems small, gray, dirty, and extraordinarily quiet. Here and there, I see the wreckage of a building or even several blocks of houses entirely flattened by the blitz. It takes us half an hour to arrive at a large, forbidding house with all its windows boarded up. There is a sign attached to the wrought-iron gate. I get out of the taxi and read: "Closed for fumigation by order of the Ministry of Health," and underneath in French, "Fermé pour dératisation."

"They could at least have put a forwarding address," I complain to the taxi driver. But my problem doesn't interest him. He replies, "You can't trust foreigners. There's a war on."

I pay him, walk up the street, and go into a small restaurant. I haven't eaten since getting off the boat and I'm starving. The food is mediocre, but I devour it with great gusto and feel much better until the waitress asks for my food coupons, which, of course, I don't have. A drama ensues. Everyone, including the owner and the other clients, gets into the act. Neither my explanations nor my passport stamped at Liverpool the day before make any impression. They continue to make disparaging remarks about foreigners and to repeat, "There's a war on," and then "We're going to call the police."

What a good idea! I pay quickly, leave a big tip, gather up my luggage, and, still under fire from the clients at the restaurant, go to look for a policeman. One of the famous London bobbies is surely going to help me out of this! The one I find will only give me the address of Carlton Gardens and tell me how to get there by tube.

At last, here I am in front of the famous Carlton Gardens FFL headquarters. The orderly on duty stops me and tells me that no one can enter without a pass and an appointment. I explain that I have just arrived from New York, so obviously I have neither an appointment nor a pass.

He insists, "If you are a French Volunteer, you would have a uniform and you could enter."

I repeat, "But I just got here. I don't have a uniform."

"Then you'll have to telephone to make an appointment."

This interesting conversation is brutally interrupted by the arrival of several important-looking officers. The orderly stands at attention, salutes, and forgets his unimpressive little visitor. I sit down on my suitcase in the middle of the sidewalk and wait, struggling against a rising panic by telling myself, "Someone or something is surely bound to come along."

An hour goes by without anyone taking note of me. Finally a short, gray-haired women in a khaki uniform comes out of the building. I literally throw myself at her and, frightened, she drops all the files she had tucked under her arm. I go down on all fours, picking up the papers that have scattered about. The damage repaired, I am finally able to engage her in conversation and learn that the French Volunteers are moving that very day from this office to another at Moncorvo House at 7 Ennismore Gardens, Knightsbridge. Delighted to have an address, I give my informant a big hug, at which she hurries off, giving me a startled look.

Now that I know where to go, I feel so relieved that I decide, with the logic of an exhausted person, to go directly to Brown's Hotel, where I had stayed with my parents before the war. I would stay the night so that the next morning I could present myself fresh and rested at Moncorvo House. The truth is that all I want is to be in a familiar place and to rest.

Outwardly, the lobby of Brown's Hotel looks the same, but it is teeming with a feverish activity unlike anything in the past. I make my way with some difficulty through the clutter of military trunks and equipment and patiently wait my turn at the reception desk. When I ask for a room with bath, the clerk looks at me with total disbelief and then doubles over laughing. "I don't know where you've been, Miss, but there hasn't been a free hotel room in London for the last three years. Only military personnel are authorized to stay here." Red with embarrassment, I leave hurriedly before he can say, "There's a war on."

A little later, pulling and then pushing my luggage, which is getting heavier and heavier, I arrive at Moncorvo House, the barracks of the women's division of the Free French Army. It is a vast, austere mansion. (Later I would learn that it had been the residence of French émigrés during the Revolution.) Inside, a half-dozen steps lead to a large, gloomy, empty entrance hall. After a moment I see light coming from under a door to my right. I knock and enter. A very plump girl in khaki sits in front of a telephone switchboard with a paperback novel in her hand.

I introduce myself once again. I wasn't expecting a warm welcome, but her gruff reply takes me by surprise: "Nobody gave me any orders. There's no room here, we're filled up. The new ones have to go to the Patriotic School to be processed. Why didn't you go there?"

I answer: "I don't need to go to the Patriotic School. I didn't escape from France. I came from New York and went through security there. My papers are in order. I am supposed to come here, you understand, HERE!"

I end up shouting at her, but, not at all impressed, she repeats, "I don't have orders and I can't bother the officers at this late hour. Come back tomorrow."

I turn my suitcase on its side and sit down on it. I have no more strength, not even enough to appeal to a pretty woman in khaki who is sweeping the steps. After a few moments everything gets blurry and then I don't remember anything.

Moncorvo Barracks

It is broad daylight when I wake up. I'm in an infirmary. There are several empty beds and a table covered with medicine bottles. A fine way to start my army life! I must have slept for hours because my watch has stopped and I am famished. I quickly dress and go down a narrow, winding stair. I find myself back in the entrance hall where I was the night before. I hear dishes clattering and, following the sound, enter the mess hall, which is filled with long tables and benches. A woman in uniform has her back to me. She is leaning over slightly, talking into the opening of a dumb-waiter. The cut of her uniform makes me think that she must be an officer. She turns around, and I am shocked to see that she is wearing very heavy make-up.

My wan smile freezes on my lips when I hear her declare in a deep and vulgar voice: "You must be the new American girl. Were you waiting to have your breakfast served in bed?"

Trying desperately to be amiable, I respond: "Indeed, that would have been very nice. But please excuse me, Madam, I was worn out by my voyage and didn't wake up. And, in fact, even though I arrived from the United States, I'm not American."

With a poisonous look, the woman lights into me: "Ah, I see you're one of those uppity American girls. But your dollars won't do you any good in the army. My job is to turn you into a soldier and, believe me, I know what I'm doing. I didn't wait until the last days of the war to sign up, not me! I have been a French Volunteer since the first day! I'm warning you, don't try one of your fainting fits again because you're not going to spend your time in the army lolling around in the infirmary."

"Of course not, Madam," I answer in a fading voice, "that won't happen again. I'm determined to do my best. But, do you think I could have something to eat?"

"Something to eat," in a simpering voice obviously meant to imitate mine. "Her ladyship would like something to eat." Then switching back to her own rough tone, "Let me tell you something, the girls who come from Brittany in little fishing boats, and the ones who cross the Pyrenees through the snow, and even those who come from the colonies don't spend their time here snoozing and making pigs of themselves. You'd better remember that you're definitely second class and that you can't go prancing around like a princess just because you come from America with your cashmere sweaters and silk stockings." And with that, she turns and leaves.

The floor is still rolling and pitching under my feet, and my brain is in a fog. I lean against one of the tables to steady myself. A girl with rosy cheeks peeks around a door at the end of the hall. With a hearty country accent she reassures me: "Don't mind her. She's like that with all the new girls and even with us. You'll see, you'll get used to it. It's the army! Now come on down to the kitchen, and I'll give you some breakfast. You're all pale."

A steep stairway leads down to a big, old-fashioned kitchen where four women in khaki are going about their chores. Lively, talkative, and motherly, they serve me a large English breakfast with coffee and hot milk. Feeling restored, I chat with the women who bring me up to speed on barracks life. Suddenly I hear my name bellowed from the dumb-waiter. I am being summoned by Captain Hélène Terré,* commander of the VF.

Having already gotten my fingers burnt once, I'm expecting the worst. But the Captain welcomes me warmly, congratulates me on joining the VF, and asks about my trip. Moved by her welcome, I answer timidly, giving the impression, I fear, of being a total numbskull. She tells me that I am to spend several days at Moncorvo. Then, after my induction, I will be sent for basic training at the ATS [Auxiliary Territorial Service] camp at Guildford where all British women army are trained.

Gathering up my courage, I tell her my secret: I want to be sent to France as a clandestine agent. With a smile, she replies that I am much too young and inexperienced. I answer that my youth seems to me an advantage for passing unnoticed and, as to my lack of experience, I hope to be selected for the necessary training. I add that I learn quickly and have an excellent memory, which would be most useful in clandestine work.

Clearly not persuaded, the Captain tells me that if I wish to make the request later, she will transmit it. However in the meantime, I must begin my basic training. Before dismissing me, she informs me that a new Liaison Officer Corps has just been created [Mission Militaire de Liaison Administrative, henceforth MMLA]. Women will be admitted into the Corps. The first entrance exam for the officer training course will take place at Moncorvo in a week, on October 7, the eve of my departure for the ATS. She offers to sign me up for the exam, and I accept her offer enthusiastically. Captain Terré warns me not to be too hopeful on account of my age (again!) and my recent arrival since "there are many candidates and only a few places. But you can always try."

My first week in the military is divided between the process of induction and working in the kitchen. Since the various offices I have to report to are in different parts of the city, I quickly become familiar with London, especially with the bus routes and the underground. I sign up officially for "the duration of the war plus three months" and receive my service registration number, 70449.

At Moncorvo I'm assigned to kitchen duty, which doesn't bother me, since the Volunteers who work in the kitchen are, for the most part, friendly and easy-going. I peel potatoes, wash dishes, scrub the floor, all the while chatting or even singing. I'm obliged to eat in the kitchen as well, which I like less, because it makes it harder for me to get to know the other Volunteers who tend to make friends during meals in the mess hall. By the time I go upstairs after the evening meal, everyone is already clustered in the big living room, which has an enormous fireplace topped by a flag-festooned portrait of General de Gaulle. Not wanting to intrude on the small groups of girls, I read the newspaper in the library and go up to bed in a room I share with five other girls.

On the evening that the MMLA entrance exam is given, there is a crowd waiting at the door. I recognize the pretty woman who was sweeping the steps the evening I arrived. She sees me and says: "Ah, so you're better." And I learn that she was the one who picked me up off the floor when I fainted and carried me to the infirmary. I thank her and ask her name. "Eve Curie,"* she answers, "and you?" Flabbergasted, I mumble my name. She smiles and wishes me good luck on the exam.

There are around sixty candidates, including several officers, taking the exam. I'm immediately at ease because I have a perverse liking for taking exams! The test lasts two hours and includes translation exercises in French and English and an essay on the steps that need to be taken to liaise in a hypothetical small French port that has recently been liberated.

I think I did all right on the exam but give up all hope when I am reminded that only six people will be admitted. The woman next to me reassures me that there will be other exams given so that I can try again after I finish basic training. She is already a lieutenant but signed up for the exam because she thinks that the liaison officers will be very quickly sent to France.

The ATS Training Camp at Guildford. October 8–November 10, 1943

On the gray, rainy morning of October 8, 1943, fifty glum young women in civilian clothes are gathered on the platform of the Guildford train station under a sign reading "ATS Recruits, Report Here." A little to the side, we French Volunteers are standing together: a gray-haired woman and three girls. We are all waiting for the army trucks that are supposed to take us to the camp. The new English recruits are dispirited and tearful. Mobilized at the age of eighteen, the more motivated ones choose the navy or the air force, while the rest inevitably end up here in the ATS. It is not a joyful gathering.

The military camp at Guildford looks like any other camp except that women in uniform stand guard. The trucks unload us in front of the barracks where we are met by a corporal who informs us that it is her job to see that in five weeks we are turned into soldiers of His Majesty's Army. The corporal is a tall, thin woman with a horsey face and gray hair in a short masculine cut. When she gives orders in her biting, clipped voice, each word is shot from her mouth like a bullet out of a machine gun. She lives by and for the army, and I wonder what she would have become if there hadn't been a war, as she obviously was conceived for the sole purpose of serving as a corporal in the ATS.

After depositing our gear on our assigned bed, we are taken to the infirmary, where I undergo my third physical exam and where, despite my protests, I am once again inoculated for typhoid, diphtheria, and tetanus. We are then marched over to receive our clothing and equipment. The army dresses us from head to toe including underwear, and the woman behind the counter is hard put to find articles to fit my small stature. I end up with a skirt that is too wide and too long, a jacket that is too small with ridiculously short sleeves, detachable collars that are too tight, and shoes that are too big. The underwear is truly atrocious: long, scratchy vests; over-sized bras; a pink corset with laces and metal stays; and an enormous pair of knee-length khaki bloomers.

Reveille sounds at 6:30. In October at that hour, it is totally dark, damp, and cold. Before breakfast, we spend two hours cleaning and polishing the barracks and our personal equipment. Making the beds is a particularly complicated affair: it is called "barracking beds," which includes folding the sheets and blankets in a fiendishly intricate way. The corporal is a stickler on the subject, and at the least false fold, she undoes everything and you have to begin all over again. We stand at attention at the foot of our beds for inspection. Two officers—a captain and a lieutenant—accompany the corporal. The first day, my back and arm are hurting, I have a fever, and my head is spinning. I curse the shots I was given and am convinced, in my sorry state, that I am going to be declared unfit and sent home. The officers stop at my place. I stay still because the corporal has warned us that, under no circumstances, is a recruit to address an officer directly. In fact, it is the corporal who acts as an interpreter and intermediary between the officers and us poor rank-and-file footsloggers, which makes me feel like some kind of vegetable or mineral. The lieutenant, a pretty blonde, asks: "Did she look like this when she arrived?" As an explanation for my pathetic appearance, the corporal responds, "She's French, Ma'am." The lieutenant approaches me, smiling (maybe she loves the French!) and tries in vain to insert her fingers between my neck and my collar. She turns toward the corporal and says severely, "Remove this collar immediately. Can't you see this child is choking? Be sure that she receives the proper equipment immediately." The corporal removes my collar. As she does, I notice that even her eyes are khaki and that she has a slight moustache. Luckily the lieutenant doesn't notice my fever so I won't be sent home. However, the corporal resents me for this ludicrous incident and continues to bear a grudge. I become her whipping boy, and from then on she assigns me all the most disgusting chores.

The dull, cold days of training go slowly by. The recruits, called the OR (Other Ranks) to distinguish us from the NCOs, run around in the freezing, muddy, soggy English countryside in brown shorts and sleeveless blaze-orange T-shirts. We are taught about the army—its ranks and regulations—and take classes on first aid and gymnastics.

The main activity is marching and drilling on an enormous asphalt parade ground. Our instructor is an actual male sergeant-major with an enormous red moustache and the voice of a lion. For hours at a time, we forward march, about-face, and stand at attention when he booms the commands. When we march in rows, we have to hold our arms straight and swing them up to the level of the belt of the girl in front of us while our legs are supposed to reach the level of her skirt. We also march out on the roads, in the countryside, and through villages. At times these activities are carried out wearing a gas mask, called a "respirator." The sadistic gymnastics instructor makes us run on the muddy roads, jump over slippery ditches, cross streams, and climb over fallen tree trunks, all the while wearing this clumsy, heavy apparatus.

Three times a day, we go on the double to the mess hall where we ingest copious, filling meals. The three-star attraction for the English is a dessert made with noodles and jam.

At night I nurse my blistered feet (my shoes are still two sizes too large) and try to sleep. Even though I am physically exhausted, the cold and damp keep me awake. Regulations forbid the use of personal clothing, but I disobey and hide a couple of sweaters under my blue-and-white striped army pajamas. Several times in the middle of the night, when the alert siren sounds, we find ourselves in a muddy trench, water trickling through our pajamas with the hated respirator covering our faces.

Finally, the long weeks of basic training are over. Before we leave, the corporal lines up our squad in front of the barracks and addresses us: "Remember," she says, "that command is a rare gift and that you owe respect to your superior officers. You probably will not reach an upper level rank, but it will always be your honor to have served in His Majesty's Army."

We Are Called the Volunteers. November 10–29, 1943

Back at Moncorvo on November 10, 1943, I am delighted to learn that I have been admitted to the liaison officer's course. Commander Terré summons me to her office and congratulates me on my winning admission to the training course. However, I first have to complete my French military training at Moncorvo before joining the MMLA class on November 29. My first thought is that the Moncorvo training will be a breeze since I have become an expert cleaner and polisher at Guildford. But I am wrong. The made-up adjutant who was unpleasant to me my first day at Moncorvo has been promoted to lieutenant while I was gone, and is apparently waiting to pounce on me.

I am bunked with seven other women, which seems pleasantly intimate after the crowds at the Guildford barracks. Indeed, my companions seem especially cheerful and lively by comparison with the ATS girls. There are two middle-aged women who whisper to each other while knitting; three very young girls who work in the office at Carlton Gardens and who break up laughing at every possible opportunity; a driver who tells us amusing stories about the officers she chauffeurs around; and the secretary of an important officer who, however, can't tell us anything about what she does since the work is top-secret.

In reality, Moncorvo is a kind of military hotel, totally empty during the day and bustling with activity in the evening. Almost everyone works elsewhere, including Captain Terré and her two adjutants, Lieutenants Burdet* and Briel.

If Lieutenant P had not set her sights on me from the very first day, I might have had a pleasant memory of Moncorvo. Unfortunately, she sets about bullying me every chance she gets, no doubt hoping that I will accumulate so many demerits that I will be disqualified for the MMLA course.

From the very first evening, my roommates warn me that Lieutenant P is a terror and that she is out to get me. It turns out that she herself failed the entrance exam and hasn't gotten over it. She has announced to everyone that the "stuck-up American" is going to have a rough time and is sadly mistaken if she thinks she will have an easy path to promotion.

Lieutenant P rules the barracks, which are impeccably maintained, and the food is excellent. As the only officer present during the day, she tyrannizes the Volunteers on kitchen and cleaning duty, who fear and detest her. Since she is the all-powerful dispenser of leaves and penalties, nobody dares annoy or cross her.

Every morning I put on my khaki work clothes and matching headscarf and am ready for the mop and broom. My work begins at eight and ends at one. I scrub, wash, sweep, polish, and lay and light the fires. Often Lieutenant P shadows me, a cigarette dangling from her mouth. She obviously enjoys seeing me slave away and often makes me repeat the same task three or four times. Diligently plodding away at my work, I am careful to respond only, "Yes, Lieutenant,"

"No, Lieutenant," "Right away, Lieutenant." My zeal and docility must exasperate her because she hurls more abuse at me every day. Since I don't understand half the filthy language she uses, her abuse doesn't ruffle me, and I resolve to take it without flinching.

Seconded by my roommates who, whenever they pass by, exclaim about the beauty of my work, I manage to avoid most punishments, but not all. Three incidents incur serious penalties, including being restricted to barracks in the evening and once for a weekend.

The first incident occurs early on while I am on fireplace duty. The preparation of the fires in the fireplaces (there is no central heating) is the worst of the assignments: you have to fetch the coal in the basement, carry incredibly heavy pails with it up the stairs, empty the ashes from the previous day, lay the fire, light it, blow on it to get it going, etc. At the end of the morning I look like a chimney sweep. On this particular day, I mistake coke for coal. As a result, a great cloud of black, greasy smoke envelops the office of Lieutenant Burdet.

Another time, I get a totally unfair penalty on account of a water leak in a bathroom for which I am unjustly held responsible. Even though I do my best to bail out the water with my pails and to stop up the leaks with rags, the water continues to course down the stairs. Finally, too late, Lieutenant P decides to call a plumber. While we're waiting for him to arrive, she blows up at me and calls me all the names in the book. I'm down on my knees futilely trying to sponge up the water; she is standing up on a stool so as not to get her feet wet. Plus she has just plucked her eyebrows and replaced them with a heavy arc of black pencil. The eyebrows and her painted mouth suddenly remind me of the wicked queen in *Snow White and the Seven Dwarves*. I can't help myself and burst out laughing. Exasperated, the lieutenant takes advantage of the fact that no one is around to whomp me in the face with a wet mop. She screams, "This will teach you not to laugh at me!" My laughter turns to tears of hurt and anger. Lieutenant P is exultant. After that, I am determined to keep total control of myself, but at the same time to try to find ways to annoy her without getting caught.

The last incident of my training period at Moncorvo takes place in the officers' mess where Lieutenant P meets her boyfriend of the moment. He is a large, florid English major. He brings two other officers with him, one English and one Canadian. They are having a candlelit dinner. The subtle light dims the outrageous make-up of the hostess, who is enjoying a great success with the gentlemen. She loves to make me serve at table, believing it will humiliate me, but she is totally mistaken. Of all my tasks, it's the one I prefer: it's not tiring, and the conversation I overhear at table is often screamingly funny. The lieutenant simpers and gives herself airs in her broken English while her guests share off-color jokes and make gross asides. Sometimes the service slows down because I am busy telling my kitchen pals what is going on upstairs. We get to laughing so hard that I have to collect myself before serving or clearing the table. Fortunately, the boss doesn't care if the dinner stretches out as long as the food is good and the wine flows. It is precisely the wine that is the indirect cause of my troubles. One evening I clumsily knock a glass full of red wine out of the hand of Lieutenant P's neighbor at table just as he is getting ready to toast her. Her uniform and immaculate white shirt are all spotted with wine. Furious, she gets up and shouts at me with her usual vigor. I busy myself preparing to sprinkle salt on the wine spots and in the process salt her head! She gets salt in her eyes, and her mascara and eye shadow begin running down her face. It's a total disaster. The lieutenant flees the room. The major is scandalized by the "salty" language of his lady-love and questions me. With a martyred air and in my best English accent I respond that I am forbidden to talk directly to an officer. When Lieutenant P returns with fresh clothes and make-up, the magic has been broken, and the major—very stiff and very English—leaves followed by his fellow guests. The lightning bolts of Lieutenant P's anger rapidly descend on me. I am assigned a week of garbage duty. But this time, it was worth it!

In mid-November I am summoned to Carlton Gardens to appear before the MMLA committee, which is very imposing. The candidates are brought one at a time into a large office where they are awaited by an august council of superior officers seated in a semicircle. Present are General Matteney, who commands the FFL, and Colonel Renouard,[*] head of the new MMLA. A lonely chair facing the committee awaits me. I have the feeling of appearing at a trial. And, indeed, these gentlemen examine me closely—in both French and English—about my studies, my past activities, my reasons for joining up, my family, etc. I do my best to answer clearly and, especially, with a confidence that I am far from feeling.

Coming out of this interrogation, I meet Lieutenant Ford, who is in charge of the women's section of the liaison officer corps. An English national residing in France, she joined the French Army in 1939, served in France with the quartermaster corps, then in the health service, and, finally, joined General de Gaulle in the ill-fated Dakar campaign. Decorated with the Croix de Guerre 1939–1940, she is the senior female officer in the FFL and the one with the highest rank.

By chance, she speaks with me and right off takes me under her wing. The very next day I am invited to dine with her and Colonel Renouard in a charming little house near Sloane Square where she lives with her father. At the end of the dinner, Colonel Renouard says in his rough tone of voice, "Vagliano, you're a stable, well-balanced woman." This unexpected compliment makes me blush with embarrassment and pleasure. It's the first time since I've been in the military that anyone has treated me like an adult. Afterwards, I would often seek refuge in the pleasant, calm atmosphere of Lieutenant Ford's little family home. She requests that I be transferred to her secretariat at Carlton Gardens. Two harried weeks follow during which I carry out my household tasks in the morning at Moncorvo and then spend the afternoon at Carlton Gardens under the orders of Lieutenant Ford as a member of Colonel Renouard's secretariat.

Plans are being made for the future role of the liaison mission between the civil authorities in France and the British and American armies. I take notes and write up reports of these secret meetings, which are extremely interesting. The plans for the MMLA are developing rapidly even though it has not yet been officially approved either by London or by the FFL in Algiers.

As might be expected, Lieutenant P is not happy with my new functions, but, since the orders come from higher up, there is nothing she can do officially. Nevertheless, unofficially she can assure that I don't have a moment's rest. When I return to Moncorvo at the end of the day, tasks for the evening await me! Sometimes I have to serve beer in the canteen until midnight; other times I wash dishes or serve dinner to the officers; or I am in charge of the coatroom, or I have to sort the cigarettes and candy that the Volunteers receive with their pay. In order not to be even a minute late returning to Moncorvo in the evening, it is imperative that I find a way to shorten the long bus and tube rides back from Carlton Gardens. Since taxis are expensive and hard to find, I buy a used bicycle and, from then on, I circulate in London at top speed, always sure to be on time.

The MMLA Liaison Officer Course

The first class begins on November 29, 1943, in the ballroom of an old private mansion on St. James's Square. It's very cold in the mansion, but the women in the class have been gallantly placed in the front row near a large black stove. There are sixty students in all, including four women.

Classes last from 9:30 in the morning to six in the afternoon. We have a two-hour break for lunch, which we generally take in the canteen. Those who have more money frequent little neighborhood restaurants and occasionally treat us to lunch with them. The atmosphere is lively and friendly. Most of the men are already officers. Many have arrived recently from France. The ones from Paris are able to give us the details, for which we are so greedy, about daily life in the occupied zone.

The high-ranking British officers give lectures in English on their army: its organization, ranks, headquarters and their function, equipment, security, communications and codes, signals, topography and map-reading, field hospitals, and social services. Our other instructors are French. Among them are several eminent members of the FFL, including Commander Maurice Schumann,* Professors Gros, Kayser, and Haas-Picard, and others who are less well known like Lieutenant Rossi, Captain Ruais, and Superintendent Stéfanini, who oversees daily instruction.

In the French classes, we are taught about Vichy, about the constitution of the Third Republic, the government and administration, including social services, police, judicial system, public services, etc.

The instruction is wide-ranging and interesting though too voluminous for my taste. I am pleased, though, to be back in school. For the most part, the men don't bother to study because they expect the final exam to be a formality. But we women work very hard. Another trainee, Lise Harbley, and I are particularly dedicated to our studies because we are determined to be promoted to the rank of officer. Her father, Lieutenant Harbley, has heard that the MMLA Committee thought that both of us are too young for the work we will have to do in France. To prove them wrong, we put all our energy into learning by heart a dizzying quantity of details about the military. Our heads are stuffed with figures, acronyms, and abbreviations. We take turns quizzing each other about weight and measure equivalences or the number of trucks and motorcycles in a division. We even converse in a code language.

Unfortunately, the conditions I have to study in are particularly difficult. My request to live outside Moncorvo was refused: too young, no family in London. I am authorized, however, to occupy a single room, which means that, unlike in the dormitories, I don't have to turn out lights at 10 pm when the curfew sounds. I am assigned a large corner room on the top floor with three windows and six beds. It doesn't take me long to figure out why this room is usually not occupied during the winter. Two of the windows are lacking windowpanes and have remained unrepaired, since new glass panes are nowhere to be found in London. The wind and rain sweep in, and the temperature inside is often the same as it is outside—that is, literally freezing. I begin by nailing blankets up at the empty windows, which I stuff as well as I can with cartons and newspapers. But every night, the blankets flap in the wind like sails, and the cartons and newspapers come loose and fall to the floor.

Next, I try transforming my bed into a tent with the help of extra covers lent to me by friends. I put on three pairs of pajamas, two heavy sweaters, a balaclava, and wool socks. Every evening after dinner, one of my pals from the kitchen slips two hot-water bottles into my bed.

Thus clothed in my cozy tent and with the aid of a flashlight, I work into the wee hours of the morning.

Everything seems to be going well until one evening when I am getting ready to get into my tent. A Volunteer bursts into the room shouting that I need to turn out the lights. Disaster! I have forgotten to lower the black-out curtains, and my windows are brightly lit since the blankets have once more fallen down. It seems the warning sirens have been sounding for a while without my hearing them, and an air raid is in progress. I am ordered to go downstairs to appear before a policeman, who is furious. After ten minutes of back-and-forth, he calms down and decides not to take me to the station for a formal statement. I am obliged, however, to join my comrades in the basement shelter until the raid is over. When I am able to go back up to my room, I discover that the last intact window has been shattered. There are shards of glass all over the floor and in my bed.

I get up early every morning at 6:30 so as to have time before inspection to stow my "tent" and the window coverings. As a result, I am sometimes so sleepy that I nod off during class, especially when I'm seated next to the delicious warmth of the stove.

In spite of my efforts, Lieutenant P continues to persecute me. In the morning I sneak around hoping to avoid her but she manages somehow to spot me and to assign me a household duty that eats up the minutes. After I am late twice to the liaison class, I receive a warning: one more lateness and I will be dismissed from the program. In spite of the morning cold and black ice, I start using my bike again. This saves me a quarter of an hour between Moncorvo and St. James's Square. Every evening, I lock my bike to an iron fence in a dark little street near Moncorvo. I conceal it as well as I can so the lieutenant will not confiscate it, but I live in fear that it will be stolen.

On Wednesday, which is payday, my time management problem becomes almost impossible. Class is over at 6:15, and I have to be at Moncorvo by 6:30. One Wednesday, the lecturer goes overtime, and, even pedaling as fast as I can, I arrive twenty minutes late. My explanations are ignored by Lieutenant P, who gives me three days garbage duty. In London at that time, nothing is wasted, so the barracks trash, gathered in a dozen enormous garbage cans, has to be sorted by hand to separate out paper, wood, bones, vegetable products, metal, and ... the unmentionable. This kind of job requiring care and precision does not, in principle, bother me, but in order to keep to my schedule, which has become an obsession of mine, I have to get up even earlier—at 5:30—in order to be in the disgusting, freezing garbage area by 6:30. At that hour, it's totally dark; I hang up a flashlight, put on some old gloves and a woolen cap, and set to work.

Fortunately Christmas is near, and we're given several days off. I retreat happily to the comfortably warm apartment of a friend of my mother's where I can work in peace all day long. The quiet house begins to bustle almost every evening at cocktail hour, when my hostess, Marian Hall,* a member of the American Red Cross, entertains numerous American Army officers. I have the good fortune to meet, among others, General Spaatz,* head of US aviation; and the famous Blood and Guts, General Patton.* On several occasions, I get drawn into vigorous political discussions about France, and I ferociously defend "my general." Blood and Guts facetiously proposes to take me to see General Eisenhower to present my case, and I answer in the same tone that it is President Roosevelt who needs convincing.

In the Brook Street apartment, I also have the great joy of seeing my uncle, Julian Allen.* My mother's brother is currently a colonel in the US Air Force. During the First World War, he enlisted in the French Army at age fourteen and served as a regular soldier. American, but French at heart, he and I get along famously. I had seen him briefly soon after my arrival in London when, in all innocence, we had dinner together. It ended badly when Lieutenant P got wind of it and restricted me to barracks for two days for going out with an officer when I was only second class. With her habitual bluntness, she silenced my protests with the vigorous rebuttal: "Your uncle, my eye! You can't pull one over on me!"

It is the end of 1943, and people are talking more and more about a possible landing in France. Will it take place in the South or in Normandy? Everyone has his opinion. Being superstitious, I don't like these discussions: in my view, the less one talks about it, the more chance it has of happening. Meanwhile, the Allies have landed in Italy. Resistance is stiff, however, and progress is very slow. In the East, Russian armies are approaching Poland.

For a couple of weeks, I've been dragging around with a cold and I feel worse each day. I'm very tired and no longer have my bicycle for transportation. Not long ago, I slipped on a patch of ice and ended up under one of the imposing London buses. I got off with minor contusions and a major fright. But my bike was demolished, and I am at a loss to find a way to hold to my schedule. I finally let Lieutenant Ford know that I have a fever, pains in my chest, and difficulty breathing. She comes to see me right away, even though it's Sunday. She arrives laden with flowers and bunches of grapes. She also brings Doctor Zimmern, the FFL medical officer. He teases me because I keep repeating like a litany, "I have absolutely to go to school tomorrow." He answers: "I don't give a damn! You're not to budge from here until I say so!" He departs with the following words: "Remember you're not in high school anymore. In the army, we don't talk about going to school!" He comes back to see me every day and gives me painful shots of a new drug—probably penicillin—which is not yet in widespread use. I improve quickly and am authorized to return to class the following Saturday.

My illness turns out to be a blessing in disguise. Learning that I have been sleeping in an unheated room open to the elements, Dr. Zimmern gives me a medical certificate authorizing me to live in town until the day of the MMLA final exam. Freed from Lieutenant P's persecution, at last I can study properly with the hope of becoming a liaison officer.

The qualifying exams for the liaison officer corps take place from January 10 to January 14, 1944. There are both oral and written components. For the written, we have to describe the evacuation of a city of ten thousand inhabitants, explain in English the requisition system in France, the British food supply chain, and, finally we have to compare the Allied and French senior staffs.

The oral exam lasts a whole day. The number I have drawn puts me last in line, so I have to wait for hours at the back of the room before I am called to take my place before several examiners. They question me one by one on the functions of French mayors, police, civil engineering, postal service, and then on military subjects such as communications and coding, and the different levels of the British senior command. I don't seem to do too badly.

My permission to live in town having expired, I return that very evening to Moncorvo where my morning household duties await me. I work at Carlton Gardens in the afternoon.

On January 20, we are summoned to appear before the MMLA committee. I wait all afternoon without the orderly calling my name. I didn't know they were following alphabetical order, so the wait causes me great anxiety. By the time I get called to appear before the committee I am on the verge of tears. But they give me excellent news: I rank fifth out of forty-two on the general exam, and second on the military section. What a relief! I am now a second lieutenant!

I return immediately to Moncorvo to pack my things since, as an officer, I am allowed to live in town. My friend Lise has also passed, and we waste no time getting ourselves outfitted in our new uniforms. I go right away to Ross and Pyke, a chic tailor in Hanover Street, where they generously allow me to set up a tab since I don't have enough money to pay until the next payday. We are going to receive 35£ a month, which seems to us a fabulous sum. I also get a warm wool overcoat in a rosy beige with leather buttons. It is very bulky, but is the ultimate in military elegance. Once I am outfitted, I am, shall we say, not unhappy to walk about looking for NCOs to return my salute.

Now I work all day at Carlton Gardens in the liaison section of Commander Merlin, who was one of our course instructors. He is calm and good-humored and particularly nice to me since he and my father went to school together. Along with Lieutenant Ford, I am assigned to formalize the organization and training of the women's section of the MMLA. I also am charged with preparing the texts for the next entrance exam. It pleases me no end to be on the other side of the desk.

Lieutenant Sonia Vagliano in her uniform.

The Mini-Blitz

The blitz recommences in February 1944. Almost every night, German bombers attack London in waves. The bombs fall seemingly at random on numerous areas of the city and its immense suburbs, but mostly on the center of town. Compared to the battle of 1940, this could be called a mini-blitz. Even so, on my now-familiar route to Carlton Gardens, past Piccadilly and St. James's Square, I often observe new damage.

One evening, while we are at Prunier toasting our new rank, plaster from the ceiling showers down onto our table in the midst of a deafening roar. A bomb has exploded in the middle of the street in front of St. James's Palace, shaking the whole neighborhood. The windows at Carlton Gardens are shattered, and we spend the following morning sweeping up glass and shaking dust from our files. One of our classmates was killed and two others wounded. The house of our co-worker, George Zarifi, was split in two and from the street you can see his clothes hanging from a section of the wall. Using a ladder, we climb up to gather his clothes and are able to reach his bedroom, which was miraculously spared. The housing situation in London is so dire that he continues to live in this truncated house.

Some evenings, we watch the air raids from a roof or balcony until the furious whistling of a civil defense warden forces us to go inside. To us, a roof doesn't seem more dangerous than any other place since where the bombs fall seems totally a matter of chance. And from on high, we witness an incredible spectacle: the silhouettes of the roofs and steeples are etched against a fiery sky, streaked with the beams of air defense searchlights. At times we see an enemy plane as if momentarily immobilized in the searchlight beams before being shot down. When this happens we applaud like spectators at a sports event. The deafening noise is then followed by an eerie quietness when the rumble of the bombers and the scream of the sirens go silent. After one of these evenings of what looks like fairy-tale fireworks, we learn that ninety German bombers had flown over the city. The toll of eight enemy planes destroyed seems to us a paltry number, but it must not be since, little by little, the bombing raids diminish in intensity and finally occur only rarely.

During the mini-blitz, we continue to go out often, and I begin to discover London by night: restaurants and bars where the music has the effect of insulating us totally from the outside world. Londoners are still using some of the tube stops as air raid shelters, and, on our way home at night, we often have to step over the bodies of the people sleeping there.

To us, the atmosphere is friendly and cordial. We go bar-hopping in a group, mostly in Allied military clubs where we meet officers from all the countries of occupied Europe. At night, London dances, sings, and has a good time. But this life, at the same time gay and tiring (since we have to work all day), will not last long.

Training. March–April 1944

The women's section of the liaison corps is being organized. At the beginning of March, a new head is appointed, Captain Claude de Rothschild.* This energetic and resourceful woman has the gift of making herself obeyed and loved at the same time. Thanks to her, we quickly become a unified group.

My friend from New York, Geneviève Tissot, joined us in December after being posted in Algeria for several months. She also did Moncorvo, Guildford, ATS, and the officer's course. We now share lodging and are following the same program. The second part of our liaison officer training is scheduled for the beginning of March. The practical part of the instruction is wide-ranging and, at times, surprising. We work in kindergartens, birth clinics, hospitals for children traumatized by the air raids, canteens in working-class neighborhoods or factories, and in a laundry. We are given courses in child care, first aid, and nutrition. We visit hospitals, including the famous center at Roehampton where amputees are fitted with prostheses. At the end of the training period, we spend almost two weeks in the Ford factory at Dagenham, where we learn about the operation, maintenance, and repair of British Army vehicles. Always, on our return to London at the end of the afternoon, we finish the day with gymnastics or swimming. At the end of March, fifteen of us are sent to Wales so that we can learn on the spot about the workings of the Citizen's Advice Bureau, which furnishes practical information and emergency aid to people evacuated from bombarded areas.

In the evenings, there are lectures by American and British officers and, more often, by members of the FFL and the French Resistance. We are particularly impressed by Lucie Aubrac,* who has an advanced degree in history and served as a member of the provisional government assembly in Algiers. This well-known member of the Resistance speaks to us about clandestine operations and the organization of the

General de Gaulle and Colonel Renouard review French volunteers. London 1944. (Press Agency Limited)

CNR (Comité National de la Résistance) in a manner that is at once lively, inspiring, and amusing. Her bravery, charm, and intelligence leave an indelible memory.

At the beginning of April, we are sent in pairs to spend several days in the country with the Girl Guides. We camp out in tents with a group of girls fourteen to fifteen years old. It brings back memories of my own scouting days, and my friend Monique Boncenne* and I take part in the games, races, hikes, and the evenings singing around the campfire. Even though it's still chilly, the weather is clear, and this little respite in the fresh air does us a lot of good.

Substituting

From time to time, as a favor, we take a colleague's turn doing work that isn't ordinarily ours. Most often, it's weekend guard duty at Moncorvo or Carlton Gardens. But sometimes it's more interesting, like the time I replace Lony Bouvier, a member of the FFL, who is about my age. He lost an arm at the battle of Bir Hakeim and has just been made General Koenig's* aide-de-camp. I'm a bit nervous about spending the day with the hero of Bir Hakeim, especially since he has the reputation of being tough on junior officers. It's Sunday, and I'm supposed to drive the general to a lunch in the country. When I introduce myself, he doesn't seem very pleased, and it occurs to me that Bouvier forgot to tell Koenig that he was going to have a female driver. As soon as he gets into the car, he closes the partition separating the driver and the passengers. I concentrate on managing an English car, which I have never driven before. On top of that, our itinerary has not been worked out in any detail. By luck, I make it through the baffling London suburbs without a problem. But then I get lost in the little, winding country roads outside of town and panic when I realize that, after a third U-turn, I'm back where we started a quarter of an hour before. When a very large American car sporting a general's flag passes me, I decide to follow it, hoping it's going to the same place we are.

A look in the rear-view mirror reveals that the general, who had been calmly reading the newspaper, is beginning to look at his watch with some impatience. Minutes later, however, still following the American car, we pull up in front of a superb country house. I just hope it's the right one! In luck! It is! Sighing with relief, I open the door for Koenig, who orders me to wait for him. Even though I'm drenched with sweat from being so nervous, I'm delighted to have gotten to our destination without his realizing the risk he was running with a novice driver who had never before driven on the left side of the road.

After a few minutes, worn out by all my anxieties, I fall into a deep sleep. Someone shakes me awake. It's the imposing butler who greeted us at the entrance. He invites me into the kitchen for a cup of tea. The other chauffeurs of various generals and colonels are seated around a large table. As the only woman, I'm given a warm welcome. We chat pleasantly until, one by one, we are called back to our cars. The return to London goes without a hitch, and, as I drop the general off at his hotel, I realize with some disappointment that the hero of Bir Hakeim spent the entire day without saying one word to me.

Another time, I agree to replace one of Boislambert's* secretaries for several days. Although I admire the colonel for his prestigious record, he is not an easy boss. He changes in a moment from being friendly and charming to being brusque and tense. It's not always easy to figure out what mood he is in. One day he bawls me out for taking too long to find a file; another for using an "unmilitary" style in his official correspondence. These reproaches don't really bother me, and when my substitute days are over, he asks me to remain on his staff.

At about the same time, I'm offered a job with Radio London. I decide to decline both offers because I don't want to risk being stuck in an office when the day of the big landing comes. Before I leave Boislambert, in a moment of optimism, he promises to look me up when we are in France for the liberation of Paris. His promise will be kept.

Wimbledon. May 8–June 18, 1944

The purpose of the Civil Affairs Staff College is to instruct British officers on how to cooperate with the local civil authorities in France. We are placed with a group of impressive officers of the ATS who are clearly older and higher ranking than we are.

At Wimbledon, we enjoy the unexpected luxury of having single rooms, served by women orderlies. The orderlies wake us in the morning with a cup of tea, take care of our uniforms, polish our shoes, and clean our room. It's like living in a palace! In addition, the Staff College is surrounded by a superb English garden where, when the weather is nice, we study stretched out on the grass, surrounded by rhododendrons. The lecture halls and the break room recall a traditional English Club. Even with all these amenities, which pleasantly mix military and university life, the regulations and schedules are very strict. The subjects we study in our classes include French administration, public services, organization of refugee camps, systems of supply, and, finally, practical problems resulting from invasion and liberation. Monique and I work very hard, trying to outstrip the English officers. We are subjected to countless oral and written exams and tests, usually unannounced. Women take the same courses as the men except for some hands-on exercises in which we are taught how to construct an open-air kitchen and how to prepare meals for the whole school.

The V1

On June 13, the weather is particularly beautiful, but since it is hot in the tin-roofed prefab where we have our class, the instructor suggests that we continue outside. Just as we are going out, a strange roar above us makes us look up. At first we don't see anything. Then we catch sight of a small airplane that appears to be advancing at a very slow speed. One of the officers says it is a plane guided by remote control. A few moments later, the airplane motor cuts off, and we hear a loud explosion. It is the first V1 over England: a German secret weapon named for its purpose—Vengeance (*Vergeltung*). On the following days, London lives under the threat of the V1s, which explode anywhere, anytime. We learn that you need to count to ten after the motor stops. If you get past this fateful number, you know you are safe. Even though they carry heavy explosives—one V1 can blow up a five-story building—these missiles, popularly called buzz bombs, cause less damage than the bombardments. They nevertheless create a kind of obsessive dread in the population of London who fear that other more numerous and more powerful death-dealing weapons will follow the V1. The British response follows swiftly: chase planes knock out the V1s over the Channel while immense metallic nets suspended from dirigibles protect the city. While I was in London before returning to Camberley, I barely escaped a V1 while I was running to catch a bus at Victoria Station. Fortunately the V1 was struck and smashed to pieces fifty yards from where I was.

During our last days at Wimbledon, we wonder anxiously whether we will ever be able to put into practice what we have learned. We're directly affected by the conflict between General de Gaulle and the Allies, in particular the president of the United States, over the administration of liberated France. This critical problem has become the unique subject of discussion among ourselves and with the British officers. In brief, what is at stake is the question of whether liberated

France will be governed by commissioners of the Republic appointed by de Gaulle and his provisional government or whether American military command will impose its control.

President Roosevelt, who has never forgiven France for its defeat in 1940, intends to subject France and the other European occupied countries to US administration. The reason most often advanced for this is military. According to the Americans, they will need to impose martial law to facilitate ongoing military operations. In their view, French public opinion is unknown and can be ascertained only when the entire country is liberated and free elections are held.

The French position, as advanced by de Gaulle, is that 90 percent of the population supports the Resistance movements, which have already provided a massive and effective assistance to the Allies. The French would not understand why they would be treated as an enemy rather than as a friend.

The English media generally defend the French position, citing the first reactions of the populace to the Normandy beachhead and also the triumphant welcome accorded de Gaulle when he entered Bayeux on June 14.

Roosevelt's refusal to recognize de Gaulle's provisional government is causing great confusion among the French and might even cause serious internal unrest, given the importance of the Communists in the Resistance. American propaganda tends to portray de Gaulle as a potential dictator even though all his actions and speeches since 1940 have promoted the liberation of France and the defense of French interests.

The American attitude is repellent to us. We don't understand the motives of Roosevelt and attribute them to a personal dislike for de Gaulle or to hidden economic considerations. Almost all of the British officers share our point of view and calmly predict that things will turn out in our favor. The European governments in exile, including the Belgians, Polish, and Czechoslovakians, all recognize the French provisional government. In fact, it is in their own interest to do so since their future also depends on this position.

Camberley. June 20–26, 1944

Back at Camberley, we are not surprised to find our comrades extremely upset. Dark rumors are circulating: the MMLA will not be sent to France as long as the provisional government is not recognized; if things don't get sorted out soon, we will be sent to Algiers. The BBC has announced that female military will not be sent to France until sixty days after D-Day.

Only a few male officers have been sent on special assignments connected to the Commissioner of the Republic, François Coulet,* installed by de Gaulle when he visited Bayeux on June 14. We try to be philosophical and prepare ourselves to wait patiently for many long weeks. But on June 26, to the amazement of everyone and to the consternation of the male officers in the MMLA, the women's section receives the order to leave for France. We are to come to the aid of the civil population in refugee camps.

Part 2

Normandy. France.

After eight months of training in England, the MMLA teams were sent to active duty in Normandy exactly two weeks after D-Day. Massive planning for dealing with the anticipated refugees in Normandy had already taken place at high command, and five hundred officers had been transferred to the American First Army Civil Affairs detachment. Although officially members of the Free French Army and therefore subject to French military command, the MMLA team in Normandy were assigned to American G5 units. Along with the welfare of refugees, one of the main concerns of the Allied command was to keep the main roads free of civilians so that the military could circulate and pursue their operations freely. In a sense, then, the camps were established not only to care for civilians but also as a support to the Allied military.

Vagliano's team of four was sent to Fontenay, the first refugee camp in Normandy, which had been set up only ten days previously. Her three-week stay at Fontenay was marked by an unfortunate incident, occasioned in part by her inexperience and naiveté, involving a group of prostitutes billeted at the camp. Their eventual transfer to a Resistance group and the harsh handling they received—having their heads shaved—foreshadowed the post-Liberation treatment of thousands of women accused of being collaborators for sleeping with the enemy.

At her next post in Cavigny, lacking the male driver supposedly assigned to each MMLA team, Vagliano took on the task, a dangerous activity, as evidenced by the many "adventures" she recounts. Also at Cavigny, at the end of July, Vagliano experienced one of the most horrific friendly fire incidents of the war.

During Operation Cobra, the first major Allied break-out campaign in Normandy, 111 Allied military were killed and 490 wounded by the two thousand bombers heading up the operation. Among the killed was a three-star general, Leslie J. McNair. Following Operation Cobra, Vagliano witnessed at firsthand the unbelievable destruction that had been caused by the Allied bombardments when she visited St-Lô, a town that lay in utter ruin.

Vagliano's burgeoning romance with a young airman also ended tragically, as did the life of their commander, Colonel Chandon. Finally, Vagliano's experiences in Normandy ended with the bizarre attempted kidnapping of herself and an MMLA colleague by a determined French Militia member who was probably collaborating with the German SS. In danger for their lives, Vagliano and her colleague took their kidnapper prisoner after a hair-raising journey through what was called "the corridor of death" in the Falaise Pocket.

❖

We Return to France

On June 28 at six o'clock in the morning, we leave Camberley forever. There are sixty of us under the command of Captain Claude de Rothschild. We are packed into an English Army truck. Dawn is just beginning to break.

British security compels us to change trucks and trains several times. We each have a suitcase and a bedroll. Bad luck has placed Monique and me in charge of all 120 pieces of luggage. In spite of all our efforts, several items get lost at each transfer. Fortunately, when we arrive at Newhaven, we still have the captain's luggage, our own, and the trunk with the company administrative papers.

We unload directly onto the pier, which is seething with activity. There are ships of all kinds being loaded with men and matériel. We launch onto the pier two by two. When the Tommies see us, they whistle and wave. One of them shouts, "The war must be over! They're sending the girls!" After ten minutes we halt in front of a kind of launch that seems minuscule. It's the famous British landing craft, LCI, number 384. In single file, we climb down into the hold on a narrow metal ladder. The ones who get down first pile up on the bunks that line the sides of the hold; the rest of us perch on our luggage. At the back of the cabin, we discover a small kitchen where we heat up our cans of C rations. We are not authorized to go up on deck until after we have left port, so we face a long wait in this confined space. Our boredom is mercifully broken, however, by the quasi-miraculous arrival of all our lost baggage. When night falls, we finally set out. As we leave the protected waters of the port, the sea becomes increasingly turbulent.

The small, crowded space we occupy in the hold soon becomes unbearable. We try to sleep; many get seasick. Monique and I go up on deck where we feel as if we're in another world: the night is clear, the stars are bright, the wind is mild, and even the sea seems calmer. We take a big breath of the sweet salt air. The only sound is the steady rumble of the engines and the lapping of the waves against the hull. We stay still for a long moment, watching the dark waves burst into white spray as they strike the prow. From time to time, in the distance, we see the sky light up. They are fighting on the coast of France while here everything is quiet and calm.

Even though it is turning cold, I prefer to stay on deck since I know it will be impossible to sleep on such a night. A young Royal Navy lieutenant we had been chatting with earlier, lends me his heavy coat. To my great surprise, he then shows me what course to follow and puts me at the helm. After a few moments of consternation, I am quickly reassured by how easy it is to maneuver the steering mechanism and mercifully forget the explosive mines that might surround us. The lieutenant dozes, stirring now and then to make sure I'm holding to course. He murmurs, "Good girl, carry on," and goes back to sleep.

If only this extraordinary night would never end. A cool, wet wind rises and makes my face tingle; the sound of the waves against the hull lulls me sweetly; the hum of the engines soothes me, and I think I have never seen such a vault of beautiful bright stars. As light begins to creep into the sky, however, I am flooded with anxiety. The coast of France is heaving into view.

At this precise moment—the one we have been dreaming about for so long—instead of feeling the great excitement that should accompany significant events, I am overwhelmed with panic. The sea turns gray. The beautiful coast of France is now an ugly beach laden with military matériel. I am suddenly paralyzed by the thought of the dangers that await us. One question keeps swirling in my mind: "What in the world am I doing here?" Fortunately, there is no time for soul-searching. The thundering voice of Captain Rothschild cuts through my reveries. I get up and manage something like a salute. She is furious: "Where were you during the crossing? Why didn't you come down to help take care of your sick comrades? You could at least have made tea!" I don't respond but rather turn to look after the baggage, which they are beginning to load onto rafts since the launch can't land on the beach.

The temporary pontoon set up for our landing has been withdrawn. I am in water up to my waist. I finally get to the beach; my boots are squelching and spouting water. Our group gathers in a circle around a British naval officer standing in front of a tent. Dressed in a heavy navy blue sweater and with a pipe in his mouth, he is engaged in an animated conversation with Captain Rothschild. We learn that he is very upset because he was expecting sixty liaison officers—not sixty women. He opines that the high command is going bonkers and that de Gaulle has been up to his old tricks again. He goes on to say that if it were up to him, we would all be shipped back to England. Captain Rothschild finally persuades him that it would be no harder to transport sixty women to Bayeux than it would be to transport sixty men. He calms down, even becomes affable, and makes a little welcoming speech that is gracious and witty. Then he offers us tea. Soon we climb into several large open trucks and set out for Bayeux in a cloud of dust that sticks to our wet clothes.

Bayeux

June 28–July 3, 1944

Leaving code-named Juno Beach near Graye-sur-Mer, we follow dusty, narrow lanes lined with hedgerows. We are agreeably surprised to find practically no destruction in the villages along the road. The inhabitants run out to greet us waving handkerchiefs and little flags. We respond to their welcome with joy.

When we reach Bayeux, we have to advance slowly because the streets are clogged with military vehicles, British soldiers, and beaming civilians. French, British, and American flags flap cheerfully in the breeze and create a festive atmosphere in the city. Piled in the trucks with our helmets on, people think we're British soldiers and shout "Welcome!" in their best English. One little boy, who has climbed up on one of the trucks, discovers our real identity and shouts to the crowd: "They're women soldiers! They're French!" Everyone presses around us to shake our hands and speak to us. The trucks are forced to stop because of the crowd. Someone shouts "Vive de Gaulle!" We set out again after this warm welcome and make our way to our destination: a huge convent behind the cathedral.

We are lodged in the Little Seminary, a misnomer because in reality it is an immense, magnificent eighteenth-century building. Dragging our gear, we cross an overgrown lawn bordered by scruffy rose bushes and strewn with tables, broken beds, packing cases, and other abandoned objects. We go up a stone staircase and are greeted at the top by a large statue of the Virgin Mary.

After we deposit our gear, we are told to clean up the place. Not a small task! Like all the other venues we later occupied, this one has not been touched since the Germans hurriedly evacuated it. We are surrounded by dirt, rubbish, and rubble of all kinds. We work until

Bayeux. MMLA teams move into the Petit Séminaire. June 1944.

nightfall, burning trash, carrying refuse away, cleaning, scouring, and polishing. We regret bitterly that we haven't brought any brooms, mops, cloths, or any of the other cleaning equipment we sorely need.

Our cleaning duties are interrupted by darkness. We set up sleeping quarters in a large room on the second floor and soon have our camp beds installed. Even though I am wiped out with fatigue, I still have to try to find a way to make my clothes presentable for the next day. Ironically, it is my suitcase that has ended up being lost, and the only skirt I have is the one I've been wearing since the landing on the beach. The dried salty water has stiffened it, and it is full of dust.

The only obvious water source is the fountain in the courtyard. But since we are not allowed to go out there after curfew, I have to find something else. After looking about, I find a large shell-shaped basin filled with holy water. It seems a little sacrilegious, but I use it anyway! I wrap up in my raincoat and put my clothes in the stoup to soak ... and promptly fall to sleep lying next to it. Wakened by the cold in the middle of the night, I wring out my clothes and spread them out between my bedroll and my cot, hoping they will dry.

It's very hard to get up the following morning at 5:30. After putting on my clothes, which are still wet, I am ordered to help prepare meals. At the foot of the statue of the Virgin Mary, we set up an oven using bricks as we were taught at the Wimbledon Staff College. We are surprised and pleased to see that the chimney actually draws very well.

Several days go by while we are busy with our cleaning and cooking duties. We get English Army rations and exchange cigarettes and chewing gum for Camembert. In order to leave the seminary, we have to apply for a special permission, and, as this is rarely granted, we begin to feel a little like prisoners in the first liberated city of Normandy. We would very much like to be free to walk about and talk to people. But the enemy lines are only six kilometers away, and we can hear the nonstop booming of artillery. From time to time, the noise increases; sometimes it diminishes, but it never stops altogether. At night, the sky is lit up by bright flashes. After a while, we don't even notice.

Several days later, we learn that our group is going to be split up into teams of four. Each one of these teams will be attached to the Civil Affairs unit of either the British or American Army. We will be responsible for refugee camps, and each team will have a small Peugeot truck at its disposal. Fortunately, we are familiar with these vehicles since they were used in our mechanics' training at Camberley. Although they have the justly earned reputation of being indestructible, they are nevertheless unwieldy to drive. To my great joy, I am assigned to the same team as my friend Geneviève. We are to be attached to the American First Army.

The last day in Bayeux is memorable. In the morning we attend high mass at the cathedral. The church is crowded with civilians as well as military. As the mass goes on, everyone is caught up in an intense fervor. Believers and nonbelievers alike give thanks and invoke divine protection for our little bridgehead and for the liberation of France.

During the afternoon, summoned by one of our female officers, I learn that I have been invited to dine with Colonel Chandon.* She visibly disapproves of the honor that has been extended to me and reminds me to look my best (which is difficult since my uniform has never recovered from being dunked in seawater).

Elated, I announce the news of the invitation to my friends. They are delighted for me because we admire Colonel Chandon unreservedly. Along with Colonel de Boislambert, he commands the MMLA in France. Even though he has a prestigious history in the military and is the companion in arms of General Leclerc, he treats us with friendly respect, which is unusual for a superior officer. He carries out his current duties with something approaching passion and doesn't seem to regard it as a come-down to be commanding a group of women. His enthusiasm inspires us so much that we later felt less afraid undertaking the formidable tasks facing us.

My friends bend over backwards to help me look presentable for this important evening. With the skirt of one, the jacket of the other, the starched shirt of yet another, and a nearly professional coiffure provided by yet a fourth, I am ready to face the evening. Leaving the seminary, I run into the officer who had relayed the invitation several hours earlier. I salute her, and she returns my salute, but it is clear that she doesn't recognize me. Reassured by this measure of my transformation, I confidently enter the restaurant at the address I have been given. I go up to the second floor and find a small, smoke-filled room where a half-dozen officers have gathered around Colonel Chandon. They are drinking champagne, and when I come into the room, they all rise, glass in hand, to wish me a happy birthday! I am totally astonished since I had thought that the dinner invitation for this particular evening was just a lucky coincidence.

The evening is convivial, and I do justice to the food, wine, and champagne. After our usual dull military rations, it is a real feast.

Our First Camp
Fontenay-sur-Mer

July 3–15, 1944

The following morning we leave Bayeux. I am driving one of the Peugeot trucks. Beside me is Geneviève, who is the leader of our team, and, under the canvas cover in the back with all our gear, are Louise and Yvonne. Our first mission makes us feel both daring and nervous. Are we going to be up to the job? What are we going to find at our destination?

Our first assignment is at Fontenay-sur-Mer, a small village about ten kilometers from Valognes. En route, we are supposed to follow an American Army truck loaded with equipment for the camp. At the beginning I have no trouble following the truck, but then a fine rain begins to fall. The road becomes muddy, slippery, and, at places, totally broken up. The windshield wipers are not working very well, and I have more and more trouble keeping up with the American truck.

At Isigny, we are halted by an MP who informs us that the bridge at Carentan is under enemy fire. We are to keep a distance of one hundred yards between us and the lead truck, start moving when we get the signal, and then cross the bridge going fifteen miles an hour. We are so preoccupied with calculating the equivalences of yards and meters, and miles and kilometers that we hardly notice that we have passed through the danger zone until the MP at the other end of the bridge drops his signal he is so surprised to see us there.

At last we turn into a long drive lined with linden trees and arrive at the front entrance of the château de Franqueville. In the large entrance hall, there is no furniture; only two typewriters, a field telephone, and a pile of khaki backpacks strewn on the floor. A door opens and several officers come in. With them is a young captain with a shaved head, wearing an American paratrooper insignia. He is the commander of the unit. For several minutes, in slang laced with grunts and swear words that are hard for us French to understand, he rants against the army, the refugees, and us. I finally understand that he was expecting a team of men and that he is not at all pleased to find a bunch of women, especially a bunch of kids like us. He goes on: the army has stuck him with eight hundred DPs and refugees, he doesn't know what to do with them, and, on top of all that, the morons don't even speak English! When he stops for breath, Geneviève says, "We are here to take care of them. That's our job. Now, if you will please just show us where to stow our gear, we will get to work."

We leave our gear in an empty, windowless room on the ground floor and set out to reconnoiter. Near the chateau we find several barracks and outbuildings set up by the Germans for foreign workers. It is in these that the crowds of DPs and refugees have sought shelter. The majority come from the region, but there are also Italians, Spanish Algerians, and a hundred or so Russian women.

As soon as word gets around that we are French, everybody wants to talk to us to get news. Our first surprise comes when we realize that these poor DPs and refugees are much more distressed by the lack of news than they are by their physical discomfort and scarce rations. We can give them some general information about the progress of military operations, but they have more detailed questions that we can't answer about the advance of the Allies, the damage to individual villages, and the duration of their confinement. We try to reassure them, note down their names and questions, and, with our beginners' optimism, tell them that the camp will be set up the next day. When we finally finish our inspection several hours later, it is still raining, we are ankle-deep in mud, it's cold, and night is falling.

We go back to the chateau. A GI is guarding the entrance. He salutes us, and then says with a big smile, "It's good you're here to look after the refugees." Then, nodding toward the chateau, adds, "They wouldn't do it. Good luck!" His words of encouragement warm our hearts, and we feel reinvigorated as we go up to our room on the second floor. By the light of a flashlight, we take off our wet clothes and set up our beds in a circle in the center of the room. Rolled up in our blankets, we dine on bread, salami, camembert, chocolate, and—miraculously—a bottle of good wine, a present from an admirer of Yvonne's in Bayeux.

Our first objective in the morning is to reorganize the barracks according to categories: families from the same village, single women, single men, and foreigners. After that, we will take whatever measures are necessary to supply food and to ensure the smooth operation of the camp.

After a few hours' sleep, we wake up at first light. We are now able to see that we are housed in a large, well-proportioned room, but one that has seen better days. The marble chimney surround is cracked; the woodwork is chipped and peeling; and large strips of plaster are hanging down from the ceiling. There are moldy splotches under the windows that are broken, and a part of the parquet flooring has apparently been torn up to be used for kindling.

Geneviève tries unsuccessfully to find the captain to tell him about our plans. But it seems he is still asleep. We decide to go ahead anyway.

It is not an easy thing to regroup, move, and quarter eight hundred people and their baggage. Some refuse to budge because they say they are fine where they are, or they don't like the people we have assigned to the same area. In one case, we try to move a family of eight who refuse to sleep under the same roof with another family from the same village with whom they have been feuding for generations.

With the help of many gestures, we attempt to make ourselves understood in French, Italian, or in our bad German. When our gentle persuasion doesn't seem to work, we resort to stronger tactics: we shout, shove, and give orders. At the end of the afternoon, everyone has a roof over his head. For each group, we appoint a leader who is in charge of seeing that the barracks are cleaned and kept in good order. Finally, we want to establish a census of the refugees with the help of the records provided by Civil Affairs. We have trouble getting access to the records, however, because they are stored in the captain's quarters. After he awakes, he seems to be in a better mood and assigns several soldiers to help us distribute blankets.

While we are getting everyone settled, Yvonne, who is our food supply specialist, has had an outdoor oven constructed in front of the barn we intend to use as a mess hall. We see her on her way to look for food in the captain's jeep, followed by a truck. If we aren't quick to provide meals, our guests will scatter in the countryside in search of food.

Yvonne is a tall, slim, attractive brunette. She has the gift of remaining calm in all circumstances. She works in the kitchen wearing a huge khaki apron, blowing on the coals, and stirring vast steaming kettles without ever getting a hair out of place. She always has plenty of volunteers, who are captivated by her smiling, quiet authority. She manages calories, kilos, and pounds with no trouble and knows exactly how many sacks of flour, potatoes, dried beans, etc. are needed to feed a given number of people each day. That very evening, we serve bread and a thick, hot soup. Even this modest meal is welcomed by the DPs and refugees, many of whom have not had a hot meal for a long time.

In addition to driving and maintaining the Peugeot, I am in charge of information and entertainment. I'm also supposed to supervise several of the barracks and to take care of whatever problems arise. We are up at dawn each day and rarely get to bed before midnight, often even later.

Our relations with the American officers are correct but cool. We are invited to their mess, but go there only occasionally when we are very hungry; generally we don't have time to sit down for a proper meal. We make friends with the local priest, who resembles an El Greco painting. He comes often to visit the camp and, on Sundays, he celebrates mass outside, standing at the top of the stairs to the entrance of the chateau. The captain, who is Irish-American, is always the first to take communion. He is somewhat less disagreeable than the first time we met him, but he is still not friendly. Our relations with him are generally restricted to receiving orders about restrictions: curfew, off-limits, non-fraternization between military and civilians, etc. His principal activity is the daily morning inspection of the camp. Accompanied by Geneviève, he inspects each refugee barracks as if he were at Camp Dix. Everybody, including pregnant women, has to stand at attention. The flimsy buildings shake when he enters, children cry, and parents are frightened. He seems to enjoy spotting an ill-made bed or running his finger in the corners looking for dust. At the door he turns and shouts, "At ease!" and goes on to the next building. My role is to run around before he arrives to make sure that everything is in order and to reassure the DPs and refugees. I tell them, without really believing it, "He shouts a lot, but he's really a good man." In fact, he has not gotten over having to leave his fighting unit to be in charge of these "flea-bitten" civilians. He soothes his wounded feelings with alcohol. Unfortunately, he is a mean drunk and is in a constant state of hostility. Luckily, we don't see much of him since he goes off in his jeep almost every day with the pretext of looking for food supplies or to try, without much success, to transfer as many DPs and refugees as possible to other camps.

My first task in the morning is to make my way cross-country to an artillery installation, where I listen to their radio. Even with earphones, it is often hard to hear what is said because of the static and the deafening noise of the nearby heavy artillery. Once I have written up notes on the news in French and English, I post them on a bulletin board that I put up near a kind of shack that I have turned into an information office. I hold regular "office hours" when I try to answer any question the refugees might have. I also post information about the camp: hours for the canteen and the infirmary, group meetings, mail deliveries for certain destinations, lost and found, child care, curfew, etc.

We take turns driving the Peugeot to Fontenay-sur-Mer to get bread at the bakery that Yvonne has supplied with flour. We like going to town because the countryside is beautiful, and we feel free, at least for a while, from the worries of the camp.

Every afternoon, we take the children out in a field to play. Sometimes the GIs break the rules and come out with us. The children are healthy, full of fun, and very excited by this new part of their life in the camp. We teach them songs and English games, which they love. One day a tragedy is narrowly averted when I find a little girl playing with a live grenade. I take it from her as quickly and as gently as possible and throw it into the woods, where it explodes without causing any human damage. Various deadly devices like mines and grenades have been left behind by the Germans and are a constant worry. Unfortunately, accidents occur frequently.

Our visits to the barracks are time-consuming and often stressful. Many of the DPs and refugees have endured unbelievable hardships. Arguments and disputes inevitably arise. We do our best to settle them quickly. But the primary cause of tension is the overwhelming anxiety among the local refugees about returning to their homes. Unfortunately, with the exception of a few unusual cases, they won't be able to return in the near future either because of war damage or because their home is located in a war zone. In an attempt to calm their worries, I post a notice on my information bulletin board stating the policy of the Allied armies, which is to repatriate both the DPs and the refugees as quickly as possible following troop advances.

On the first day we numbered the barracks and divided up responsibility for routine inspections. The majority of the barracks assigned to me contain families: one houses an entire village including the priest and the mayor. But I also have the Russians and the single women.

The visit to the families is the most trying because they always have a million and one questions. They want news not only from the front but also about the outside world. They ask me about life in England and about the "great men," Churchill, Roosevelt, and, of course, de Gaulle. They want to know if I've ever seen him, what he's like, what he's going to do. I hand out little printed pictures of him and a few precious copies of newspapers like *France Libre*. I am also often asked whether there is a secret understanding between de Gaulle and Pétain, a question that is very surprising to me. Conversely, I am fascinated to hear their accounts of the dark years of the Occupation and regret having to cut them short so I can carry on with my other work.

We all have our favorites who, for one reason or another, have emerged as individuals from the mass of DPs and refugees. The first day of our arrival at Fontenay, I had noticed a rather fat woman nursing her baby surrounded by a brood of young children. Behind her stood a skinny little man dressed in his Sunday best. With him was a toothless old woman with a shawl over her head. When I approached them to get information from them for our refugee count, I realized that big tears were coursing down the mother's plump cheeks. As soon as I spoke to her, she stood up very rapidly for a person of her size and literally threw the baby into the arms of one of her other children. With a resounding "Praise God" she enfolded me in her strong arms and launched into her story. It turned out that the air raids had driven her out of Caen with her children, husband, and mother-in-law. After several days and nights on the road, they were finally picked up by an American truck that brought them to Fontenay. As soon as they had gotten into the truck, however, she realized that her little son, Victor, was not with them. Since then, which was three days ago, she has been trying to tell the officials what had happened, but nobody spoke French and nobody would listen to her. With a final great sob, she cried: "If only we had lost my mother-in-law instead of little Victor!" I tried to calm her by declaring—without wholly believing it—that I would report her missing child to the Americans who would surely look for him.

By a piece of extraordinary luck, he was, in fact, located forty-eight hours later in a neighboring camp. It is my job to go fetch him. The famous little Victor in no way resembles the "magnificent child" his doting mother sees. Small for his nine years, afflicted with a severe squint, he immediately takes a dislike to me because he has been happy with his newfound independence and has no desire whatsoever to be rejoined with his family. I lure him into the truck with candy and chewing gum. During the drive to Fontenay he alternates kicking at the side of the truck and sticking his tongue out at me.

The family reunion is emotional and noisy. After hugging the prodigal son to her ample bosom and covering him with kisses, the mother gives him a good swat for wandering off. Victor begins to howl, his brother and sisters join in, and I take advantage of the general confusion to slip away.

After that, each time I visit their barracks, I have to submit to the effusions of the mother, who adores me, and to the kicks given to me in secret by Victor, who detests me. Since he refuses to speak to me, he always gets slapped, and the visit inevitably ends with his shrieks.

When I leave, I am almost relieved to go to the barracks of the Russian women. After the backbreaking labor they were forced to do by the Germans, life in the camp seems wonderful to them. It is hard for me to converse with them since our only way of communicating is through smiles, gestures, and a few words of German. They never ask for anything and seem satisfied with the food and living accommodations. They don't venture farther than their doorstep except to go as a group to the mess hall, where they do not mingle with the other DPs and refugees. They spend their days taking care of the babies they seem to have acquired during their peregrinations, and in chatting, singing, and coloring eggs and little wooden objects. Whenever I come, they give me little presents. I learn a few words of Russian but my pronunciation must not be very good because when I try to speak, they double over laughing. At the news that they are going to be evacuated to England, they are dismayed and beg me to let them stay because they are happy at Fontenay. I let them know that I will do my best to let them stay but that the decision depends on the American officers.

Originally I thought that the barracks occupied by the single women would cause less trouble than the others, but it didn't work out that way. The women divided themselves into two groups and marked out their separate territories by hanging up a canvas left over from a German tent. They even drew a boundary on the ground with chalk. I start with the group of twenty young women and girls, almost all of them from the local area. They are less pleasant than the other group because they won't stop asking to be transferred out of the barracks. For one thing, they are driven crazy by their noisy neighbors on the other side of the curtain. It is tiresome to have to explain every day that a transfer is not possible, that space is at a premium, that it won't be long until they can move on, etc.

By contrast, on the other side of the curtain, the women have formed a jolly group. They welcome me with open arms, offer me flowers, fruit, cigarettes. They wear short, ultra-tight skirts, junk jewelry, and lots of cheap perfume. After I extricate myself from their effusive welcome, my first action is always to open the windows and to ask them, once again, to go easy on the perfume, which bothers their neighbors. They laugh, shrug their shoulders, and direct impolite gestures at the other end of the barracks. They call me their "sweet little lieutenant," and I can't help feeling a kind of affectionate gratitude toward these unfortunate women who remain cheerful in such distressing circumstances.

The head of the group is a certain Madame H. Tall, plump, and recognizable from a distance by her ample bosom that looks like a combination of a shield and a feather pillow. This imposing, dark-eyed brunette acts like a grand duchess in her chateau. After a time I recognize what their neighbors have already clearly understood: these women from Caen are the working girls from a brothel. When I understand this, I also understand why Madame H is so insistent about returning to Caen as soon as possible. With the Germans gone, she is hoping for new clientele among the British soldiers.

Shortly after installing the women in their barracks, I have to be away for most of a day and miss the commotion in the camp caused when several of the women go into the woods near the American artillery installation with the hope of exercising their profession. After I return to camp, Madame H, all smiles, politely requests permission to follow up that evening in the barracks on some work they had begun the previous day while I was gone. Totally ignorant about what is going on, I naively grant her the permission she requests.

That night, catastrophe strikes. Apparently the news about what was planned has spread like wildfire. Around three in the morning, the camp sentinel reports to his unit commander that the GIs are lined up at the entrance to barracks number 3. From there things go from bad to worse. Geneviève and I are summoned to report immediately to the American captain: "You are the ones responsible for number 3 barracks? And so it's you who gave permission to Madame H to use the barracks as a brothel?"

"Never!" I answer.

Without giving me time to explain, he continues: "I'll never understand why the army send us staff as naïve and idiotic as you! You would do better taking care of the little girls in your parish! What in the world happened? What was in your mind? Whatever it was, Miss, let me inform you that the whole army already knows about this ridiculous affair, and we are a laughingstock and worse. When it got around that there is a brothel in my camp, I haven't stopped getting calls from regional headquarters." Boiling over with rage, he adds, "And I'm expecting at any moment to be called to the First Army HQ."

After that, the women don't dare go out and they keep to their barracks. I stop by to comfort them and bring them food. This continues until we receive the order to take them to Montebourg, a nearby village, where there is a camp run by the French Forces of the Interior for people suspected of collaborating with the enemy. We transport the women, who have to stand up so that we can fit them all into one truck. They are so pitiful that Geneviève and I feel as if we're in the Revolution, delivering condemned prisoners to the guillotine.

Montebourg is almost entirely destroyed. A large French flag flutters above the town hall as we pull up. Waiting for us are several men talking and smoking. Half appear to be military, the others civilians. They all have knives and revolvers stuffed in their belts. It is our first encounter with Resistance fighters who have now been assigned to the FFI. When the women see the men, they begin to wail. Their cries turn to screams when the men treat them roughly as they get them out of the truck.

I go up to a tall bearded man who appears to be in charge. He is standing immobile and silent, hands in his pockets, a cigarette butt dangling from his lower lip. I ask him what's going to happen to the women and request, timidly, that they not be treated badly. Without dropping the cigarette butt, he sneers and mutters through clenched teeth: "It's easy to see, Sweetie, that you weren't around when the Fritz were here."

That is the end of the conversation.

We decide that it is useless to stay around to see what's going to happen. As we are turning the truck back toward Fontenay, we see two men grab one of the women while a third begins to shave her head. The sound of our motor doesn't blot out the poor woman's terrible screams that sound like the shrieks of an animal being slaughtered.

All the officers of the army unit kid me about what happened. I pretend not to pay attention but I am furious with myself for being so dense. Except for the children, all the DPs and refugees are angry and resent me.

It is not long before I get into trouble again. This time Colonel de Boislambert, head of the MMLA, is furious with me for planning a Bastille Day celebration as part of my job as director of entertainment. He is outraged and dresses me down. It is, he says, totally inappropriate—"indecent" is the word he uses—to hold a celebration in the middle of a war zone where people are fighting and dying. Unable to confront the American captain, who is off drinking, Boislambert calls for his driver, hurls himself into his vehicle, and disappears in a cloud of dust.

In spite of his objections, we go on with the planned July 14th celebration. After a mass, races for the children, and other activities throughout the day, in the evening we all gather in a giant barn on the property. The barn is decorated with garlands and flags and portraits of Eisenhower and de Gaulle. The American captain is seated in the front row with other officers from HQ and nearby units. The barn is bursting at the seams, and many spectators who can't get in are watching at the doors.

I go out on the improvised stage and announce that we will observe a minute of silence in honor of those who died during the Normandy landing. I add a few words about the ongoing battles and our compatriots who are still suffering under German occupation. The captain joins me, says one or two sentences in an incomprehensible French, then finishes in English. Everyone applauds wildly. We yield the stage to the volunteers from the camp who have planned entertainment. There is singing and dancing, ending with a French cancan. Finally we all stand at attention for the playing of the Marseillaise and the Star Spangled Banner.

The next day, our team gets orders to go to Cavigny, near Saint-Lô, where we are to set up a forward transit camp. We are pleased to leave Fontenay, especially since it means going to the front with the troops. And maybe, with a little distance, we will be able to avoid the fallout from the bordello affair.

Cavigny near Saint-Lô

July 16–August 15, 1944

Compared to the trip to our first assignment at Fontenay, the drive from Fontenay to Cavigny is easy and pleasant; there is no rain and the Peugeot is purring along. At Carentan, where fighting was going on two weeks ago, we find a sunny, peaceful village. In spite of the frequent stops at MP checkpoints, we make good time. Soon, however, the calm, pleasant countryside changes aspect. We see more and more demolished houses in the villages and dead cows in the fields lying on their backs with their feet pointed skyward. They give off a horrible stench. Our destination is about ten kilometers from the front, which currently stretches in a line from Périers to Saint-Lô. The roar of artillery fire becomes so loud that it drowns out even the noisy Peugeot engine. We finally arrive midafternoon at Cavigny and find a charming, small chateau surrounded by trees and fields.

Our job here is to process the refugees from the combat zone and to evacuate them within twenty-four hours toward Cherbourg, which was liberated by American parachute troops on June 26. Our military unit is already in the process of moving in. We find a group of GIs in the basement gloomily eating their K rations: chocolate, cookies fortified with vitamins, and instant coffee in packets. Our former unit commander has been replaced by another who is quite a bit older. Bald, with a fringe of gray hair, he looks a little like a monk. This is our first impression of Captain Gibb. As the days pass, we realize that in spite of his grumpy manner, he is really an appealing person; he gives us free rein and grants our requests as long as they are presented according to protocol. His only requirement is that we turn in a daily report. In reality, we are a kind of shield for him; officer in the active service, he really doesn't want to know anything about the DPs and their problems because he too regrets that his life in the military has taken this turn. We usually see him only when we turn in our report because otherwise he is closed up in his office or on the road to HQ.

There are already dozens of refugees waiting on the lawn in front of the chateau. While two of our team distribute K rations and water, we look around the property. Hidden in the trees behind the chateau we find several German barracks and, a little farther away, several farm buildings grouped in a rectangle around a kind of courtyard. To our dismay, we discover that everything is in a state of unimaginable filth and decay. There are all kinds of abandoned objects including broken dishes, old farm machinery, and a wrecked piano. But the worst is the acrid odor of dead cows mixed with the disgusting stench of the human excrement that the Germans have left behind everywhere—both inside and outside the buildings.

We spend hours counting and feeding the refugees and spraying them with DDT. There are more than two hundred of them. We organize teams to clean the barracks and the farm buildings and to dig latrines. Louise sets up an infirmary under a tree. The refugees are suffering not only from hunger and thirst but also from sunburn, blisters on their feet, and infected wounds. Most come from the region around Saint-Lô. Fleeing their homes and farms, they were often forced to spend several days hiding in ditches or woods, trapped by artillery fire and by bombs falling from the summer-blue sky. Many traveled for miles, carrying their children and dragging whatever belongings they could manage to take with them. Some were eventually picked up by an American army munitions truck returning empty from the front.

My official job as a driver means that I frequently have to leave camp on various missions. The first assignment is to scout out farms in the area that could provide us with provisions. My job also takes me to St-Jean-de-Daye to the First Army HQ. In addition, I'm often called on as an interpreter to help resolve problems arising between the American military and local civil authorities such as mayors, doctors, and priests. Lastly, my favorite task is to take refugees back home after they get authorization from the camp commander and a permit from the First Army.

Getting around is difficult because the main roads are crowded with fast-moving convoys that we are forbidden to cut through. As a result, we often have to make do with little side roads that form a tangled web and that all look the same. Finding the way is made harder by the fact that there are hardly any road signs, and the ones that are left have all been turned the wrong way to confuse the enemy.

When I'm taking refugees back home, they usually can direct me. But the trip back to camp is not so easy. I develop the habit of stopping every now and then on the way out to mark a tree or rock with blue chalk (like Hansel and Gretel!) so I can find my way back. Even with all my equipment—compass, chalk, maps—I still manage to get lost fairly often.

Since the mines have not all been removed from the roads, we also have to stop often to check suspicious bumps in the road, especially when they are located at the approach to a bridge. While most of the little roads that I take have not been mined, there is another danger: steel wires strung across the road at the height of a rider in a jeep. During the first several days after the landing, quite a few GIs were decapitated. Now, all jeeps have been equipped with an iron bar attached to the hood that cuts through the trip-wires. I don't need this apparatus on my Peugeot, however, since the body of the truck protects the driver and front passenger.

For the first week, our schedule at this forward transit camp is determined by the arrival and departure of the trucks: the arrival of trucks from the front bringing the refugees that we keep for a few hours or a few days at most; and the departure of these same trucks evacuating the other refugees to a camp further back from the front lines. We thought we were overworked at Fontenay. Here we are quite simply overwhelmed. We take turns night and day waiting for the trucks, loading and unloading them, making our rounds in the camp, and trying to fend off the problems and dramas that are bound to occur. Eating and sleeping are a catch-as-catch-can affair. Some days, the boom of artillery seems particularly menacing, it is so close by. But we no longer even notice. We live in a kind of closed world and are oblivious to everything else.

At the end of three or four days, things calm down. The refugees who arrive are less exhausted and, on that account, more demanding. They begin to complain. And I have to admit that in spite of all our efforts, the living conditions and food are barely adequate. At the beginning, they were happy just to have shelter even if it meant sleeping on straw in a barn. Little by little, however, the tone begins to change: "I'm not going to sleep in this pigsty with my family!" We explain, we cajole, we reason with them, and, usually, they end by accepting the situation.

In contrast to the complainers, the majority are unbelievably patient. We even receive generous help from a family who refused to leave, wanting to stay as close as possible to their farm. It's absolutely against the rules to let them stay, but they persuaded us and, since the American commander never visits the camp, we are not likely to be caught. These admirable people help to install new arrivals and, what's worth even more, are able to procure fresh foodstuffs including lettuce, potatoes, eggs, chickens, and even a pig. I take the father with me looking for provisions, and we always come back loaded with food. The commander gets wind of our expeditions and is furious. We calm him down by offering him lettuce and two chickens. It seems he too is sick of K rations and so he decides to close his eyes to our infringement of the rules. Thanks to the help of this family who call us "de Gaulle's girls," the material situation in the camp improves daily. We organize games for the children and, in the evening, the adults gather in groups. They dance and sing. Life seems to be beginning again.

The Landing Strip

In the middle of our camp, right behind the latrines, there is an artillery installation and a long, narrow field used as a landing strip for two Piper-Cubs, called Watch Dogs. The mission of these planes is to monitor enemy movements, to scout out targets, and to report on the firing range of the artillery and the results of the bombardments. We see Watch Dogs all day long rising in the air like giant dragonflies. When they land, the strip is so short that it looks as if the trees are swallowing them.

Landing strip at Cavigny.

Captain Gibb, who seems to prefer prohibitions to directives, has placed the artillery battery and landing strip strictly off limits for everyone. Of course, the off-limits rule is immediately and frequently disregarded.

Soon after our arrival at Cavigny, as I am passing close to the landing strip, I am terror-stricken to see a plane come down so fast that I am sure it is going to crash. But it stops short as if by magic. Looking more closely, I see that they have installed a trip-wire across the strip that catches onto a hook under the plane's fuselage. I begin to return to my work when a voice emerges from the bushes and, in English, asks: "Do you know how to play gin rummy?" Sitting cross-legged under a tree, one of the pilots is serenely playing a game of solitaire. Astounded, I reply without thinking, "Yes," and find myself sitting on the ground facing him, shuffling the cards. He is very handsome, although a bit old (at least thirty), tanned, and with light-colored eyes. He reminds me of a popular movie star. After we play a while, I say, "You're not very talkative."

"Why talk about this mess we're in?" he replies.

We continue to play until the honk of a truck reminds me where I am.

"I have to go."

"Come again, girl."

The next day, I learn that he is called "Professor" by his buddies, so when I arrive I greet him by saying, "Hello, Professor."

"Please don't call me that. My name is Timmy."

"But why are you called Professor? Is that your profession in civilian life?"

"No. My buddies call me that because I don't drink, the funnies bore me, and I happen to read a book now and then. But come on, let's play!"

The following days, we spend less time playing cards and more time talking. Timmy is a born storyteller and he gets me laughing with his tales. By talking about films, theater, and novels, we escape to another world, at least for a little while. Inevitably, these lovely interludes and the emotional tie that is growing between us are brutally interrupted by the events of the war that we try so hard to ignore but that ends up engulfing us.

Visit to First Army HQ

The day after our arrival at Cavigny, Captain Gibb informs me that I have been ordered to appear at the First Army HQ, which is located at St-Jean-de-Daye. I am to report to Major Lewis, who is head of G5, the unit responsible for liaison with civil authorities with respect to displaced persons. The HQ is only ten kilometers away but the traffic on the roads is so dense that I have trouble making my way. As I wait in the long line of vehicles, I become increasingly apprehensive about this meeting. Major Lewis is a Presbyterian minister who has the reputation of being tough about rules and work performance. He is considered a terror by all the members of our unit. He had come twice to Fontenay on inspection tours and apparently was very displeased about the Barracks #3 affair. To top it all off, he is from the Middle West and is known to detest foreigners in general and the French in particular, as well as women in uniform and Roman Catholics, whom he calls "Papists."

An MP stops me at the entrance to the camp. He checks my orders and then calls another soldier to replace him while he personally accompanies me to the major's tent. While we cross the camp, the GIs honk and whistle approvingly. "Everyone is jealous of me," the MP says. "Believe me, it's not every day that we have the chance in this hole to ride with a pretty girl. I'm going to hear about it later it at the canteen!" This raises my morale no end and, by the time I get to the major's tent, I get out of the jeep feeling much more sure of myself.

There are two men in the tent, one standing and the other busy with something on a hotplate. "Welcome, Lieutenant," says the first man. "Thank you for coming so promptly. Usually the women who come here get lost because they don't know how to read a map." I don't answer.

The major goes on: "Given that you are a liaison officer, I assume that you speak English, which is good because I can't stand Frog talk." I still remain silent.

He continues, "Tell me, Missy (later on he would often call me this, especially when he was not pleased), are you deaf and dumb or maybe you just don't understand me?"

"I understand you perfectly well, Sir, but I didn't think your comments required a response. I followed orders to appear here thinking that you would want to talk about our work in the camps and to give us instructions. But if you really want to know, I am perfectly capable of reading a map and driving a truck. I also speak English."

The major bursts out laughing, all the while holding on to his pipe, a permanent fixture clenched in the corner of his mouth. He calls to the other man, "Come over here, Sergeant. Let me introduce you to Lieutenant Vagliano. And bring us some tea. We're going to sit and talk."

We sit down on some wooden crates in a corner of the tent beside a folding table covered with maps and papers. The sergeant serves us tea in fine white porcelain cups. The major is tall and heavy, around fifty years old. With his bushy eyebrows and iron-gray eyes, he looks quite fierce. It's easy to see why he is feared, but for some reason I sense that he regards me in a kindly way. We begin talking, and he expresses surprise that I speak English so well. He says that I have a New England accent and that I could pass for an American.

"How old are you?" he asks suddenly.

"Around twenty-five," I lie with all the assurance I can muster.

"Why did you join up?"

"Because I was in France when the Germans arrived, and I was disgusted to see German soldiers strolling in Paris as if it belonged to them. It would be too long to explain it all, but, in short, they were there in our city, and it was unbearable. As far as signing up is concerned, I wanted to be useful."

"You must be very sure of yourself to imagine that a little girl like you could be useful in this immense war machine! It's a man's war, a brutal war."

The major's comments irritate me no end but I respond as calmly as possible: "Exactly. Your officers and GIs are not capable of looking after a DP camp where most of the people are women, children, infirm, and elderly. Your men don't speak French and they think the work we do is an attack on their dignity as men and soldiers."

"Don't get upset. You must know that since there are not many MMLA girls, there are several camps that get along fine without your precious help."

"That must be a fine mess!" I blurt this out and wish immediately that I could take it back.

"I'm going to surprise you, my little lieutenant, by saying that I rather agree with you. I'm fair play and recognize the enthusiasm and ability of your teams. But that's not what is bothering me. You're women, young women for the most part, in a man's army. It would be much easier for me if the liaison officers were men. You girls are surely going to cause me problems because romantic situations with my men are inevitably going to occur. And in this case, I'm warning you, I will take steps immediately. If I hear of any monkey business in my units, the whole MMLA team will be sent home!"

"The whole team?"

"Yes, the whole team."

"Understood. But as for my team, I don't think you have anything to worry about. Frankly the men in the unit are nothing to write home about."

"This is no kidding matter. What I am asking is a commitment from you on the part of your whole team."

"But I'm not a team leader. Why don't you address this concern to our captain who can then issue orders?"

"I didn't bring you here to get a lecture on military hierarchy. Your officers are far away, and you're here. In my judgment, it is more effective to warn you personally so that you can inform your comrades. I'm counting on you."

"Yes, Sir."

I salute him and head back toward the Peugeot. Standing outside the tent, he calls after me, "Try to cause less disturbance on your way out than you did coming in!"

Fortunately the camp is almost empty, and I have no trouble getting to the main road. I immediately get stuck, however, behind an enormous and bizarre military apparatus. Going twenty miles an hour, I have plenty of time to reflect on my conversation with Major Lewis.

Thanks to my time in the US, I feel that we actually got along pretty well. He annoyed me at times but didn't frighten me. When all is said and done, he seems very human, and I appreciate his ironic brand of humor. In the meanwhile, I can't wait to announce to my friends that I have become the guardian of their morals!

The Refugees Return to their Homes

It is always a joyous event when a displaced family gets to go back home. Those who are staying behind in the camp gather around the ones who are leaving. They hug each other and promise to stay in touch. When they leave, the refugees often give us flowers or little presents they have made. Occasionally two of us can accompany them, but usually, as the driver, I am the only member of the team to go with them.

Goodbyes said, we set out, the father of the family in the front seat to give me directions. The women, children, and baggage are in the back. I am always uneasy about these returns because often we find that their house has been ransacked or damaged by artillery. During the trip, the sight of houses that have been demolished or burned dampens the joy of my passengers, who go silent with worry. Once in a while, as if by miracle, we find their houses and farms intact. But that is the exception.

Six weeks after D-Day, the front between Saint-Lô and Avranches is unstable. With the objective of securing the towns and ports that are communication centers, the Americans have made way along the principal arteries. But in the tangled web of little roads and country lanes, there are still pockets of motorized German units. Some of the Germans attack isolated US groups; others are just trying to get back to the main body of their army. Knowing that the Americans occupy various localities around Cavigny, I don't even suspect that there are any Germans remaining in our sector. My ignorance almost costs me dearly.

At the very beginning of our stay at Cavigny, after I dropped off a family at their farm, I lose my way in a dense woods. I attempt to retrace my steps back to the farm where I dropped off the refugees but realize I am going in circles. I stop and try to get my bearings with the help of a compass. With some difficulty I manage to turn the truck around on the narrow little road I am on and find a more promising road further on. Thinking I am going in the right direction, I cover several kilometers and finally see some habitations: a farm building, a house, then another. Relieved, I say out loud, "At last. A village. I'm saved!" As soon as I say these words, a man hurls himself in front of the truck waving his arms. I brake as hard as I can to avoid running him down. He leaps to the side of the truck, opens the door, and jumps in beside me shouting, "Quick! To the left!" Instinctively I obey, speed across the courtyard of a farm and go into a barn whose doors are wide open.

I cut off the motor. The man gets out and quickly closes the barn doors. It is dark and completely quiet. I finally decide to get out of the truck, grab my gun, open the door, and step down. I can see the man flattened against the door. It is somewhat reassuring to see that he is rather short and totally out of breath. I try to sound lighthearted as I ask, "What's going on? Is this a kidnapping?" Silence. All I hear is the sound of his breathing, which gradually calms down. He turns, and I sink back as he hisses at me with deep scorn: "Imbecile! The Krauts are still in the village!" I am speechless.

He goes on: "When I heard your motor, I thought the American Army scouts were arriving and I ran out to warn them that a heavily armed German unit is still occupying one end of the village. They have armored vehicles and maybe even tanks. But what in hell are you doing here in this jalopy with flags flying and 'France' written all over it?"

"I am a liaison officer and work in a camp for DPs and refugees at Cavigny. I was returning a family to their farm and got lost. It was really stupid."

"You can say that again! It takes a girl to get lost at a time like this. Come on, follow me to the house. We'll be safe there. If the Krauts had spotted us, they would be here by now."

"You go on. If it's all right with you, I would rather stay here."

"Not on your life. You're coming with me. And leave the gun, it will only get in the way."

He cracks the door and points to a house on the other side of the courtyard. We start out running bent over but go the rest of the way crawling on our stomachs. At the house, we cross through several cellar rooms, climb over a woodpile, squeeze through a narrow opening, and finally fall down hard on a dirt floor. We are in a small cellar room. The only opening is a window with bars that lets in a dim light. In a corner, some sacks of potatoes look like they've been used as a bed; food and bottles are strewn about; a few books.

My companion, who I now see is young and good-looking, gets up and signals me to be quiet. He climbs up on a crate and looks outside. After a few moments he gets down and motions me to get up and look. The window opening, which is level with the sidewalk, looks directly out on the central square of the village. Although nothing much is going on, I am nevertheless shaken to see several German soldiers nearby. I see boots going by on the sidewalk and, in the square, a German leaning over a sidecar. I can hear voices but am able to catch only a few words. When a pair of boots stops just a few inches from my lookout, I get down in a hurry. My companion whispers in my ear, "Don't worry. They can't see us. But just don't make any noise!"

Since we arrived in his hideout, he seems more relaxed, even friendly. He tells me he is a law student in Paris and a member of the Resistance. He has been hiding in this house for several days because the Germans are looking for him. My surprise arrival put him in danger just a few hours before he hoped to be rescued. I now understand the rage he expressed before and try to apologize. He shrugs without saying anything. I ask him his name, and he answers, "Paul." The conversation stops there. He paces back and forth checking on what's happening outside. Time passes very slowly.

The sudden roar of motors makes us jump. Paul turns around and cries out, "They're leaving!" He jumps down from the window, burrows down into the sacks of potatoes, and uncovers a radio transmitter. I can see him talking but can't hear what he's saying. When he finishes the transmission, he carefully covers the radio up again. I ask him if we can go out, but he answers, "Not yet. We have to wait for the Americans to get here. You never know; the Germans could begin shooting or try to set fire to the village."

We wait for what seems a long time. Paul walks in circles, looks out of the window, sits down, gets up again, runs his hand through his hair, asks me for a cigarette. I tell him I don't smoke. He shrugs, and, yet again, I feel useless. At last he stiffens, cocks his ear, and says, "They're here!" I can hear motors too. We go back through the opening, over the woodpile, across the cellars, and up a stairway into the house. We can hear the shutters in the village clattering as they are opened. The streets and the square are filled with GIs and villagers. Already French flags are hanging in several windows.

Wild with excitement, Paul runs out into the street and disappears in the crowd. I am getting ready to go get my truck when the front door of the house opens and a rifle barrel pokes through followed by a GI. The GI looks at me with astonishment and then calls out, "Lieutenant, look what I found!" The lieutenant arrives and eyes me dumbfounded: "Who are you and what are you doing here?" I introduce myself and explain briefly what happened. I ask for permission to leave with my vehicle but he tells me to wait. A Counter Intelligence Corps (CIC) officer arrives, asks some questions, and looks at my papers. He calls HQ to verify my identity.

Suddenly the room is full to bursting. Bottles appear, people toast, they drink to my health as the first to liberate the village. Everybody is talking at once so I can slip out without being noticed. I find the Peugeot where I left it and, with a pass provided by the CIC, return safely to Cavigny.

Interlude

After the onslaught of the first week, the flow of refugees has slowed. For the first time we can take some time out for writing letters, taking care of our clothes and equipment, and doing some personal grooming. I have caught scabies for the first—but not the last—time, and Louise treats me with some kind of sticky cream. Also, over my protests, she cuts my hair down to the scalp. She comforts me by telling me that I'll look just like Ingrid Bergman in *For Whom the Bell Tolls*. But the result is a disaster—my hair looks like it was chewed on by a rat and, to add insult to injury, the ointment has turned it green! I am mortified and furious. I threaten Louise with the same treatment. Our team leader has to intervene to separate us. At least I am able to get some new shoes—the ones I have are held together with string—by trading chocolate and chewing gum with one of the displaced persons for her shoes.

The morale of our unit is high. There is talk of a major offensive ending with a swift march on Paris and German surrender. The quartermaster, Lieutenant Schurr, who is ordinarily very anxious, fantasizes aloud about his heroic entrance into Paris and his future romantic conquests. Others are already talking about their return home and looking forward to seeing their families and sweethearts. Swept up in the general optimism, we think the worst is behind us without suspecting that what we are experiencing is the calm before the storm.

Having heard a rumor that the reconnaissance unit is going to leave, I go down to the landing strip to see Timmy. He is whistling as he works on his plane. He confirms that his group is soon going to be posted near Avranches. He seems so happy to be leaving that it annoys me.

"You seem to be very glad to be leaving."

"Of course I am. The farther we advance, the sooner it will be over. I'll finally be able to take care of serious business."

"Like what?"

"Like you."

"Like me?"

"Come on. We like each other, I think, although with you it's not easy to be sure. Sometimes I think if I were a refugee you'd be more interested in me."

"That's ridiculous. I do my work as well as I can. That's all there is to it."

"An eager beaver, that's what you are. Believe me when I say that in the army it's better not to go all out. The road is long and war is a dangerous game. If I weren't worried that it would end up reflecting badly on you, I would have cornered that idiotic captain who sends you out alone to drive all over the place in a combat zone."

I don't say anything, especially since I have avoided telling anyone about my recent misadventures.

Timmy continues: "One of these days you'll get lost and end up in the arms of the Germans, and do you know what will happen to you in your French uniform and truck draped with flags? They'll shoot you down like they do with the Resistance fighters or they'll send you to a prisoner-of-war camp. Please promise me to stop these absurd expeditions."

"I can't promise you that! If Captain Gibb orders me to take refugees back to their homes, I have to do it. But I do promise not to volunteer for these trips anymore. At any rate, everyone says that we'll be in Paris by the end of the summer."

Timmy frowns and says: "People will say anything. The less they know, the more they talk. A lot can happen between now and then, and I admit I am not as optimistic as you." He leans toward me and takes my head in his hands. I think he is going to kiss me but instead, after gazing at me for a long time, he smiles and asks: "What happened to your hair?"

"Oh nothing. It must be the chlorine in the water. And Louise cut it a little too short. You must think I look really awful."

"Not at all. It's funny, that's all. Don't look sad, I think you're marvelous. When we get to Paris, I'll take you to Maxim's for dinner. You'll wear a gorgeous dress, and we'll dance all night. The next day you'll show me all the monuments and museums."

"And if everything is destroyed the way it is here?"

"You're being a pessimist all of a sudden. It's not like you."

"But I don't know where you'll be. I don't even know your last name!"

"It'll all work out. It will be easy for me to find you. When I'm up in the plane, I'll look down and as soon as I see a group of refugees, I'll dive down, and there you'll be. But seriously, we'd better exchange our military addresses. Come back tomorrow evening and, in the meantime, don't do anything silly. So long, kid." Timmy gives me a friendly pat on the head and goes off.

Bombardment of July 25–26

That night it is very hot. We don't hear any artillery. Lying on my back, eyes wide open, I am startled to hear the drone of a German bomber passing overhead. Almost immediately a violent explosion shakes the walls and loosens plaster from the ceiling. I get up and put on some clothes. I am slowed down by the fact that my helmet, which I use as a washbasin, is filled with soapy water. By the time I leave our room, there is nobody left in the chateau; everyone has gone to the farm where the refugees are housed. The sky in that direction is lit by an immense yellow glow. A bomb has made a direct hit on the barn only a hundred meters from the farm courtyard. There is total confusion. The refugees have run off, but fortunately the damage is not as bad as it looks. We spend the rest of the night looking for the refugees who panicked and fled and bring them back to the camp. They thought they were fleeing to safety but, in fact, they were risking much more crossing the fields, which are still riddled with mines.

It is dawn by the time we get everyone settled and return to the chateau. Just as we are eating breakfast, we hear the dull roar of planes. We run outside to find the sky filled with a giant armada of Allied planes. They look like flying fortresses. They are flying so low that we can easily spot their bomb bays. I have never seen such a sight. The refugees have come out as well, and we all exclaim to one another that this is the beginning of the final attack. Lieutenant Schurr, who becomes especially bellicose when he knows he is not in danger, shouts to no one in particular: "That's it, guys. This time we're going to wipe out the Krauts!"

Once again, he has spoken too soon. We see a bomb fall, then another and another until the sky is full of them. It looks like the planes are laying giant eggs that tumble end over end just beyond the tree line. Fear stirs in the crowd. A GI standing beside me says, "It must be an optical illusion." But the din of the explosions, the shaking of the ground, the shock waves that knock us to the ground and break the chateau windows are not illusions. As if hypnotized, we watch the bombs continue to fall. Then there is only the sound of the planes, and then silence.

The birds are the first to come back to life. Their chirping wakes us out of our trance. The refugees crowd around us asking for explanations that we are unable to give. What is clear is that a colossal mistake has been made—the planes have dropped their bombs several kilometers from their target—and that we have come close to being pulverized. How could they make such an error in full daylight? Speaking through a loudspeaker, the sergeant asks everyone to remain calm and to return to the farm. For the rest of the day bad news continues to pour in, and rumors begin to circulate. In the midst of this chaos, it is hard to tell what is true and what isn't.

The road to Saint-Lô, which runs near the chateau, is filled with all kinds of vehicles: ambulances, trucks, jeeps filled with soldiers, tanks. There is no doubt: this is a retreat! An MP calmly directs traffic while a young officer with a bloody bandage around his head sets up a table beside the road. I ask him what is going on, and he answers,

"Don't worry, Miss, we are not retreating, we are regrouping." Soldiers form a line in front of his table, and he notes their name and regiment and tells them where to report. I bring out coffee and sandwiches while at the chateau they serve drinks and food to hundreds of soldiers. By a lucky coincidence, we had brought in lots of supplies the day before. Most of the men are exhausted and stretch out on the lawn to sleep. Some have minor wounds, which Louise tends to with the help of Jim, the unit nurse.

During the afternoon, soldiers start crowding in from all directions. Most of them have lost touch with their units and ask us where they should go. We learn that the regiment that was supposed to attack after the bomb raid has been decimated: the road they were on was cut in two by an explosion; a general has been killed; a munitions depot exploded; and the Germans counterattacked. One soldier who seems particularly haggard and disoriented grabs me by the arm and says in a hoarse voice: "Get away from here, kid. The Krauts are coming."

Toward the end of the afternoon, I go back to the Saint-Lô road and find the traffic has not abated. A truck loaded with civilians stops. The driver is looking for our camp. I climb up beside him and direct him to the chateau. The refugees on board are wearied by thirst and by the heat and dust of the road. Some are wounded. We do our best to take care of them and move them into the chateau instead of the farm to avoid alarming those who are already there. Meanwhile, artillery is making an infernal noise, and an infantry detachment is beginning to dig trenches in the chateau lawn. We are told that enemy soldiers are close by. We hear gunfire all night long.

The next morning an animated discussion is going on in the mess hall. Lieutenant Schurr asserts that the army has forgotten us. In a grandiose whine, he takes this supposed abandonment as a personal insult. Reminding us that he was drafted in spite of his ulcers and bad eyesight, he declares: "Look at what's happening: we're in the front lines, the infantry is camping out on our lawn, there is gunfire from all directions, and the army doesn't bother to provision or evacuate us. It's a scandal!"

Another officer, the one we call the "Southern Lieutenant," sees in the situation a chance of rejoining his fighting unit and is delighted by the turn of events. He laughs and says, "Don't get upset, my friend, if you knew something about artillery, you would realize that we're not in the front line, we're between the lines." Schurr goes pale, shrugs, and repeats: "It's still a scandal to leave a DP camp in this place!"

"Pull yourself together, old buddy, you can always write to your congressman to complain. And if you go up to the top floor of the chateau, you'll probably be able to see some Germans, and, who knows, when it's all over, they'll give you a ribbon, and you can tell your children all about your exploits. With just a few adjustments to the story you can be the family hero!"

Indignant, Schurr gets up and announces gravely: "I'm going to check our reserves. With all these soldiers to feed, we'll soon run out of provisions. Since we're forbidden to leave the camp, what will become of us? Will we be taken prisoner?"

"Don't panic. Look at our girls. They're not upset. Take a page from their book."

"They're crazy," replies Schurr. "Crazy and witless."

"Thanks a lot, Lieutenant," I respond.

"Oh, excuse me. I didn't see you there."

"Thanks all the same."

Deflated, the lieutenant leaves.

"People say that women are hard on each other, but you were really rough on Schurr. He's really not bad," I say to the Southern Lieutenant.

"Schurr is a crybaby. I want to be transferred out of here as soon as possible so I don't have to deal with guys like him."

The captain, who had remained silent through all this, announces that he has finally been able to get in touch with HQ. We are not going to be provisioned or evacuated. It seems that German soldiers have infiltrated the area around Cavigny, and we are hemmed in on all sides. "So what are we going to do?" asks one of the officers. "Nothing," the captain responds. "The sector is going to be cleaned out. We'll be OK in a few hours."

The few hours turn into two days and nights. The time passes very slowly. Apart from feeding and taking care of the refugees, the only thing to do is wait. I'm worried about the ones we had moved into two houses at the end of a field about eight hundred meters from the chateau. I ask the captain about them, but he says he doesn't have any news and assumes they must still be there. I decide to go check on them.

A GI from the infantry camping at the chateau stops me. I explain that I am going to get some refugees who are in the houses that I point out to him. He warns me not to go there because the end of the field where the houses are located is under enemy fire. I am astonished to learn that the Germans are so close. I still insist because I know that the families there have several young children. The GI tells me that I have to wait for authorization from his lieutenant. When I don't move, he grumbles and goes off to warn his buddies not to shoot at me.

As soon as he is gone, I walk quickly through the tall grass at my end of the field. Then there are three hundred meters that I have to cover crawling on my stomach. My helmet keeps falling down onto my nose, which is very painful. But I arrive safely at the house, which is providentially surrounded by a tall, thick hedge of hawthorns. I open the door and call. No answer. I check from the attic down to the cellar. Not a living soul. Before going back to the chateau, I rest for a few minutes, crouching low in a corner as far as possible from the windows. I start laughing to myself when I think about the posters in the London tube: "IS THIS TRIP REALLY NECESSARY?"

I get back safely and am weirdly reassured to be between the lines; it's as if we were in the calm eye of a storm. The GI is at the same spot, leaning against the same tree. "Where are the refugees?" he asks indignantly.

"Not there," I answer curtly.

"They are probably the ones who passed by here at daybreak. My buddy thought they were Germans and shot at them, but he didn't hit anyone. Lucky for them he's a bad shot. He couldn't hit a football at ten yards."

"Ah," I say, furious. "You and your buddies are quick on the draw."

"OK, you're right. But the important thing is that you got back all right. Someone shot at you, did you know that? My buddies were able to spot the shooter and, from what I hear, they took him down. It was a piece of luck; if you hadn't crossed the field, we wouldn't have gotten him."

"I'm glad to hear that some of you are good shots."

"We're not all top marksmen, including me, but think about it, the Kraut could have hit you if he had had good aim!"

Cavigny is still cut off from the outside world. Captain Gibb isn't even allowed to contact HQ. Wild rumors circulate: the Germans have broken through our lines and are advancing on Cherbourg; they have new rockets like the V1 but more deadly; they are going to start using poison gas; there are German spies among the DPs and refugees; the Allies are giving up and going back to England. It's impossible to know where these rumors are coming from, and in the tense atmosphere at Cavigny we don't know what to believe.

Meanwhile, our stocks are diminishing in spite of the strict rationing imposed by Lieutenant Schurr and Yvonne.

Another giant squadron of bombers has flown over the camp. This time they must have hit their target correctly because the explosions we hear sound far away but the earth still shakes under our feet.

Captain Gibb advises us to wear civilian clothes and gives us cigarettes, chocolate, and canned food to use as a means of exchange. Lieutenant Schurr is irate to see his stocks raided; he has been hovering over them like a mother hen. To kill time we play cards and hopscotch, but the captain, annoyed to see us playing this child's game in front of the chateau, puts a stop to it. We try to read or write letters, but in the strained atmosphere, it is hard to concentrate.

In spite of the off-limits, I go twice to the landing strip. The planes with their wings folded up are hidden under the trees, and several dead cows camouflage the strip. Timmy is playing cards with the other pilot and grumbles about the idiot bombers who managed to miss their target.

The next morning a counterintelligence officer arrives on foot at the chateau. He is looking for collaborators and spies who might be among the refugees. He demands to interrogate them. We propose to be present for the interrogations under the pretext that it is normal for a French officer to do so. The officer doesn't buy our story and proceeds on his own. Around ten in the evening he comes back to the chateau with a man and a woman whom he places under armed guard. He joins us in the canteen where we're playing bridge and announces that he is going to remain in camp until he receives further orders. Unusually closemouthed, he tells us nothing about the capture he has made, and we never find out whether or not they were actual spies.

At nightfall, the GI who was on duty at the field comes in, gun drawn, with three German soldiers. The lieutenant arrives and requests permission to lock them up in the chateau. If things continue this way, our refugee camp will soon turn into a camp for prisoners of war. The German soldiers look like kids dressed up in military costumes. They appear to be so young and harmless that I find myself feeling sorry for them.

The capture of the three German soldiers marks the end of the siege. In several hours the American army reappears in force on the main road to Saint-Lô. We are once again overwhelmed by refugees, who arrive by the hundreds. Since we don't have vehicles to evacuate them, we go out on the road and thumb rides for them in munitions trucks coming back empty from the front. The captain doesn't approve of our improvised system but, unable to provide any alternative, he lets us continue.

Saint-Lô

Saint-Lô is entirely destroyed.

The Germans have left. The American troops have moved on. The pitiful inhabitants who weren't able to get out in time are buried under the ruins. Apparently, however, there are a few hundred people left who are to be evacuated immediately because of the risk of disease. Captain Gibb orders me to load the Peugeot with provisions and medical supplies. I leave Cavigny accompanied by the Southern Lieutenant, who is in a very good mood because he has at last been reassigned to a combat unit.

The closer we get to Saint-Lô, the worse the roads are. I do my best to avoid the biggest holes but our truck gets stuck, and we have to get out to place planks and sacks of potatoes under the wheels. All of a sudden, the lieutenant looks ahead and exclaims, "Good God! There is nothing left!" As we go down a hill approaching the city, in effect, all we can see through a cloud of acrid, yellow dust are the remains of what once was a city: not one house is left standing, only a few fragments of wall, and, on our left, a lake that is not supposed to be there. We soon realize that the lake was formed by the river water, which was plugged up by giant piles of stones and debris of all kinds, forming a kind of dam. The lake covers a whole section of the town. On the surface of the lake we see innumerable black objects floating. When we get near enough, we see that they are bodies.

The stench of death is horrible. We don't see a living soul. There are no vehicles moving about. Finally we see an MP standing beside a jeep. A scarf covers his nose and mouth. He directs us to a high point near the edge of town where he thinks the inhabitants who are left have probably gathered. It's not far but we have a great deal of difficulty getting there because our truck keeps getting stuck, and we have to get out at least a dozen times to clear away the stones and wooden beams from the wrecked houses that block our way. We come at last to a little square miraculously left intact. As soon as we arrive, people begin to appear. Seeing our French flag, they press around us to shake hands and hug us. Everyone is talking at once.

The Southern Lieutenant is delighted to be given a hero's welcome. I go in search of the person I am told is in charge of the civilians and find a tall, thin woman with salt-and-pepper hair. This is Mademoiselle Bertha. Unlike the others, she does not seem pleased to see me. She doesn't say anything, and her silence and cold stare intimidate me. I ask hesitantly what I can do to help. She answers in a brusque and imperious manner: "There is only one thing for you to do, and that is to keep the Americans from evacuating us. We stayed in Saint-Lô during all the bombing raids; the Germans didn't succeed in driving us out, and now the Yanks want to make us leave. We've been hiding out in the tunnels under the Citadel, and now we want to stay here in these houses. All we ask is authorization to remain here and to receive the provisions that you would, in any case, be obliged to give us in your camp."

"Unfortunately, Madam, the decision is not mine to make. The American military ordered me to organize your evacuation. You can't live here."

"Listen to me, Miss. Some American soldiers already tried to get us to leave. I refused and the rest of the group here agrees with me. I asked to speak to a French officer, and here you are. It's your job to persuade the Americans. Our town is destroyed, but we won't leave. This is our home, and we intend to rebuild it. The sooner we get started the better. So go tell that to your chief and be sure to say that we are not going to budge."

"Personally, I understand your position. But let's be practical. Even if we could feed you, we can't furnish safe drinking water. And all the water here is polluted. There is a big risk of epidemic. No high command can take responsibility for that."

"Water is not a problem. There is an artesian well a few hundred meters from here."

"I will try to explain your position, but if you remain here all the inhabitants of Saint-Lô will want to come back, and you'll be overwhelmed."

"But that's exactly what we want—for everyone to come back and share in the work. After so much suffering we don't admit that our city could simply be erased from the map."

With a look of despair, she opens her arms, letting fall the shawl she has been clasping to her chest: "I don't speak English well, but if only I could speak to the Americans myself I think I could convince them. I would tell them what Saint-Lô was like in the old days. Then I'd tell them about the Occupation and the bombs. I lost everything: my mother, my father, my younger brother, my house. And there are many like me. We refuse to leave. A city can't live without its people."

She speaks with such conviction that I feel almost ashamed to have to answer: "You are doubtless right. But an army in the midst of combat can't afford to take feelings into account. The military have to give first priority to security, health, and provisions. I'm afraid that the high command won't allow you to remain in the middle of all these ruins."

Her disdainful look turns me to ice, and I'm almost afraid that she is going to spit in my face. It pains me to have to take the rational point of view in the face of so much suffering and passion. I stammer: "I'm going to do my best for you. I can't promise anything, but I'll try." I leave hurriedly with the feeling that her eyes are burning holes in my back.

During the drive back to Cavigny, I can't stop thinking about Mademoiselle Bertha and her eloquent pleas. I decide then and there to go immediately to the HQ at Saint-Jean-de-Daye to talk to Major Lewis.

Since I had not been ordered to appear, the major is very surprised to see me burst into his tent. I offer my excuses quickly so he doesn't have a chance to interrupt. I then launch into an account—probably incoherent—of the experience at Saint-Lô: the ruins, the refugees, Mademoiselle Bertha. When I stop, out of breath, he reminds me with a stern look: "Lieutenant, in the army you have to respect the chain of command. Your request may be legitimate, but it needs to go through the head of your team and then the captain of your unit, who will pass it on. In future, you must respect . . ."

I take the liberty of interrupting him to respond: "That's all very well in normal circumstances, but this is an urgent problem. To speak frankly, Captain Gibb is slow to come to decisions. I came to see you directly because you need to go to Saint-Lô right away to see Mademoiselle Bertha. If not, for sure a young infantry officer will come along and ship everyone out."

"Thank you, Lieutenant, for telling me what I should do, but I am a very busy man . . ."

"Excuse me, Major. I think I didn't make myself clear. You should go yourself to Saint-Lô and see these people clinging to their city, the city that we have destroyed."

I feel my eyes filling with tears so I turn and leave in a hurry. But the major follows me and, to my surprise, says: "OK. Let's go." We climb into the jeep. Feeling weary and intimidated at the same time, I don't say anything. After several kilometers, the major takes a khaki-colored handkerchief from his pocket and says: "Here. Wipe your face. There's a flask of water under the dashboard." I do as I'm told and only then realize that my face is caked with a thick layer of yellow dust. He looks at me and says: "That's much better. Now, drink the rest of the water." I am in fact extremely thirsty and down the remaining water in one gulp.

We enter Saint-Lô. The major is murmuring to himself, no doubt moved by this abominable spectacle of destruction. We arrive at the square where we find the same group of people who excitedly crowd around the vehicle. I take Major Lewis to see Mademoiselle Bertha and play the role of interpreter. At one point, inspired by the understanding attitude of the major, Mademoiselle Bertha starts beaming and begins to speak in English. I leave them and sit on the front steps of the house to wait. After ten minutes or so, the major comes out and gets immediately into the jeep. We set out. I don't dare question him about what happened. Once we get clear of the debris, he says: "You were right to come get me. Mademoiselle Bertha is a remarkable woman. We'll help her. I told her that her group will be annexed to the Cavigny camp until the Saint-Lô unit moves in and can look after them. Until then, you'll have to get provisions to her on a daily basis."

"Major Lewis, you are terrific!"

"That's the first time that anyone in the military has said that to me," he says with a sardonic half-smile.

Back at HQ, he becomes stern once more: "In future, Lieutenant, you must respect the chain of command and go through channels!" And for the good of his aide who comes running up with what must be an urgent message: "Young people are always in a hurry, Sergeant. Sometimes, they're right..."

Danger! Mines!

While Cavigny was surrounded by the Germans and for several days afterwards, I was pursued by a young farmer from the region who kept after me with heartrending arguments for why I should take him home to his family. I finish by yielding to his pleas and obtain permission from Captain Gibb. Once we are under way, I can't help reproaching my passenger when I realize that the farm is much farther away than he had led me to believe.

After an endless trek on dusty, damaged roads, we stop at a white gate. The farmer, who is riding beside me, cries out for joy and points to a pretty little thatched-roof house in the middle of an apple orchard. The house appears to be in perfect condition and even has geraniums at the windows. The only indication that there is a war on is the presence of two large dead cows near the house. The farmer opens the gate and runs toward the house. I yell after him to stop: "Watch out! Don't go in! The house might be mined!"

I get out of the truck, and we circle the house several times looking for concealed wires. I am just about to open the front door when my companion calls out, "Look, Madam!" It is then that I see an electric wire strung along the ground, hidden by the leaves of a honeysuckle. The wire runs up along a window and into the house.

Mines inspire a holy terror in me. When we were at Camberley, an English mine-clearance specialist taught us how to identify and disarm antipersonnel mines, or, as he called them, booby traps. I was terrified even when I was clearing artificial mines, and just the idea of touching a real one gives me cold chills.

Being a coward, I suggest that we go get a specialist technician at the nearest HQ, knowing full well that this is probably not going to work. The farmer absolutely refuses my suggestion and insists that we deal with the problem ourselves. He was in the war in '40 and never was caught out by the Fritz and is not going to start now. So I go to work with a pair of clippers, saying silent prayers all the while. When I finish and crawl into the main room, my breath is taken away by a ghastly, fetid odor. I see two, then four soles of enormous boots. They belong to two German soldiers who are well and truly dead and in the process of decomposing. My guess is that they were killed by a mine meant for the Americans. We haul the bodies outside and cover them with a tarpaulin.

My farmer friend disappears for a moment and comes back with a bottle.

"Here, take a drink. It'll do you good. You don't look so great. It's good Calvados," he adds sniffing the bottle. "Ten years old. I thought I would never find it again."

He wants me to carry the bodies away in my truck. I refuse absolutely to do this, but promise to alert the Americans at the post in Tessy-sur-Vire. We say goodbye. I promise to come back if I can and, with great relief, head away to Tessy.

On the Vire Road

At Tessy-sur-Vire I stop at the Office of Civil Affairs to turn in the ID tags of the two dead Germans and to explain where they are located. The American officers are very friendly and invite me to stay for lunch. Their mess is in a local inn. The good food and wine quickly make me forget the tribulations of the morning. After lunch, I accompany one of the officers to a forward post where refugees have been gathered together in a field. He wants me to help him communicate with them because it seems that his American Army interpreter is an academic type who knows only medieval French. He understands not a word of current French and gets lost when anything differs from *Le Roman de la Rose*.

The Germans are still holding the town of Vire fifteen kilometers away. We are in range of their batteries, installed on a hill outside of town. They are trying to buy time by forcing civilians onto the roads, thus creating a human shield. The sound of nearby shelling and bombardments is deafening. We have to shout at each other to be heard. The civilians who managed to escape are exhausted; many have crawled along the road for several kilometers, keeping low to avoid being hit by machine gun fire. They were picked up by American trucks and brought here, but the location provides only relative security.

After speaking with them and assuring them that they would soon be evacuated from the front line, I leave for Tessy and Cavigny. By hook or crook, I make my way to a point about twenty kilometers south of Saint-Lô. I was supposed to be away from camp for only two hours, so I am in a hurry to get back. However, after proceeding for just a few more kilometers, I am stopped by a jeep. A young lieutenant of the 88th Division asks me very politely for permission to borrow my truck so he can pick up refugees who are blocked on the Vire road.

"We have to get them out of there," he says. "The division is moving up for an attack on Vire."

I explain to him that I am the only one authorized to drive my "jalopy," as he calls it. We get into an argument. He emphasizes the danger: the Germans fire on anything moving on the roads; there is one area that is especially exposed, etc., etc. It seems clear that he has no confidence in either me or my vehicle, but we are all he's got.

I respond resolutely: "You will not take my truck. It belongs to the French army. And it's not my job to go pick up these people, but I'll go if I have to."

He says he will drive, but, of course, he can't manage to get my temperamental Peugeot started. I get it going for him.

"OK, you take charge of this junk heap. I'll show you what we need to do." He spreads a map out on the hood and shows me where the refugees are hiding. I ask him how many there are because the Peugeot will hold only fifteen at a time, and that many only if some of them are children. "I have no idea. Maybe a hundred."

"A hundred! And you think . . ."

"Don't worry. Other trucks will arrive soon. But until they do, these poor people are running an enormous risk."

I let him persuade me and take the Vire road. The GI rides beside me with a tommy gun braced between his legs. He is not the ideal road companion since he is a big oaf whose intellect is inversely proportional to his set of muscles. I try to engage him in conversation but succeed in eliciting only grunts that seem to be either "Yes" or "No" depending on the intonation. I finally give up talking but the lieutenant never stops grumbling and swearing under his breath.

We are secure for the first five kilometers. After that there are three kilometers where we are exposed. The instructions of the lieutenant are to "zigzag like hell." In spite of my efforts to avoid holes while zigzagging, we hit a pothole at top speed. The truck bucks up and makes an alarming cracking sound. On top of that, I am bothered by the lieutenant's helmet, which he insisted I wear instead of my own "ridiculous object," as he so gallantly put it. But his helmet is much too big, and every time we hit a bump, it falls down over my eyes.

The road and the helmet preoccupy me to the point that I am almost surprised when we arrive without incident at our destination. I turn off on a little dirt road and stop. There are about thirty people sitting and lying down in the grass under the trees beside a large rock. They are happy and relieved to see us. Very quickly, with the help of the GI who impresses them with his submachine gun, I load up the youngest refugees, including several mothers with their children and a pregnant woman who looks as if she is about to give birth.

The trip back seems much longer. I only hope that my truck will hold up under a load that is close to the maximum. The American trucks still haven't arrived, but I feel more sure of myself on the second trip since the first one went all right. As I look around I notice a wooded hill with flashes of light emerging from the trees. This troubles me but I just try to concentrate on the road. Once at our destination, we load up a priest with several young boys and some elderly people who have trouble climbing up into the truck. The boys start singing a Boy Scout song and seem to be in a good mood, which is more than I can say for myself. We get to a spot about one hundred meters from the place that I had identified with the help of my odometer as being inside the safe zone. At the same moment, I hear an enormous noise that sounds like a speeding train. Then, on our right, an explosion. The truck shakes; stones and dirt rain down on the hood and the canvas covering in back. But everything holds. I keep my eyes glued on the road and floor it. Even though I have the impression that we are not moving, at last we arrive.

The radiator is leaking in two spots. I make a temporary repair with some chewing gum. The canvas cover has some holes in it, but nothing major. The lieutenant who recruited me for this lovely mission has disappeared. I'm disappointed because I wanted to point out to him that my truck and I weren't as useless as he seemed to think.

The captain of the unit arrives and says he wants to telephone to Cavigny to thank his colleague for my help. "If you don't mind," I say to him, "please don't do it. No use advertising that I'm in this sector where I'm not supposed to be. It would just get me into trouble. Thanks all the same."

When I finally get back to Cavigny, they are in the process of evacuating a truckful of refugees. I try to mix in with the group and look busy. The captain arrives and calls me over. "What were you doing?! We looked for you everywhere. It's not acceptable to leave for such a long time."

"But you know, Captain, I was returning a family to their home. You gave me the order yourself this morning. I was delayed by engine trouble, but I've been back for quite a while. Now that I see you, I'd like to request authorization to take my vehicle to maintenance so they can repair the radiator."

Cavigny from Above

The next day, which is the beginning of August, it is very hot, and in the middle of the day, the camp is unusually quiet. "Everybody must be napping," I say to Timmy, who is tinkering with the engine of his plane. I tell him that I have once and for all given up taking families back to their homes. "That's good timing," he answers, "I was just about to propose that we take a little ride." My worry about the rules is quickly swept away when I learn that Geneviève, my team captain, just took off in the other Piper Cub.

We climb up into the little plane and take our places. When the engine turns over, I note that the fuselage vibrates and shakes even more than my little truck. In no time, we are up in the sky above Cavigny. From here everything is beautiful, clean, and orderly. The refugees look like little black ants; Louise and the children playing in the field look like confetti scattered on the grass; and the dead cows camouflaging the landing strip resemble toys. As the plane gains altitude, the camp disappears and a fantastic scene stretches out below us. It is a perfectly clear day; surrounded by the dark blue water of the Channel, the Cotentin peninsula unfurls like an immense map. From here I realize how tiny our little bridgehead is. The movements of the troops remind me of a slow-motion ballet. I think about Saint-Exupéry and experience the marvelous sense that pilots must feel of belonging to another world, far from the suffering and pettiness of the earth below.

Huge numbers of small craft are lined up on the beaches perpendicular to the shore, while the roads converging on the sea are animated by the endless to-and-fro of vehicles.

We fly toward Cherbourg, and I recognize Carentan, Sainte-Mère-l'Eglise, Montebourg, and the trees grouped around Fontenay. On the right, Bayeux. Farther away a brownish cloud covers Caen. Above Valognes we turn around and go toward Saint-Lô. We follow the main road that I know so well; it looks like a ribbon covered with trucks and jeeps, which from here look like snails inching along. And then, all at once, I see the tanks, armored vehicles, and khaki jeeps of the US Army and the dark gray vehicles of the Wehrmacht. They advance toward each other almost concealed by a large cloud that covers Saint-Lô. From time to time, I can see flashes of light followed by puffs of smoke, but I hear nothing. Seen from on high, the combat seems reduced to a match between unreal players miraculously unaware of the horrors of war and the fear of dying.

Just as I begin to notice that almost all the German vehicles have a red cross on their roofs, the plane nosedives, then climbs vertically, and then, after a few seconds, turns to the right and then to the left before plunging again. The plane seems to have gone mad. With alarm, I realize that these acrobatics are maneuvers to avoid the shelling of enemy artillery. After a last, alarming dive toward a tuft of trees, we make a bumpy landing on the Cavigny airstrip.

Very relaxed, Timmy helps me down out of the plane. I lean against the fuselage to hide the fact that my legs are buckling under me, and I take off the pilot's helmet Timmy lent me with what I hope looks like a nonchalant gesture. As Timmy talks to me for the first time about his work, I listen fascinated, slowing regaining my composure.

Geneviève's plane lands right after ours. Just as we are setting off to share our impressions over a drink at the canteen, a GI runs up and announces that Captain Ford is at the chateau and is impatiently waiting for us. "She knows that you went up and she's furious." Captain Ford is commander of the Normandy group and is making an inspection tour of all the teams. As our bad luck would have it, she chose this day of all days to appear at Cavigny.

With a coolness that I will always admire, Geneviève speaks first: "Captain Ford, we're very sorry we were not here to welcome you, but we thought we should take advantage of a unique opportunity to do reconnaissance from the air. It's by far the best way to check the movement of the trucks carrying refugees."

This gem of an excuse does not impress the captain, who gives us a terrible dressing-down: we broke the rules; we are irresponsible, foolish, unworthy of wearing the French uniform, of being officers, etc., etc. To end it all, the captain decides to remain at Cavigny to supervise us. We are confined to camp for a week and are strictly forbidden to speak to the pilots.

War Is a Dangerous Game

For the next several days while Captain Ford is at Cavigny, we are well-behaved and stick to our work in the camp. Even so, I invent all kinds of tricks to see Timmy. He is impatiently waiting for orders to join another group near Avranches. Currently far from the front, the Cavigny pilots go out on reconnaissance missions only now and then. Since the area is calmer, Timmy invites me to take another ride in the plane, but I have to refuse because Geneviève and I have been warned that, if we repeat our joy ride of the other day, we will be sent back to England.

On August 6, Colonel Chandon arrives unexpectedly to inspect Cavigny. We haven't seen him since Fontenay and are especially pleased with his visit since he will be able to give us news of the outside world and our MMLA colleagues. He is optimistic about the progress of Allied military operations and predicts that we will be in Paris before the end of the summer.

Accompanied by two of our comrades, Marie Dumas and Marie Fréchou, the colonel is on his way to Coutances to scout out new locations for camps. He invites me to go along with them. I am disappointed that I have to decline the invitation and even more embarrassed to explain that Geneviève and I are restricted to camp. I tell him about our escapade, which he finds very amusing, and he leaves quipping that the punishment fits the crime since it will keep me from "flying away" with him.

Two days later, August 8, I am humming while sorting out the refugees' registration cards and, at the same time, trying to figure out a way of seeing Timmy, who is due to leave the following day. The door opens, and a young MMLA officer comes in. "What a nice surprise," I say to him, "have you just arrived from Camberley?" The grave expression on his face stops me, and I ask what has happened. "Colonel Chandon has been killed, and the two women with him are seriously wounded. I'm not sure they're still alive."

"But they were all here the day before yesterday. I can't believe it. There must be some mistake. Maybe they got lost . . ."

"Exactly. When they left here for Coutances, they must have taken a wrong turn because they ended up in a zone where there are pockets of Germans left. The Germans are trying to get back to their units and meanwhile they hide out and fire on any Allies that come along. The driver escaped and told us the whole story. The trouble is he isn't sure where they were because the colonel was navigating."

"What happened?"

"A hail of bullets from a machine gun hit the car. The women, who were riding in the back seat, were hit right away. The colonel first told the driver to get out of there fast, but when he realized the women were seriously wounded, he told the driver to stop. The colonel got out of the car waving a white handkerchief. Some German soldiers and their SS commander surrounded them. Speaking German, Colonel Chandon asked the officer to look after the wounded and then he surrendered and handed over his revolver. The Germans led them toward a barn near the side of the road. Then the SS officer cold-bloodedly killed Chandon with a shot to the back of the head. God only knows how, but the driver managed to escape. He got to Bayeux yesterday in a sorry state. He doesn't have any idea whether the women are still alive or not."

Distressed beyond measure, we shake hands without saying anything. Since I'm on duty, I continue to go about my work but I feel like an automaton. At last I'm able to rejoin my comrades and tell them the tragic news. We are utterly crushed and think that being shot down like a dog is a cruel way for such a fine soldier to die. We know that the Germans don't make any distinction between the members of the FFL and those they call "terrorists," that is, fighters in the Resistance. For our part, we feel forsaken because we realize that nothing will be the same without this commander to whom we were so deeply devoted.

To try to console myself, I decide to go see Timmy earlier than planned. When I arrive at the landing strip, I realize immediately that something is wrong: only one plane is there, and it's not Timmy's. Even though I keep repeating to myself—"No, no, it's not possible. Not all at once. Not the same day"—I have a sense of foreboding. The other pilot sees me and comes toward me. He stops and looks down at his feet. I know what he is going to say. Finally, still looking down, he blurts out, "The Professor got shot down this afternoon." He stops for a moment and then continues: "His luck ran out. It was just a routine flight. The shell had one chance in a million of hitting the plane..."

Without really believing it, I say, "Maybe he parachuted out, maybe he's a prisoner."

"No. I saw everything. They got him."

I sense that he is ready to give me more details, but I can imagine only too well the Piper Cub as small as an insect in the huge blue sky, the yellow flash, the plane falling slowly like a toy, followed by a long trail of black smoke. All I want is to get away but my feet feel like lead. Trying to make things better, the pilot says: "Come and have a drink. It will do you good."

"No thanks."

"Well then, come over to his tent. You can take something to remind you of him. There are a whole bunch of books..."

"No thanks. Really."

He probably thinks I'm callous but I don't care. I say goodbye and thank you (thank you for what?) and leave in a hurry.

The following days are difficult. It's very hot and humid, and we are constantly tormented by clouds of mosquitos. The refugees are still arriving in large numbers, and we continue to evacuate them as quickly as possible.

Cavigny is now far from the front line, and we are waiting impatiently to be moved closer to the front. We were beginning to think that we had been forgotten when, on August 15, Captain Gibb at last receives the order to move to Mortain, sixty kilometers south of Saint-Lô.

Mortain-Falaise

August 17–23, 1944

My memory of our arrival and the first twenty-four hours at Mortain is not a good one. Indeed, it is only on August 19 that we can really begin to move in because the town, recently liberated by the Americans, is recaptured by the Germans in a brief but fierce counterattack. We are forced to return to Cavigny and to remain there until the Americans retake the town. As soon as the fighting is over, we go back to Mortain and begin to set up in a sumptuous twelfth-century monastery called the White Abbey, which has miraculously survived the bombardments.

We enter through a courtyard surrounded by massive buildings that in normal times serve as a seminary for future missionary priests. Our admiration for the huge buildings is tempered, however, by a touch of anxiety when we think of the hundreds of refugees we will have to lodge in them.

We are disappointed to learn that the American soldiers in our detachment have not had the chance to clean the premises since the Germans evacuated the abbey only the day before. So, after hastily depositing our gear in a huge room on the second floor, we set to work. For the time being, there are only a hundred or so refugees here; some twenty of them pitch in and help us with the tasks that have become routine: clear out, clean, inspect and number the rooms, set up the canteen, etc.

The first night at Mortain turns out to be eventful. We are too exhausted to set up our beds, so we camp out on the floor. Around midnight, an enormous noise of explosions wakes me up. The flashes of light are so bright that it looks like broad daylight in our room. Shaking with fear and convinced that the Germans are returning, I shout to my comrades to hurry down to the cellar. Geneviève grabs my

The White Abbey at Mortain. (Photo courtesy boblenormand. *Abbaye blanche 1.* https://commons.wikimedia.org/wiki/File:Abbaye_blanche_1.jpg. Creative Commons (CC BY-SA 2.5). https://creativecommons.org/licenses/by-sa/2.5/deed.en)

arm and tells me to "shut up because the enemy attack is only a thunderstorm!" Totally mortified, I lie back down and, for once, have trouble going back to sleep. It's silly, but the storm alarmed me more than any bombardment I had witnessed!

Our first concern is the inhabitants of Mortain. There are around two thousand of them. Some have returned to try to clear out their houses in the town, which is almost totally destroyed. But with the help of the priests, most of them are housed in the monastery. In spite of all their losses and suffering, these people impress us with an optimism and determination that we were not to witness anywhere else. Is their amazing morale due to the abbey, which has become a place of refuge as it was in the Middle Ages? Or maybe the large, white statue of the Virgin Mary that seems to look out for her flock from the top of a hill? Or is it due to the example of the devotion on the part of the Father Superior and his monks whose courage in the face of the enemy is

Jean-Claude, the Mortain refugee who wanted to go with us to fight the war.

already legendary? In any case, we all have the feeling that the White Abbey is a special haven of calm.

During the years of occupation, the Germans requisitioned the main buildings of the abbey, but the priests remained in quarters near the chapel and the cloisters. When the bombardments made it impossible to stay where they were, the Father Superior led the inhabitants to an old quarry where they have remained dug in for two weeks. We need to transfer the eight hundred people who are still there back to the Abbey.

The whole morning of August 20 is spent transferring the Mortain inhabitants and the little baggage they have from the quarry to the abbey. We make it just in time before the military trucks arrive, filled with their human cargo. The trucks come in quick succession. The courtyard is never empty; at times there are as many as thirty trucks lined up under the trees.

In the evening, the morale of our team hits a low ebb because Geneviève receives orders to leave immediately for Brittany, where she is to head up a new team. We are miserable that our close-knit group is going to be broken up. We blame Commander Ford, who has just arrived at the abbey to keep an eye on us, or at least that is what we think.

Several days later, a big front-wheel drive vehicle bursts into the abbey courtyard and screeches to a stop in a cloud of dust. A woman in navy blue wearing the tricolor armband of the FFI and the badge of a captain gets out and yells: "Hey! You there, tell me where I can find Lieutenant Vagliano!"

"No trouble, Captain," I say smiling and saluting, "it's me."

Thickset with dark hair and a cigarette dangling from her mouth, she looks me over with surprise and a little contempt. I note that she is wearing a high-caliber pistol at her waist. Without another word, she hands me an envelope with my name on it. In it are orders from the MMLA signed by Colonel de Boislambert to leave Mortain immediately with Captain L, to pick up Monique Boncenne at Falaise in the British zone, and to proceed to HQ at Le Mans. Without news of the advance of our troops, I am astonished to hear that our forces are already at Le Mans, and say so. The captain shrugs, raises her eyes to heaven as if to say "Oh help!" and orders me to hurry and get my gear because we have to leave immediately. I explain to her that this is impossible because I have just been made head of the team and we are overwhelmed with work. The captain replies that orders are orders and that she doesn't give a f—— for the refugees and that I had better hurry and obey. When she adds that the colonel lent her his own car so we could go as fast as possible to Le Mans—and then to Paris—I waste no time getting my gear, saying goodbye to the team, and presenting my orders to the American commander. He protests vigorously, saying that it is highly irregular, that he hasn't received any instructions through the First Army chain of command, and that... But I leave him in mid-sentence, run to the Citroën, and get in the back seat.

I have to admit that my regret at having to leave my team is quickly dissipated by the excitement of being on the way to Paris. Comfortably settled in the back, I catch my breath, and appreciate the luxury of being driven for once. After a few minutes, I try to engage the captain in conversation. Since we left Mortain she has been talking in a low voice to the driver. He also is in navy blue with an FFI armband. From where I'm sitting, all I see are wide shoulders, a thick neck, a massive head, and large, hairy hands on the steering wheel.

In a voice that I hope is both friendly and self-assured, I ask the captain when and where she joined our group because I had never heard of her before. She spins around, visibly annoyed. The dark, bright eyes she turns on me strike me as being very hard. Neither pretty nor ugly, with a matte complexion and thin lips, it's hard to tell how old she is. In a disagreeable tone of voice, she answers that she was in the Resistance and is now Colonel de Boislambert's personal adjutant. Then she challenges me: "Do you want to see my papers?" I say no, but she takes a paper out of her pocket and sticks it under my nose. I see a name: Yvonne L, member of network X, the colonel's signature, several stamps, and the cross of Lorraine.

"You don't need to show me that. I take your word for it,"

"You're wrong to do that, but it doesn't surprise me. You seem very young and naïve. It's easy to see that you English don't know what real war is like."

"You're right," I say humbly. "As a matter of fact, I would like very much to hear about your group and what you did."

In a tone of voice that is a little less hostile, she launches into a quick and somewhat garbled account of her activities. She becomes animated, and her pale complexion takes on color as she describes the ambushes, the bridges blown up, the secret meetings, the escapes in the middle of the night, etc. I am dazzled by her story but she suddenly stops and says, "That was real war. DP camps, that's nothing. All those pathetic people are a pain in the ass." The captain, full of hate, hurls abuse at me in a series of gross insults. To believe her, I'm the lackey of "Judeo-capitalist Anglo-Saxons" and the least of my defects is to be a "stupid idiot." Her look and tone are poisonous, and she is beginning to scare me. The driver tugs at her arm and in a harsh voice speaks a few words to her that I can't make out from the back. She turns back away from me. I try to tell myself that she has perhaps been driven crazy by being tortured and that I need to excuse her outbursts on that account. I say nothing more.

We finally get to Falaise in midafternoon after going through numerous villages and towns in ruins, but also every now and then a place that seems to have been miraculously preserved. With the pedal to the floor and honking at everything and everyone, we pass interminable motorized columns and groups of miserable refugees. When we pass from the American into the British zone, the difference in the uniforms, road signs, and vehicles of all kinds creates the impression that we have gone from one country to another. The ruins and the misery are, however, the same everywhere.

We enter Falaise on a long, straight road bordered by wide sidewalks. The facades of the buildings are still standing, but they are empty shells. The captain reprimands me because I don't know the location of the refugee camp. I ask a British soldier and, following his directions, we easily find the army barracks where the refugees are gathered. I am more than happy to find Monique whom I haven't seen since Bayeux. Like me, she is both astonished and delighted to learn that we are to go to Paris as quickly as possible. While she gives instructions to her team, the captain becomes increasingly impatient. Scowling, she chain-smokes and paces around the car.

After consulting the British colonel, Monique informs the captain that we can't go on the roads at night and that, therefore, we need to stay over at Falaise. Even though I had warned Monique about the captain's nasty temper, she is still surprised by the violence of her reaction to this news. Monique responds calmly that you can't fool around with the British command and that there is no way we can leave this evening. If the captain wishes to go on her way, she will be shot at and, in any case, we will not go with her. After calling us "yellow cowards" and "chickens," and the British Army "a bunch of Boy Scouts," she shrugs, tosses her cigarette away, climbs into the car, and leans on the horn. The driver comes running and, upon hearing the news of the delay, says that our arrival in Paris is now in doubt.

We wait next to the car as Monique explains to me that the Falaise Pocket, which has just been closed, is far from being secured and that there is a significant presence of enemy troops near the town. Many minutes pass before the captain lowers the window and asks to be taken to the place where we are to spend the night, a charming, half-timbered Norman house in the middle of a garden filled with flowers.

The evening is a happy one. While Monique shows me around the chateau where the British officers are quartered, we stop to have a drink with them and then go back to dine with the team. The team members are intimidated by the MMLA captain, and our efforts to converse with her fall flat. She doesn't speak at all but eats and drinks in large quantities. Soon we forget about her, and an animated conversation with the team ensues. We have so much news to exchange! The captain and her driver retire early, and Monique and I decide to do the same since we have to leave at daybreak in order to get to Le Mans by noon.

It is barely light when Monique and I come down, but Captain L is already there looking at a Michelin map while the driver is tinkering under the hood. We greet them, and I ask as politely as I can if I could take a look at the route we are going to take.

"Certainly not," the captain replies, "I'm in charge here." She grabs the tommy gun that is propped against the car and gets into the front seat, the gun between her knees.

"So charming," I whisper to Monique. "She's the last person that should be handling such a powerful gun."

"She does it to look tough," Monique answers to reassure me, because I told her earlier that the captain scares me to death.

We sit in the back seat chatting about our activities of the last few weeks without paying attention to the route we are following. Our conversation is abruptly interrupted by the enraged voice of the captain hurling abuse at the driver. She calls him an imbecile, a traitor, etc., and orders him to obey without question or else.

We are following a little, winding, dusty road through a thicket when we pass a convoy of military vehicles of all sorts: trucks, jeeps, half-tracks, and other armor. The column has stopped, and we're driving on the shoulder to get by. Shaken up by the bumpy ride, with windows closed and in a cloud of dust, we can still see the astonished looks of the soldiers as we pass. We have the impression that some are signaling us to stop, others hailing us, but we can't make out what they are saying. We continue to advance at a crazy speed until we come to a sudden stop behind a large truck that is blocking the road. The captain lets loose a stream of curses and opens her window. A sergeant approaches the car, leans in the window, and says coolly: "Excuse me, Ma'am, I don't know where you're headed but I have to warn you that if you keep on this road, you'll fall right into the hands of the Jerries."

Dumbfounded by this news, I blurt out in English: "We are going to Le Mans."

Immediately the captain yells at me to shut up. Then speaking to Monique, she asks her to explain to the sergeant that we are lost and then, without having been asked, she hands our orders to the sergeant. He looks them over attentively and then, saluting, hands them back. After that, without any explanation, he orders us to turn around. The sergeant clears the road enough for us to maneuver, and then in spite of his orders to go back the way we came, we go forward at a good speed, passing several jeeps, until we come to a clearing. The driver finally slows down, and we think he's going to turn around when the captain says, "Straight ahead and make it fast!" Suddenly very friendly, she explains that she is familiar with the area and that we're going to take some little lanes that she knows so we can avoid the traffic on the road. We go faster and faster and don't see any more military vehicles.

"Did you see?" I say to Monique, " Those were Canadians."

"Yes, I noticed. They are the ones who are clearing out the Falaise Pocket, and if we continue straight ahead, we'll be right in the middle of it!"

After a few minutes, without any apparent reason, we turn into a track through a forest and then, going a little more slowly, follow a road shaded by trees on either side. In spite of myself, I think, "What a nice place for a picnic this would be." But I am quickly brought back to reality by the horrible tension and fear that Monique and I are both feeling. We're back on a paved road, and I am pretty sure that it is the same road we were on when we met the Canadians and that we are still going in the direction of the "Jerries."

We are suddenly out of the forest. Before us is the Corridor of Death, a scene from the Apocalypse. On our left, as far as the eye can see is a field literally covered with burned-out German vehicles and dead soldiers and horses in grotesque positions. Some of the horses are still harnessed to their wagons. A shattered body is hanging from the opening of a tank; its arms seem to be moving. Dozens of bodies are heaped up in the ditches on either side of the road. This horrendous massacre must have taken place recently to judge from the smoke still swirling above the field as well as from the burning smell that covers the acrid odor of the dead.

We are forced to stop because an enormous dead horse is blocking the road. When the captain jumps out of the car, the driver, who has never spoken to us, turns and says in a hoarse, urgent voice: "Stop her! Make her go back! Don't tell her I'm on your side. You are in mortal danger!"

With one mind, Monique and I get out of the car, our eyes on the captain, who is standing with her back to us, her tommy gun in her hands. She looks at the huge carcass, gives it a kick, doubtless wondering how she is going to get it out of the way. We take her by surprise, both leaping on her at the same time. In a few seconds Monique has come up with her revolver, and I have the tommy gun.

She looks at us very calmly and says, "OK, girls. Drop the toys. You don't know how to use them and somebody's going to get hurt."

"Don't be fooled. We know very well how to use them. Now, we're in charge and we're going to Le Mans."

The driver has already turned the Citroën around. We get back in the back seat and tell the driver to get moving. It's only now that I realize I am shaking like a leaf. Even so, I have a firm grip on the gun. We are relieved to see that our prisoner has collapsed, motionless, on the front seat. Monique and I, speaking quietly, ask each other whether we will shoot her if the need arises. We agree that, yes, we will, but hope that it won't come to that.

We are soon back to the column of Canadians. Some of them recognize us and wave. We think about turning the captain over to them, but we are in a hurry to get to Le Mans and Paris and decide that it would be better to hand her over to the French authorities. We now realize that she intended to take us into an area that had not yet been liberated so that she could hand us over to the Germans. We feel sure that she is a German spy and wonder how she managed to infiltrate our group and fool the ranking officers.

After Alençon, we have to stop for gas. I get out with the driver to fill our fuel cans while Monique stays in the car to guard our prisoner. After we start up again, the woman turns toward us and very calmly declares that we are going to be in big trouble for mistreating a superior officer, that we will have to appear before the discipline board, and that we will surely be discharged and probably put in prison. "But," she continues, "if you will be reasonable and stop playing soldier, I promise that I will not report you. That way, we can all be friends and continue working together."

Monique answers equally calmly, "We'll see about that later,"

But that doesn't stop her, and she goes on in the same amiable tone: "You know, if you hadn't lost your head, we would already be in Paris without having to stop in Le Mans. Imagine getting to Paris before everyone else. The welcome we would have! And you ruined all that because you can't stand the sight of blood and the dead. It's too stupid! Now, not only will you not get to Paris, you're going to have a plateful of trouble. Believe me."

Our "captain" then turns to the driver and demands to know what right he has to disobey her. She calls him a traitor and says he'll end up with a bullet in the back. The driver only shrugs and says nothing, keeping his eyes on the road. There is silence again.

We arrive in the suburbs of Le Mans. It seems like a miracle to see clean streets with no soldiers, the houses intact with actual panes in the windows, and civilians going about their business. We feel as if we're in another world.

At HQ our prisoner is led away by two soldiers, while a third takes charge of the driver. An information officer questions us at great length. He ends by asking us not to say anything about what happened.

Several months go by before I learn that our false captain had an important post in the French Militia and that she was the mistress of a colonel in the SS. Even after I learned this, I wondered why she wanted to take us to Paris and why she wasn't more pleasant with us. If she had only treated us with a minimum of consideration, who knows, we might have gone along with her.

And what about the driver? My supposition was that he must have worked for Yvonne L for a long time but that he preferred to cast his lot with us in the middle of our crazy escapade to improve his eventual position with respect to the Allied military authorities, especially since he could claim that he saved our lives.

In the midst of all the commotion at Le Mans HQ, we quickly forget our weird adventure. We are disappointed to learn, however, that we have missed the first convoy to Paris. They promise us that we will leave in the next one at dawn the following morning.

The other good news is that our colleagues Dumas and Fréchou were liberated by the Americans from the German hospital at Coutances. Transferred to an Allied military hospital, they are now out of danger, although Marie Dumas is still in a serious condition. The same SS officer who killed Colonel Chandon shot her when she was already wounded. It scares me in retrospect to think that I have been in the same kind of danger more than once.

Part 3

Paris. Belgium.

In the five months covered in this section, Vagliano experienced the liberation of Paris, a friendly fire attack, and the Battle of the Bulge. Reunited with her family in Paris, she describes the universal joy in the city at the departure of the Germans, followed by a gigantic hangover when resentments, divisions, and reprisals came to the fore.

After a short stay in the spa town of Saint-Amand-les-Eaux, the MMLA teams received permission to follow their units outside of France. No longer just a team member, Vagliano was now given the responsibility of overseeing a number of teams. Resisting being tied to a desk at HQ, Vagliano was paradoxically saved from that fate at the end of an epic confrontation with her commanding officer, Major Lewis, by her unconventional decision to bunk her teams in a brothel.

Her assignment took her to the Sainte-Claire Institute, a convent and school in Verviers, an industrial town of some sixty thousand in Belgium, only thirty kilometers from the German border. It was here that she experienced being strafed and bombed by American P-38 fighter bombers on October 11, 1944. Two months later, in the midst of a brutally cold winter, Verviers found itself in the midst of the Battle of the Bulge, the largest and bloodiest battle fought by the United States in World War II. When her American Army detachment was ordered to leave Verviers, Vagliano was left in charge of over a thousand refugees and DPs in a camp without water, heat, or food. They scrounged meat by cutting up the frozen cadavers of cattle left dead in the fields. They were unable, however, to protect themselves from bombardments of the camp and the town. By the end of her tenure in Verviers, in March 1945, Vagliano was in charge of fifteen MMLA teams spread out in the region, a job that entailed her spending many hours on the road, a challenging and sometimes dangerous activity.

❖

Le Mans–Paris

August 25–September 10, 1944

The billet at Le Mans reminds me of Moncorvo—only smaller and livelier. The same disciplined schedules for getting up, going to bed, meals, showers, work. We are impressed to see how elegant our comrades are with their polished shoes, careful coiffures, and knotted ties. I feel disoriented and unfit for barracks life. I miss my friends. On the other hand, I have the happy surprise of finding my suitcase that I thought was lost forever. It is sheer happiness to take a hot shower and wash my hair, and to sleep in a real bed with real sheets. Passing by a mirror (not broken), I feel as if I'm looking at a stranger. I note with a certain satisfaction, however, that my silhouette is slimmer and my complexion tanned. My hair has grown in, and my natural color has returned. A colleague from London passes by, her arms weighed down with files. She is wearing thick glasses, looks pale and wan, and has dark circles under her eyes. She comes straight to the point: "At least you had an easy time in the camps: nothing much to do but lie around and sunbathe. What a nice life!"

I answer with not a little sarcasm: "Right! It's really nice in the camps. You should request a transfer."

While we are preparing for the great return to Paris, selecting our clothes and vying for the only iron, our joyous demeanor belies the deep worry we feel. Without news from our families for months, and in some cases for years, we can't help being anxious about what has happened to our loved ones. Are they sick? Dead? Prisoners? Deported? Or, miraculously, well? Several of our comrades who are Jewish know already that everyone will be gone and that they are facing agonizing searches for them.

In addition, we are not certain about the Allied advance on Paris. For the last few days SHAEF has not published any bulletins on military operations in order to avoid giving any information to German command, which at this point often doesn't even know the location of their own units. As usual in such cases when there is no hard information, rumors fly. People are saying that the city is intact but that the Germans have mined the bridges, sewers, and monuments and that they are preparing to blow everything up. We also hear that famine and epidemic have struck and that thousands of inhabitants have been evacuated and are being used as human shields by the Germans. What we do know is that General Leclerc's division has reached the southwestern suburbs of Paris and is advancing toward the center of the city, fighting street to street. Even though we are one hundred kilometers from Paris, we can see dense smoke in the sky, which causes us great concern.

August 26, the day our convoy leaves for Paris, remains indelibly imprinted in my memory. As we leave at dawn we have no idea what we are going to find. As for me, my mind is still full of the crazy rumors we heard at Cavigny, but I try to remain calm and cling to the bits of good news that have come our way.

We race toward Paris. The traffic is light, and we don't see any destruction. We finally enter the suburbs by the road from Chartres but have to drive slowly because the streets are congested with people. Our vehicles are often totally immobilized by the crowds who shake our hands and talk with us. We learn from them that the military governor of Paris, von Choltitz, has, just the day before, signed the surrender of the German garrison and that General de Gaulle has already appeared on the balcony of the Hôtel de Ville to greet the population of Paris. We had no idea where de Gaulle was and are thrilled to learn that he is in Paris.

Our little group of four trucks decorated with French flags and the cross of Lorraine finally comes to a halt at the top of the Champs-Elysées in front of the Claridge Hotel where we are to be quartered. I set my foot down practically at the same spot where four years earlier I was saved during the student demonstration of November 11, 1940, by a street cleaner who used his broom to smack the German soldier who had grabbed me and was dragging me off. But this is not the time for reminiscences...

Our trucks are instantly recognized and surrounded by the jubilant Parisians crowding the street and sidewalks. Everybody wants to shake our hand, hug us, talk to us, touch us. They even help unload our baggage. I disentangle myself from the crowd as quickly as possible because all I want now is to get in touch with my father and sister, who are in Paris. After the commotion in the street, the hotel lobby—quiet, luxurious, smelling deliciously of beeswax polish—is a haven of calm. The concierge is imposing in his maroon uniform embroidered with an insignia of gold crossed keys.

"Welcome, Miss. How can I be of service?"

"I want to find my father," I stammer.

I am amazed to learn that the telephones are actually working. The distinguished concierge leads me to a booth in the lobby. Although it is imprinted in my memory forever, I have to dial the number three times my hands are shaking so hard. The telephone rings three times. Someone picks up, and I hear the familiar voice of my father. Tears are streaming down my face but I manage to control my voice.

"Papa, it's me."

"Where are you?"

"At Claridge's."

"In London?"

"No, Papa. Claridge's in Paris."

"Is everything all right?"

"Yes, everything is fine. And you?"

"Everything is fine."

"I'll be right over. It's not far."

"Wait for your sister. She'll come on her bicycle. It'll be quicker that way. In fact, I think she already left. I just heard the door slam."

I quickly try to tidy up and then rush outside. I don't see her coming; suddenly she is just there in front of me, tall, dark, tanned, beautiful. She hasn't changed a bit.

"Hi."

"Hi."

Our family is not very effusive but that doesn't mean that the feelings are not there. Lally and I kiss, a rare event but certainly fitting for the occasion. Instinctively we revert to the language of our youth. The years melt away.

"You haven't changed at all."

"Neither have you."

"Is Mummy all right?"

"Yes, I had a letter from her yesterday at Le Mans. She must be fuming that she's not here with us."

"You certainly took your time getting here. We were really getting sick of the Germans."

"I know. But it wasn't all that easy."

"Where are you coming from?"

"From Normandy. We landed at the end of June and since then we've been setting up camps for refugees and DPs."

"Was it bad?"

"Not too bad. There were ups and downs. But you must have had a worse time of it."

While we are talking, Lally climbs on her bicycle and I straddle the luggage rack in back. We move at a fast clip, zigzagging around the pedestrians while Lally shouts at them to get out of the way and rings the bell on her bike, which is particularly loud.

We were inseparable before the war. Now she is a mother, and I am an officer in the army. When I start thinking about it, I burst into tears again and wipe my face on the back of her dress.

"I see you are still the same crybaby."

"No, I don't cry much anymore, but it's just so good to see you."

"It is wonderful to be back together, especially since we have come out of it pretty well, so you can stop crying. By the way, do you still faint at the sight of blood?"

"No, luckily I'm much better about that but I can't promise that it won't happen again. The important thing is to keep busy, and so far, that has been the case."

"Good, but I'm sure none of your friends knows how to keep you in line. I'll have to fill them in."

"You're right. There's no one around to bully me anymore."

We arrive at our house. My father is waiting in front at the big green door. I rush into his arms. It's so good to be home again.

We learn that General de Gaulle is going to march down the Champs-Elysées, and we hurry out again on the bicycle. L'Etoile is mobbed. Thanks to my uniform, the crowd lets us through. Everyone is cheerful and excited. One joker pulls off my beret, no doubt as a souvenir, but the people around me are outraged and start yelling insults at him, even calling him a "collabo." They get my hat back for me and then start pummeling him. But we have already moved on, carried by the whirlwind of frenzied Parisians.

We work our way into the area behind the official retinue. I can just catch sight of the general's kepi, which looks as if it is bobbing like a cork on the sea of heads in front of us. What a day this must be for him! By the time we get to the Place de la Concorde, we are exhausted and decide to go home, which now seems impossibly far away. We go toward an American jeep parked on the sidewalk. Two young women are sitting on the hood, and three others are perched on the back with their feet resting on the seat. I sense that I'm not going to be popular with these girls but I don't care and am relieved when the two GIs agree to load up the bike and take us home. After a jolly "We'll be back," to the girls, we set out. Our drivers are happy as clams; it is the best day of their lives, and they seem to be floating, buoyed by the festive welcome they have received. One of them keeps repeating, "Fabulous, fabulous!" Each time he says it, he adds emphasis by hitting the steering wheel with his fist, making us lurch wildly. The other is more talkative and tells us he is glad there are so few Americans in Paris because, that way, the ones who are here receive special hospitality. He has already been invited into several French homes, and when we get back to the house, we invite them in but they have to pick up their colonel at the Carlton. They drop us off and leave with a last "Fabulous!"

The gathering that evening is touching, comforting, and extraordinary all at once. All evening, relatives, friends, FFL soldiers, and Americans come by. Champagne is flowing, and we talk as if we could catch up on so much lost time in one night.

Around two in the morning, I realize that I never went back to the Claridge and never requested permission to be absent. My father says he doesn't think it is safe to be out at this hour especially since we hear gunshots from time to time, apparently from snipers on the rooftops. Someone says that there were shots fired along General de Gaulle's route on the Rue de Rivoli and also when he arrived at Notre Dame. I suddenly feel very tired and upset, afraid that I'll be put under arrest. My father reassures me, reminding me that it's not every day that Paris is liberated. He is right, of course.

An American officer takes me back to the hotel in his car. The concierge hands me my key and, with a hint of reproach, says: "You are the last to come in, Miss." In my most dignified although slightly slurred voice I answer: "It's not every day that Paris is liberated."

The following days are like a dream; time and the war seem to have stopped. The atmosphere in the city is joyful and full of hope. An unusual sense of camaraderie prevails, and people who don't know each other talk together and even invite each other to their homes. There is very little traffic. No American troops are around except for a few officers and members of the general staff who are quartered in hotels. As soon as they appear on the street, they are surrounded by applauding admirers. The Leclerc Division is bivouacked on the Avenue Foch and neighboring squares. People bring them flowers, wine, gifts.

I crisscross the city on my motorbike with my sister or Monique on the luggage rack. As we revisit bridges, monuments, and avenues, people ask me about the FFI and de Gaulle or they want to tell me about their war experiences. The weather is splendid—warm and sunny. With red, white, and blue French flags everywhere along with those of the Allies, Paris has never been so beautiful.

Food supplies are nonexistent, but, for the moment, nobody cares. People know they have been liberated and that they just need a little patience until the new administration gets up and running. The stores and restaurants are supposed to be closed, but, in fact, there is lots of activity going on behind closed doors. Apparently in some restaurants, gourmet meals are being served at astronomical prices. Electricity comes on around 8 or 8:30 pm, and in some areas not at all. Our neighborhood is still in the dark because the Germans blew up the local power station. Everybody is bringing out the last reserves of food they had stocked up for an emergency, anticipating that they will no longer be needed. At home, we finish up the last of the canned food my mother had put aside before she left for the United States. Our steady stream of visitors soon depletes our stocks. Some of our guests bring military rations, and, when those run out, we compensate for the lack of food with champagne.

My unit is transferred from Claridge's to the Château Frontenac. At first we are told that we will be helping to distribute food. But since there is none to be had, we are given three days of liberty. Monique has no family in Paris, so she comes to stay at the house and shares my room. We spend our days strolling in Paris and, especially, window-shopping on the Rue du Faubourg St-Honoré. We are dazzled by the beauty, luxury, and price of the items on display. After the austerity we witnessed in London, this extravagance astonishes us.

The festive atmosphere of the Liberation lasts about three days. After that, a collective hangover sets in. Little by little, the envy, resentment, and hatred built up over the years of occupation rise to the surface. Fierce opposition between the Communists and anti-Communists in the Resistance breaks out. We don't know what is going on outside of Paris, but we hear tales of atrocities, summary executions, even massacres. These stories make us realize that everything in this damaged and divided country depends on the authority of General de Gaulle, backed up by the Resistance and the presence of the French and Allied troops.

Occasionally I meet people whose comments shock me profoundly. Some are still Pétainists and talk as if it were still 1939; they are rabidly opposed to the Resistance fighters, whom they consider to be outlaws. I am astonished to learn that they fear the Communists more than the Germans. Others consider the war over, now that Paris has been liberated, and complain that the Americans are not bringing in enough food and that the bread they distribute is inedible. I tell myself that there are always complainers, but it is still depressing to listen to them. Fortunately, I also meet many other people who share my view that, thanks to de Gaulle, a new France will emerge.

"The festive atmosphere of the Liberation . . ." (Photo by Malindine E G [Capt]. Courtesy of the Imperial War Museum; from the War Office Second World War Official Collection)

On August 28, my father, who is usually vague with us about his activities, asks me to pick him up at the Rue Séguier after a meeting of the Resistance Committee. There I meet Alexandre Parodi,* who takes me to a meeting of the FFI at the Place St-Michel. An old friend, Louis de la Garandière, is also there. He is now heading up a group of snipers. I feel as if I am finally among my soul brothers, which consoles me for the unpleasant exchanges I have had with those who, in my estimation, haven't understood or learned anything in the past few years.

My father takes me to the internment camp at Drancy, where he has been going regularly and which has just been liberated. We take food and cigarettes to the internees who are still there. A number of them who are foreign or stateless don't know what to do or where to go. Sadly, some of their group had been sent off in the last trains to Compiègne and Germany.

These errands and meetings make my inactivity seem less burdensome. I report every day to the Château Frontenac, but there's basically nothing to do aside from a few hours of guard duty, secretarial work, and the disbursement of pay—the first since our landing in Normandy! At my request, Captain Rothschild agrees to see me. She confirms my impression that, in the midst of the current confusion, the command doesn't know what to do with us. In spite of all her efforts to obtain orders for new assignments, she has not been successful.

I am sorely disappointed: "We can't just stay here twiddling our thumbs when there is so much to do!" She explains to me that things have gone so fast that the command is overwhelmed. We have to be patient.

I can't understand why our teams don't automatically follow the American and British units we have been attached to. As far as I understand, they are already moving toward the eastern front to receive and repatriate military and political prisoners. Captain Rothschild informs me that she has been denied permission to send our teams outside of France. For me this is the last straw. She laughs at my indignation and says: "Fine, go tell these gentlemen that the refugees and deportees should be handled by the French. Up until now, I haven't been able to get through to them. Maybe if there are two of us, we'll have more success."

In the following days, I knock on many doors and manage to get in to see a good number of superior officers. Everybody seems to agree with my position but no one can or will make an official decision. Finally, I see André Diethelm,* Minister of War and associate of Henri Frenay,* Minister for Prisoners, Deportees, and Refugees.

I report in to Captain Rothschild to tell her about these meetings. She has also been busy making the rounds. We agree that nobody seems to know what department we belong in and, therefore, who is responsible for making decisions about our future assignments. To be honest, the military administration thinks we're superfluous—we don't belong in their world—and they can't understand why we aren't content to remain quietly in Paris with nothing to do.

So we wait.

Suddenly, and much sooner than we expected, all obstacles seem to be removed, and on September 10, I am ordered to Versailles with fifty of my comrades. We spend the night camped out in the Royal Stables.

Northern France

The following day, September 11, I am ordered to appear before Colonel Ryan of the American 12th Group. He gives me orders attaching us to the First Army G5 along with three teams for which I am to be responsible. We leave in three of our Peugeot trucks—they're still running!—for the north of France. On the way we stop at Compiègne, where my family spent many vacations. Our villa is half-demolished and totally looted: the plumbing, including the toilets and even the huge furnace, has been torn out. The tall fir tree where we used to hide out is nothing but a stump. With a heavy heart, I regret having come to see this ruin. The view of the city, which was almost totally destroyed by the bombardments in 1940, also reminds me that a war is on, something the festivities in Paris had momentarily made me forget.

My teams are stationed at Valenciennes, Charleville, and Saint-Amand. For two weeks I circulate from one camp to the other. The teams clear out, clean, and arrange enormous, gloomy barracks intended by the Germans to house French prisoners of war. While my teams do their job, I work hard to smooth relations between the American military and French civil authorities. I also go to Huy in Belgium to the First Army HQ and back to Paris to try to get authorization to follow our American units outside of France. Getting this permission is urgent because our American Army detachments are scheduled to move very soon.

The euphoria of the rapid Allied advance convinced us that we would need to have welcome centers operational in a few weeks. In fact, that wasn't the case, since prisoners weren't liberated until March, April, and May of the following year. But in September 1944, the American military believed that the Germans would surrender soon and that everyone would be home for Christmas.

Road Adventures

I don't lack for adventures during my road trips. Having learned from my Normandy experiences, I always carefully study my itinerary before setting out and often consult the map to avoid getting lost. These precautions do not prevent me, however, from getting stuck in the mud or having numerous flat tires. Each time, I am lucky to find helpful American military who pull me out of ditches with their jeeps, change my tires, and, more than once, tow me to the nearest maintenance station.

I now have my own car. When I didn't succeed in obtaining either an American or French army vehicle, my father yielded to my pleas and lent me his Onze Chevaux Légère. The car has now "joined up" and sports large white stars on the doors, with flag insignias and the inscription MMLA and FUSA (First US Army) on the windshield. On the front fender a little tricolor with the Cross of Lorraine flaps in the wind. I am quite proud of my official look, which has the advantage of keeping me from having my papers checked. The GIs are very respectful; they salute and address me as Ma'am or Lieutenant because I now have two stripes (they are provisional, but no one can see that) and the Military Cross. The officers are often more insistent, trying to invite me to their mess, but since I am always in a hurry, they don't press the point.

One evening at dusk, I leave Charleville to go back to Saint-Amand. I am driving through the dense, eerie La Capelle forest when the motor stops. I am out of gas! I get out to fetch the emergency gas can I keep in the trunk. It isn't there. With a sickening feeling, I now remember that I had passed it on to the Charleville team because they were out of reserves. I wait for a while standing in the road, hoping in vain that an American vehicle will come by. Then I notice a light shining intermittently on the other side of the road. With my flashlight in hand, I find my way to a little house hidden in the trees. I knock, and a bearded giant, rifle in hand, opens the door with a violent tug. A thundering "Who's there?" just about makes me take to my heels, but I stay and, after a timid "Good evening, Sir," explain my plight. He asks me into what is visibly the only room in the house where a candle stuck in a bottle is burning. We talk, and I discover that under the rough exterior he is actually very pleasant. He goes down into the basement and comes back with a liter of gas.

"It's from before the war. I've been keeping it, just in case of bad times."

He walks me back to the car, pours in the gas, starts the car, and says: "With that you should be able to make it to La Capelle. There are plenty of Yanks there."

I thank him profusely and promise to replace the gas as soon as possible because he wouldn't let me pay for it.

At La Capelle, there is not one drop of fuel. Supplies still have to come from Normandy and, until the northern ports are opened, gas is a rare and precious commodity.

I take refuge in an MP post located at the intersection of my road and what they call the Red Ball Route, which is reserved night and day exclusively for the trucks carrying fuel from Normandy to Belgium. I am dozing on a chair when a lieutenant from the Air Force comes in. He is very nervous and says he has got to have some gasoline because he is AWOL and needs to get back to his unit right away or he will be in big trouble. I suspect that he's been on a binge in Paris. When he notices me, he comes over and asks what I'm doing there.

"Ah, we're in the same boat, but you have some cards up your sleeve that I don't have," he sneers.

I find him very unpleasant and, somewhat taken aback, I don't reply.

"Come on, come on, you're not going to spend the night sitting in that chair waiting for gas to fall from the sky." And then, in a more agreeable tone: "I have a fantastic idea. All these trucks going by busting our eardrums are filled with gasoline. You go stand out on the road like this," and with one hand behind his head and the other on his leg, he strikes the pose of a pinup girl hitchhiking.

"Absolutely not! I refuse to do anything like that."

A heated discussion ensues. The lieutenant becomes increasingly insistent, appeals to my generosity, and reminds me of the court martial awaiting him if he doesn't get back to his base by dawn. I relent and agree to try.

The trucks are going by at a terrifying speed, their headlights replaced by small slits they call cat's eyes. I yell to the lieutenant: "They can't see me. I'm going to get run over."

"Be brave. Atta girl, remember we're in a war."

I go to the side of the road and take the prescribed pose. Two mastodons pass one after the other with a deafening roar. I am practically blown over. The lieutenant comes over to me, and I say: "You see. It's not going to work. It's too dangerous. They can't see me."

"It'll be fine. I thought the French were more on the ball. You need to stand in the middle of the road and hike up your skirt a little more. Right now you look like a scared little English miss."

Even though I'm exasperated by his remarks, I go out to the middle of the road and try to take an appealing pose. The noise of grinding brakes sends me into the ditch, but a truck has stopped. I go up to the driver's side, and before I can say anything the driver shouts at me: "What the f—— are you doing? I could have run you down!"

As sweetly as I can, I beg him to give me some gas. He says he would rather take me along with him. I persist. He finally gets out and brings me two beautiful jerry cans filled with gasoline. I thank him warmly and, as he drives off, he calls back: "We guys never leave a damsel in distress."

When I proudly show my spoils to the lieutenant, instead of thanking me, he remarks: "If you had only flirted a little, he would have given you more."

This puts me over the top, and I shout at him in French, "Tordu! Maquereau!" [Pervert! Pimp!]

But he is already running toward his jeep with the precious fuel can. In any case, he wouldn't have understood my French. Philosophically, I take my can and fill up the Citroën with the help of an MP who witnessed the whole scene.

I finally get back to Saint-Amand without further incident, but I will always regret that, in spite of several attempts, I never could find the little house in the woods.

Saint-Amand-les-Eaux

At Saint-Amand we join up again with our Normandy detachment led by Captain Gibb. A group of French reserve officers has also arrived: two captains—Mousset and Deloche de Noyelle,* and two lieutenants—Trouvé and Bouchez. They are part of a team responsible for the repatriation of prisoners and deportees. Luckily, two of my teams have arrived as well, so the French are present in force.

While I was making my rounds, a camp has been set up at Airain, a nearby spa where we are all lodged. The three-story Victorian hotel has seen better days but it is still possible to imagine the elegant patrons strolling about under the trees with their long dresses and parasols. Soon it will become a welcome center with the capacity of lodging fifteen hundred prisoners of war. Now, however, in the chilly, damp autumn weather, its former elegance is replaced by peeling paint, ravaged gardens, and crooked or missing shutters. A thick layer of dead leaves covers the walks and lawns. Everywhere—both inside and out—there is a dank odor of decay.

I find my comrades in boots and overalls, along with thirty or so young men and women from teams organized by the French. They are clearing, cleaning, and burning rubbish with joyful exuberance. Upon inspection of the site, I find hotel rooms suitable for four or five persons, a large salon that will serve as a rest area or perhaps a dormitory, a large mess hall, and a well-equipped kitchen with a vast oven, a relic of the old days. There is even running water in the numerous bathrooms.

Not far from the hotel, the concert pavilion has become a storage facility filled with beds, mattresses, blankets, and other furniture "liberated" from a German depot. Everything is going so well that we will be ready for business in just a few days.

The spa building with its baths might have been useful but it is now in total ruin. The old swimming pool next door is filled with black, stinking water. Louise is persuaded that there are German corpses on the bottom. I tell her if there were they would have floated to the surface.

"Not necessarily," she counters, "if they were wearing boots and had rucksacks. In any case, the pool is disgusting. We have to empty and clean it."

"Fine, but now we need to go back. It's almost dark."

In our hurry to leave this reeking, lugubrious place, Renée, one of the team members, slips on the wet leaves. I hear a shout and a splash. Renée is thrashing about in the water shrieking, "I don't know how to swim!" I lie down on the ground and, with someone holding on to my feet, I manage to grab her hand, which is slippery with pool slime. I begin to pull her toward me but lose my grip, and she slithers away from me. Her head disappears under the water. Her boots are weighing her down, and she can't manage to come up again. Shouting to no one in particular, "Quick, help me," I take off my boots and jump into the frigid, nauseating water. I manage to get under Renée and push her to the surface. My comrades catch hold of her, pull her out, and then help me out in turn. Louise begins artificial respiration on the poor girl who begins to spit up water and dead leaves. In spite of my efforts not to breathe, I swallowed a lot of water and begin throwing up as well.

Numb with cold and fear, we run back to our quarters. The team goes off to get hot water, towels, and dry clothes. I am immobilized in the middle of the salon, covered with mud and leaves, a large puddle of water spreading out at my feet. At this exact moment, I hear an American voice say, "Come in, Colonel, I'll introduce you to the lieutenant in charge of the liaison teams."

My instinct is to hide under a table, but before I have time to move, the head of town civil affairs, called the Town Major, comes in followed by a lieutenant colonel, who is, without doubt, the most handsome and elegant man I've ever seen. What a disaster!

"What happened?" inquires the Town Major when he catches sight of me. "Where is Lieutenant Vagliano?"

"It's me, Commander. I fell in the pool. It's nothing."

When I open my mouth to speak, water sprays out with several leaves. The impeccable colonel laughs and says, "It's not a good time to go swimming, Lieutenant."

I don't feel like laughing and leave the room as decorously as possible while making a curious squelching sound and leaving behind a trail of muddy water. My team takes charge of me; and soon, washed, warmed, dressed, and perfumed, I return to the salon where all the officers of the unit have gathered. I learn that the handsome officer is named Colonel Litton and that he is the counterpart of Colonel Lewis in the Advanced Section Communication Zone (ASCZ). We are now attached to this unit since the First Army has already moved into Belgium. I'm angry that I am meeting him for the first time in such circumstances, and his ironic smile irritates me. I sense that he will not delay making a comment about my age, and I'm waiting for him. He comes over to me, delicately picks a leaf out of my hair, which is still wet, and says affectionately, "A water baby!" I answer brusquely, "Old fogies don't win wars."

I notice that he is wearing a medical badge and ask him, more courteously, if he will check on Renée whom we have put to bed with a grog and a hot water bottle. Even with these remedies she is still shaking from head to toe. I drop into a chair and begin to feel much better when one of the officers serves me a stiff drink. The colonel returns: "It's not serious. I gave her a sleeping pill and some aspirin. After a good night's sleep, she'll be fine. And now, you should go do the same."

"I'm fine, thank you, and I'm not thinking of going to bed at this early hour. Besides, I'm taking care of myself by drinking this whiskey, even though I dislike it intensely." The evening turns out to be very jolly, perhaps too jolly. The whiskey goes right to my head, and I begin to feel better and better. After dinner, Colonel Litton awards me a large lifesaver's medal made out of cardboard by my team. After that, the only thing I remember is talking nonstop and dancing on the table.

The next morning I wake up with a major hangover and a massive head cold.

Belgium

On September 27, I finally receive authorization for the MMLA teams to follow our army units outside of France. The very next day our convoy leaves Saint-Amand. While we are loading our trucks, I notice that my team members have accumulated an unbelievable quantity of souvenirs: German helmets and swords, lace, lamps, brightly colored pillows, etc. After shouting at them, I make them leave the most cumbersome of their treasures and remind them that we are military, not Gypsies. They are not pleased and look sideways at me all morning. The day thus begins badly and goes from bad to worse.

Our destination, the Belgian city of Verviers, is almost 250 kilometers away. We go through Mons, Charleroi, and Namur. At Liège we are held up for almost an hour by a V1 attack. We finally arrive at Verviers. Even though it is after dark, the streets are still crowded with military cars and trucks. We have trouble making headway, especially because the MPs have not seen many vehicles like ours and stop us often to check our papers. Fortunately a false air raid alarm empties the streets, and we finally find the Civil Affairs Center. My sense of relief does not last long, however. The officer on duty, who is overwhelmed, has never heard of a refugee camp at Verviers and adds with a sarcastic smile: "I have enough trouble with the army. I don't need civilians to take care of." He is sure I have mistaken my destination and advises me to return to Liège because there are absolutely no available beds in Verviers. When he sees how crestfallen I am, he tells me to try the hospital, where there might be some spare beds in the nurses' dormitory. But when I tell him there are fifteen of us, he gives a hopeless shrug and says there is nothing he can do for us.

I take my cold and exhausted team to a large hotel that I noticed earlier when we drove through the city, hoping that they might let us camp in the lobby or reception rooms. But they tell me there is absolutely no room. I leave my team huddled in the bar, where at least it is warm.

Determined to find shelter, I ring at several doors and am greeted with nasty remarks about the hopeless mess of things in general and my personal incompetence in particular. Finally, over the strong protests of the madam, a corpulent woman in a flowered bathrobe, I requisition a brothel where, with great relief, we spend the rest of the night.

An Unfortunate Incident at Verviers

The next morning, I order my team to remain indoors while I go to Spa, a health resort ten kilometers from Verviers, where the First Army has set up its HQ. I find Major Lewis pacing up and down in a small office, puffing on his ever-present pipe while his faithful sergeant types away in the corner. The major, who is in a vicious humor, points out to me that I am a week late and that, because of my delay, the barracks that were supposed to serve as a refugee camp have been taken over by another unit. I answer as calmly as possible: "It's not my fault if you couldn't hold onto the barracks. You should have installed one of your units or some DPs."

"Your advice is useless, Lieutenant. I can't run a camp without personnel."

Understanding that the major is in a really bad mood, I try to answer in a conciliatory tone: "I'm sorry for the delay, Sir, but we couldn't come any faster. As soon as we received your instructions, we set out immediately. But our arrival in Verviers was complicated by the fact that the Civil Affairs Center knew nothing about the existence of a refugee camp and couldn't even provide us with lodging for the night. I had to requisition a brothel in town with some false papers."

"You should know better than to arrive in the middle of the night in a strange city. There's a war on, and we're fifteen kilometers from the front. What were you thinking?"

He stops for a moment to speak to the sergeant, who has stopped typing to listen to our conversation. Then, drawing slowly on his pipe and visibly embarrassed (his Methodist [sic] pastor side gaining the upper hand), he continues: "Why would you spend the night in such a place (he can't bring himself to say the word)?"

"Quite simply because it was midnight, and we were out on the street. In those circumstances, you take what you can get. We actually spent a pleasant night there."

"That's enough, Lieutenant. No need to be provocative. I'll take care of your transfer immediately. But we need to talk about serious things. One of your teams will be attached to the D3F1, which will be under the orders of Captain Ball, who is a very competent officer."

"That'll be a change," I murmur under my breath.

"Excuse me?"

"Nothing. I suppose that my team will join them. We're used to working together."

"I have to thank you again for your advice, but I'm the one who makes assignments here. It happens that I came to the same conclusion. The D3F1 will be responsible for the Forward Transit Camp at Verviers. We managed to get hold of a convent there. Unfortunately it is much smaller than the barracks we hoped to have, but it will do, especially since I've decided that the DPs will stay there only temporarily before being sent on to a much larger center near Liège. The second team will go to Eupen, and the third to Malmédy, where we are going to open more transit camps. In addition, another team is on its way and should arrive at any time. As for you, you'll be assigned to our HQ so you can supervise your four teams as well as the others that I hope will arrive soon. You already know the sergeant; he will show you your room, the officers' mess, and the rest. We don't have much room in this office but I'll have a work table moved in next to mine so we can collaborate closely."

I am made speechless by the prospect of being stuck at HQ, far from my comrades and condemned to spend my days in Major Lewis's office, where I'll have to account for all my comings and goings. Taking my silence for assent, the major stands up, shakes my hand, and declares solemnly: "Welcome. I'm happy to have you with the G5 of the First Army."

"No, no. It's impossible," I answer resolutely.

The major sits back down and responds with some weariness: "To tell the truth, I was surprised that, for once, you didn't raise any objections. But let me point out, this is an order."

"I'm very sorry, Major. It's not that I don't want to work with you. On the contrary, that's why I'm here. But in addition to my job as liaison between you and my teams, I am still responsible for my own team, the Normandy team that will be at Verviers. I need to stay with my comrades. How do you expect me to be up on the problems at camp when I'm sitting here at a desk, making inspection tours only now and then?"

"That's exactly what I do," the major retorts, furious. "In your opinion, I don't understand anything about the problems on the ground?"

"That's totally different. You're the big boss, and my role is to report our activities and the problems we're having to you. I'm sure that you want things to be organized as efficiently as possible for the smooth operation of the camps. That won't happen if I'm at HQ bogged down in paperwork."

"You don't seem to realize, Lieutenant, that this is not like Normandy where you had only one team. Now you need to inspect all the teams. In addition, you will have a number of administrative tasks that you will be able to carry out more easily here. In addition, you will have comfortable accommodations and all our infrastructure at your disposition, including transport and communications. You were named supervisor of the MMLA teams attached to the First Army. You will remain here, that's all there is to it."

"But I can get my administrative work done perfectly well in camp and then come here often for the rest. I'm sorry to mention this because I know it will irritate you, but I got official instructions from Paris to remain with my team and to liaise between you, the teams, and Paris (in truth I never got explicit instructions like this, although they were implicitly understood)."

"I was surprised that you hadn't yet invoked orders from the Frogs. Their instructions don't surprise me. If you remain at HQ, you'll risk being contaminated by the Americans. It's very convenient for you, Lieutenant, to play both sides against the middle!"

"You may think it's easy. It seems pretty hard to me!"

Just then the telephone rings. It's for the major. While he's talking, the sergeant brings me a cup of coffee and gives me a reassuring tap on the shoulder.

As the major listens on the phone, his bushy eyebrows begin to twitch, and he turns to scowl at me. After a moment he hangs up and says: "You have caused a major scandal, Lieutenant."

"What? Me?"

"Yes, you. That was the town major on the telephone. He's livid. The place you selected to quarter your teams is strictly off limits for all troops, including your MMLA team. You've disobeyed orders and are liable to be called up before the First Army Discipline Committee. What do you say to that, Lieutenant?"

"I didn't know. How could I have known?"

"A particularly clear and visible notice is posted on the door of the house."

"But there was no way I could read it in the dark."

"So you did see it?"

"In fact, I did see a small notice, but I didn't read it. With the blackout, you can't see a thing."

"You must realize that you have placed yourself in a serious situation, very serious."

"I understand, Major, and I'm extremely sorry. But what else could I do? I wasn't going to leave my teams to die of the cold overnight in our little trucks. If the American Army had found quarters for us, this wouldn't have happened. Frankly, this doesn't seem so terrible. After all, there's a war on (I'm rather pleased with myself to be able to throw his favorite phrase back at him)."

"The whole town is talking about it. The people of Verviers are claiming that the American Army set up a brothel to service our troops and that a group of French women in uniform were brought in as 'staff.' Right now, I wouldn't give much for your reputation. In your place, I would start by taking the situation seriously."

"What do you want me to do? Should I go to the town major and explain what happened?"

"Especially not that! There's no use in aggravating the situation by criticizing his system of billeting and making your usual remarks in bad taste. I prefer to take care of this myself. To start with, I'll transfer you without delay to the refugee camp."

"Thank you, Major. I really appreciate it."

"I want you to know, Lieutenant, that you may have lost your reputation in the space of the last few hours, but I've become the laughing stock of the First Army. It's very disagreeable, exceedingly disagreeable. What's more, the town major told me that a crowd of GIs was in front of the house this morning and that your women came to the windows to talk with them. They told the GIs that they had orders from their officer to stay inside and keep the door closed. The town major felt he had to intervene, so he sent MPs to guard the house and to clear the area of GIs. One thing is sure, your arrival in Verviers did not pass unnoticed!"

"I'm truly sorry to have caused you all this trouble, Major. What are you going to do? Send us back to Paris?"

"No . . . never. If you think I'm going to be bullied by all these smut-minded imbeciles, you don't know me. Wait here, I won't be long."

With that, the major gets up and goes out, leaving me with my thoughts that run the gamut from consternation to glee. He returns with a satisfied look on his face. I take a deep breath. He hands me a paper officially authorizing us to stay in "our house" until the next morning.

"Tomorrow," says the major, "you will all go to the Sainte-Claire Institute. Here is the address. I advise you to go by there as soon as possible to clear the details of your team's arrival with Captain Gibb. We'll take care of the other problems tomorrow. I'll expect you at 1700 hours."

"Thank you, Major. You're terrific! And what about me? Do I stay here?"

"Not for the moment. We'll talk about that another time. Goodbye, Lieutenant."

"One more thing, Major. I bet that the beds in the convent will be less comfortable than the ones in the brothel."

"I said goodbye, Lieutenant. I have work to do. Now get out of here."

And so it was that the unfortunate incident at the brothel ended up getting me exactly what I wanted.

Sainte-Claire Institute

When we arrive at the Sainte-Claire Institute in the afternoon of September 29, there are already two hundred DPs in the huge courtyard, sitting, standing, or lying down in little groups. They are Russians for the most part, half of them women with babies and children. There are also nineteen French, fifteen of them STO. In addition there is a scattering of Poles, Czechs, Serbs, and Dutch. There is no food, no beds, no mattresses, no blankets. The place is very dirty, but at least the buildings are intact, the windows are not broken, the electricity is working, and there is running water and central heating. We need most urgently to clean the area and to find food supplies and blankets. These poor people haven't eaten for several days and have walked dozens of kilometers in the cold and rain, sometimes under fire. For the first time I don't have to participate directly in the cleaning and organizing tasks; when all is said and done, I'm not entirely displeased to be giving the orders.

My team gets established in the building, where a few nuns are still living. Each of us has a cell that is so small it is almost entirely filled by a camp bed. After we get moved in, I go to Spa. Major Lewis is in an excellent mood and offers me a cup of tea. Since he doesn't mention my being domiciled at HQ, I think—wrongly, it turns out—that the question is settled; in the ensuing four months that we are in Belgium, he never lets the issue drop.

It's dark by the time I get back to Sainte-Claire, and I am relieved to see that the courtyard is empty and that the whole unit is already dining in the mess hall. The DPs have been registered, dusted with DDT, fed, and put to bed. The team was able to get supplies from a storehouse left by the Germans and also from the American Army quartermaster. It's extremely pleasant, after all the chaos, to find everything in order and to be able to sit at table and be served my dinner.

Along with looking after the DPs' lodging, food, and health, my duties as head of the MMLA group include overseeing my teams—their work, health, and smooth integration into their G5 units. I also have to deal with personnel problems including conflicts in the teams or, inversely, romantic attachments. New recruits keep arriving until, in the beginning of 1945, there are fifteen teams, comprising almost sixty women of different ages and backgrounds.

Things start off well. I am able to procure for my teams the superb, warm winter uniforms of the American Army. This success, however, is at the price of numerous road trips and bargaining sessions with HQ in Brussels and even Paris, since neither the Americans nor the French want to cover our equipment expenses and keep bouncing the ball, that is me, back and forth between them. Naively, I begin by paying from my personal funds and very quickly find myself in a catastrophic financial situation as I end up paying not only for uniforms but also for repairs to our vehicles. The American maintenance shop refuses to take care of our little trucks, which they consider no better than heaps of scrap iron. Since they don't have replacement parts in any case, we are obliged to use local Belgian mechanics, who insist on being paid upfront. Every day I wait in vain for the paymaster and end up having to borrow money from my American and Belgian friends. I finally get afloat by winning at cards. It's not exactly the most moral way of dealing with the situation, but it works!

Mission to Verdun

At the beginning of October, Major Lewis, who is exasperated by not being able to get through to our HQ in Paris, orders me to find and bring back the team that was supposed to arrive some time ago. We've had no news of them, so I go to Verdun to the HQ of the 12th Group, where I quickly discover that the Third Army has taken over the team and that there is no way we will get it back.

The return trip is long, and I begin to tire of the interminable solitary hours I have to spend on bad roads in bad weather. I no longer get lost, but am frequently troubled by mechanical problems. The radiator overheats so often that we baptize my car the Gurgler. I always carry an extra can of water, fan belts, and other replacement parts to make repairs. But these incidents make me lose a lot of time.

On the way to Spa, I stop off at Namur to relate to Major Litton the news I got at Verdun about the departure from Charleville of one of his teams. The HQ of the ASCZ is well equipped, and I am treated like a queen in the officers' mess. After dinner, they put me up in a comfortable, well-heated room in a big hotel. Feeling much better after a restful night, I set out on the road that goes through the Ardennes forest. It's a nice day, and the autumn colors are splendid. The Gurgler is purring along. When I get to the outskirts of Marche, I am stopped by a dozen bearded, well-armed Resistance fighters. These Belgian partisans are searching for German soldiers who are hiding in the woods and targeting American military vehicles. This very morning, one driver was killed, and another wounded. Without asking permission, they pile onto my car, riding on the fenders and the hood. After about five kilometers, they get down and spread out in the woods as merrily as if they were going game hunting. Shortly I hear submachine gun fire and what sounds like a handful of gravel raining down on the back window of my car. It happens so quickly that I don't have time to be afraid, but I get out of there fast and feel safe only when I'm out of the forest and stuck in a reassuring traffic jam.

When I get back to Spa, I'm very happy to learn that Major Lewis is gone for the day; I don't feel like getting into another discussion with him. I ask the sergeant to tell him that the prospect of getting the extra team is nil, but that, in compensation, the team headed by my friend Matthews will arrive at our Malmédy camp in two days.

The Attack of October 11

At Verviers, we are about twenty kilometers from the front. We can hear the roar of artillery more or less clearly depending on the direction of the wind. Air alerts are frequent, but more often than not they are false alarms or, if real, they are usually due to an isolated bomber dropping a few random bombs. Sometimes at night we can hear an Allied air squadron on its way to Germany. Habit makes us less and less aware of the noise of war, until October 11.

I had just returned from Spa, where I had a rather ill-tempered discussion with Major Lewis about some German DPs, and my refusal to lodge them at our camp. I am chatting with my comrades in the institute courtyard since, for a change, the weather is superb. All of a sudden we hear the sound of an airplane engine. It gets louder and louder and finally becomes deafening. The plane heads right for us. I shriek: "He's crazy! It's a kamikaze!"

A comrade shouts back, "No, it's American. Look, you can see the insignia on the fuselage."

As if mesmerized, we continue to watch, beginning to wonder if it might be one of our aviator buddies. Then the plane veers off, almost touching the roof. It's so close I can see the pilot's face; his mouth is open and twisted as if he were shouting something. At that moment, his machine guns spit fire, and the bullets hit all around us. We flatten ourselves against the nearest wall. A second plane, then a third, repeats the same scenario before disappearing into the blue autumn sky.

The panicked DPs run in all directions. The members of the military unit try to herd them into the basement. We pick up a woman whose leg is wounded and start to take her to our infirmary. But suddenly a whole wave of bombers arrives and releases its death load on us. There is a deafening noise, and we are plunged into an opaque cloud of dust. The attack lasts several minutes and then stops as suddenly as it began.

We are lucky at Sainte-Claire. There is not too much damage: twenty people slightly wounded, many broken windows, a cistern of drinking water transformed into a fountain, and the hot-water pipes split. But around us, things went less well. The factory next to the institute is destroyed, and several houses nearby are obliterated. People from the area come running to ask us for help for the victims of the raid. Louise, Renée, and I set out in our truck. Belgian doctors are already there, and we help to clear debris and to transport the wounded to the hospital. This is exactly the kind of situation that I have feared the most. My stomach in knots, a lump in my throat, I am afraid I will be sick and make a fool of myself. But having to act, to make decisions, keeps me going and in control until I move a rock and see a child's little hand. I take hold of it gently and call for help. They clear away more debris while I keep holding onto the hand. Then, my self-control falters, and I collapse on the ground. Somebody shakes me. It's a Belgian doctor: "Come on, Lieutenant, on your feet. We have to take the wounded to the hospital, and your truck is already loaded."

I get up and walk unsteadily toward my vehicle. Once I'm behind the wheel, I come to my senses and focus all my attention on avoiding the ruts and debris on the road so as not to jostle the wounded.

Back at Sainte-Claire, somebody hands me a glass of cognac that I swallow with great relish. Louise cleans a cut on my temple that I didn't even notice and that had begun to bleed. It hurts. And when I swear about it, everything returns to normal.

Major Lewis arrives a little later, very relieved to find us alive because he had been told at HQ that the Sainte-Claire Institute had been totally destroyed and that the team and the DPs were buried under the rubble. I rush up to him and indignantly demand to know why our harmless camp had become a military target.

"Easy, Lieutenant, easy. Let's not be so aggressive. I share your feelings, but I assure you it wasn't me who ordered the bombardment!"

To tell the truth, arriving from HQ, the major is not on the same wavelength as the rest of us whose emotions are running high after what we experienced in the last few tense hours. After a moment, he announces that he will have the enormous red cross the Germans painted on the roof removed: "The Germans doubtless put it there because they wanted to conceal something or someone in the building, and it makes an easy target that led to this horrible mistake. The cross is coming off."

Paris. October 12–16

In a moment of weakness, doubtless due to the emotions produced by the air raid, Major Lewis agrees to give me orders for a mission to Paris accompanied by two of my comrades. The very day after the air raid, we leave early for the capital.

Unfortunately, I'm not able to profit personally from my presence in the city because I am obliged to spend my time in various offices negotiating for money and written instructions for dealing with administrative problems. I encounter many nit-picking functionaries, and the whole experience is depressing. The people here seem to think that the war ended with the liberation of Paris, and they are all immersed in their little problems.

An example: Champing at the bit, I have to wait in a hallway while the officer who is supposed to meet with me finishes polishing her nails. Finally, I am ushered into the office but she doesn't take my proffered hand ostensibly because her nail polish isn't dry yet. She makes an unpleasant remark about my somewhat dusty, untidy uniform and reproaches me for not having requested an appointment twenty-four hours in advance. Enraged, I manage nevertheless to contain myself because I have to go through her to reach the next higher echelon.

After this first unpleasant contact, things go somewhat better. On the one hand, I am easily able to obtain written permission to stay with my team rather than to be stationed at HQ. On the other, I spend countless hours getting authorization to deal directly with staff permissions and transfers without going through Paris. The reimbursement of my expenses and an advance on future costs are also knotty problems, it seems. I end up getting most of what I request, but the problem of uniforms for my teams is not resolved. No credit, no equipment. Somehow I'm supposed to cope on my own. This infuriates me because I observe that the pen-pushers who sit across the desk from me are all sporting new uniforms.

I go to SHAEF in Versailles after loading my car with two cases of champagne that I got while passing through Rheims, several bottles of cognac cadged from my Paris friends, and a half-dozen German helmets—all to use for bargaining. The officer I was directed to turns out to be very understanding and gives me the papers I need to have access to the WACs' stocks, and I leave with my truck loaded with uniforms. This experience convinces me that if you want something done, you have to do it yourself.

After collecting my two team members, I leave Paris. But the return to Verviers does not go well. The trouble begins with a faulty induction coil that stops us in the middle of a convoy barely twenty kilometers from Paris. Then it's the radiator, which stops functioning due to holes caused by shrapnel during the attack at Sainte-Claire. And to top it all, not one, but two flat tires. We finally arrive at Verviers in the middle of the night after two days on the road and, to our shame, being towed by a jeep.

As soon as I arrive, I learn that Captain Gibb has been replaced. He is going to be court-martialed for leaving his post for two days without permission to go to Brussels ... with two of my team members. I spend a short, sleepless night anticipating the fury of Major Lewis.

Indeed, the next morning, he gives me a very chilly reception because I have been away for five days instead of the three that were planned. I counterattack immediately, accusing Captain Gibb of taking advantage of my absence to go off with two of my girls, even though I suspect that they were the ones who pushed the poor man to take them with him to Brussels so they could meet up with their boyfriends. I affirm, in total bad faith, that he ordered them to accompany him so that they could get supplies of powdered milk, medicine, and clothes for the children in the camp. A lively argument follows. The major ends up abandoning his intention of reporting my team to Paris in exchange for my promise to discipline the guilty parties and to make sure that it wouldn't happen again, etc., etc. In turn, I bawl out my team, feeling more and more sympathy for Captain Rachel Ford, whose fury we had endured in Normandy. I give them a week's restriction to camp and threaten to send them all back to Paris for the least infraction of the rules. After that, totally exhausted, I sleep until the next morning.

The Organization and Administration of the Verviers Camp. Captain Ball's Circus

After Captain Peter Ball* replaces Captain Gibb in mid-October, there is a dramatic change in our daily routines. Before, there had always been some uncertainty about how things should be done, and, as a result, we had to improvise constantly (I took advantage of the confusion to arrange things as I saw fit). Now, organization, discipline, and foresight are the order of the day.

By October 20, 1944, the Sainte-Claire Institute harbors almost seven hundred DPs and refugees. Everything is clean, calm, and orderly. The courtyard is washed down regularly; the rooms and hallways smell of soap and polish; brightly painted signs mark the welcome center, the refectory, the infirmary, the laundry, the shelters, the off-limits, etc. Bells announce mealtimes and curfew, and loudspeakers broadcast practical information and news in several languages. Access to the main office is reserved to the heads of the various national groups by appointment only. No more noisy groups bursting in unannounced. As for my team, their tasks are clearly defined and allocated. The daily meetings at 9 a.m. attended by all the liaison officers are presided over by Captain Ball, who assigns the day's work. In special cases, the convent bell calls staff to the office for urgent meetings.

Captain Ball is an excellent administrator. Unlike most of his colleagues from Civil Affairs, he believes that our role is important for military as well as for humanitarian reasons. During our four months at Verviers, Captain Ball manages, with a firm hand, to turn a diverse group of people into a united and effective team. Sainte-Claire becomes a model camp visited by superior officers of various army units as well as by future directors of other camps. We also receive visits of reporters from the major American networks. Throughout the winter I and my team are ordered to supplement our regular work by making presentations about the organization of the camp to several hundred British and American officers at the HQ of the First Army. The BBC and the American Army radio service also call on us and on Captain Deloche to record informational and morale-boosting messages intended for French prisoners in German factories and work camps.

Our basic military detachment comprises three US officers and six soldiers, and liaison officers from Belgium, Holland, and Poland, plus our team. The staff is enlarged over time by auxiliary volunteers recruited on the spot. The first to join us are two Belgian doctors who

"We are a united and effective team."

work with our team. Then there is a group of ten young Dutchmen who had been deported to Germany. Finally, DPs of all nationalities work as nurses and nurses' aides, interpreters, secretaries, painters, carpenters, electricians, plumbers, cooks, guards, etc. When the day comes in the beginning of March to leave for Germany, there are three hundred of us. A waggish American officer gives us the nickname "Captain Ball's Circus." The name pleases us and sticks. Soon that's what everyone calls us.

Shortly after our arrival in Verviers, I call Captain Ball's attention to the fact that our staff is too numerous to be lodged at Sainte-Claire. Predicting that the front line will not budge over the winter, he thinks we should keep everyone here and put our energy into using this period for education and training. The goal is to mount a sizable, experienced group capable, at short notice, of administering the camps of the twenty to thirty thousand DPs he expects to encounter in Germany. While talking with Captain Ball, I realize with humility that our activities up to this point have been amateur endeavors. Fortunately, this doesn't seem to occur to Captain Ball, and he continues to consult me about all kinds of problems, considering me an expert!

Verviers. The Staff

At the start, I serve as intermediary between Captain Ball and the liaison group because he finds it difficult to communicate with them. Most of the officers assigned to our detachment are imbued with the prejudices of their caste or military training. As a result, they have trouble adapting to our unconventional unit, dedicated to nonmilitary activities.

The English Captain Walters has nothing to do since there are no British DPs. He becomes Captain Ball's adjutant for administrative affairs and accompanies me on my local inspection tours. While we travel through snow and over black ice on damaged roads, his solid, taciturn presence is a great comfort to me, especially because he loves to tinker with cars and is an ace at changing tires. His morose demeanor disappears as if by magic the day he encounters a Finnish refugee whom he recruits as his aide. Once his buttons, belt, and shoes begin to shine again, he becomes a devoted officer of His Gracious Majesty in spite of the gloomy place to which the accidents of war have brought him.

The Polish Captain Kapinski is an old-school aristocrat. His English is as incomprehensible as his French is perfect. In his grand style, he calls us "the young ladies" or "de Gaulle's young ladies," and bows and clicks his heels when he greets us. Totally paternalistic, he is generally followed by three or four aides and considers the Polish DPs a band of naughty children whom he punishes and rewards by turns. His overwhelming generosity means that he is always broke. When, after several months, he finally gets paid, he invites his friends to a dinner complete with champagne and caviar. Two days later, after a bad night at poker, he admits sadly that he is once again penniless.

The Dutch Captain Koldewey is one of our most agreeable and effective officers. He is always ready to help even if it means delousing a refugee. But we all know not to disturb him when he sits down to a game of solitaire.

At the beginning, there are three French liaison officers. For us on the team, it's three too many. We don't like them treading on our territory and give them the cold shoulder. We have won our independence and think that whatever concerns the French should be our affair. In addition, the idea of having a superior military authority on site does not please us. But our prejudices turn out to be totally unjustified. Members of the reserves, these officers volunteered with the Ministry for PDR (Prisoners, Displaced Persons, and Refugees) to help with the repatriation of French prisoners of war. Assigned to units of British and American Civil Affairs to prepare them for the liberation of camps in Germany, they take advantage of this phase of their service to establish contacts with the American command and to familiarize themselves with the working of its administration. One of them is in charge of Intelligence and interrogates all the French DPs who transit at Verviers.

The highest grade officer is Captain Mousset, whom we call Képi-Head because he is never without his military cap. He also wears riding boots and carries a swagger stick. We find him old school and have the impression that he systematically scorns women in uniform. My polite but cool relations with him become strained because Major Lewis continues to consult me about all problems concerning the French. Poor Képi-Head, who is already offended by not being in a normal unit more befitting his dignity, spends his time writing interminable letters to high command in the hope of a transfer, which, in fact, he obtains after two months. We soon make friends with the other officers, who are much more pleasant. Captain Deloche has to deal with the difficult problem of transport behind the lines and often accompanies refugee trains headed to various rail stations or to other camps. The culture, intelligence, and cheerful disposition of Lieutenant Trouvé make him a dynamic colleague, always ready to do a favor. His experience in public service makes him particularly skillful at resolving numerous problems with the French civil authorities, especially ones relating to the railroads.

The American detachment includes most of the same men who were in Normandy. Under the leadership of Captain Ball, the plaintive Lieutenant Schurr has suddenly gained self-confidence. With Yvonne, his collaborator, he crisscrosses the countryside searching for abandoned German supply trains and storehouses. Thanks to them, we have the rare privilege of enjoying excellent food at our mess, to the point that many of the DPs, who have never been so well fed, are reluctant to leave the camp.

The belligerent southern lieutenant, transferred at his request to a combat unit, has already been killed. He is replaced by Lieutenant Helm, a frail, bespectacled young man in charge of transportation, including our rapidly growing fleet of vehicles. Sensitive and extremely nervous, later he will be repatriated from Germany suffering from severe depression.

In spite of our distance from home, the dismal environment, the bombardments, the intense cold, and other adversities, there is a warm friendly atmosphere in our group. A real team, we stay together until the German surrender. Returning to camp after my long, solitary, difficult, sometimes dangerous trips, I have the happy feeling that I am coming home to my new family.

Verviers. The DPs

The number of DPs at Sainte-Claire ranges from seven hundred to twelve hundred depending on what is happening on the battlefield. The various elements of the refugee population are not always easy to manage. Russians are the most numerous of the national groups. Depressed or full of high spirits by turns, they complain neither about the crowding or the cold (they've seen it all before) and relish the food we serve. They rarely mix with others and do everything as a group: talking, laughing, singing, and, of course, making love. Their main recreation is to provoke the Poles. Since the Poles reciprocate their feelings, we house the two groups as far apart from each other as possible. At night, the doors are locked and patrolled by armed guards. Alcohol is strictly forbidden, but the Russians always seem to find a way to nick some or, worse, to concoct some dreadful brew that puts them in the hospital or the morgue.

In spite of all our efforts, rules, and punishments (being held in the basement or ejected from the camp), the Russians and Poles manage to get together and settle their differences with fists, clubs, and knives. These incidents keep our doctors, nurses, and social workers busy. On the occasion when someone is gravely wounded, we take him to the city hospital. The men go willingly, but the story is entirely different when we try to take a Russian woman in labor to the hospital. They absolutely insist on taking care of things themselves and even block the door to keep us out. We are forced to wait out the delivery and hope things go well. (I am touched to note that two out of three girl babies are named Sonia—but then I have to admit, it is a common Russian name.)

When the Russian DPs arrive at camp, we have a lot of trouble carrying out the admission procedures even with the help of a Belgian interpreter who speaks excellent Russian. The women often act as if we're taking them to the slaughterhouse, rolling their eyes with fright and moaning when we merely ask their identity. By contrast, many of them are incapable of signing their name without help, and when we try to guide their hands, the process provokes gales of laughter. When they first see our DDT sprays, they mistake them for instruments of torture and resist with shrieks and sobs. Later we find two large, solid Russians to hold them still while we delouse them. Once we've finished, they relax again and entertain themselves by watching the ruckus raised by new arrivals.

The Poles are totally different. They snap to when Captain Kapinski gives orders. Whenever a new incident occurs, he never fails to remind us that Russians are "animals."

A few French arrive at the camp every day. They are, for the most part, prisoners of war, escapees, and workers deported to Germany for slave labor. We are mostly successful in evacuating them within twenty-four hours. They are surprised and happy to be received by women in the FFL and are grateful for our efforts to make their transit through the camp as quick and easy as possible.

I go on tours with Major Lewis, inspecting our operational camps and looking for possible new locations. On one of these tours, I am distressed to observe that my teams' camps at Malmédy and Hombourg are filled with German DPs. It is easy to identify the Germans by their discipline and the quality of their clothes. At the outset, circumstances made it unavoidable to mix Germans in with other nationalities: an unfortunate situation that provoked conflicts and, sometimes, bloody fights. Since then, the military at the front have received orders to separate the Germans and take them to special camps. Some camps, however, remain mixed, and, in one of them, the Americans make the Germans wear a yellow armband.

On the way back from one of our tours, I remind Major Lewis that the MMLA teams were assigned to the First Army to look after DPs, particularly repatriated French refugees, not German DPs. To my surprise, he answers amicably that he anticipated this objection and adds, "The German DPs should be shipped as quickly as possible to camps behind the lines."

We then go to Spa where there are modern, clean barracks, totally empty, but that won't last long. When I return several days later, there are already two thousand DPs there. The barracks, built for five thousand, will soon house eight thousand DPs.

Winter Sets In

November seems endless. The weather grows colder and colder, and the snow and black ice turn the shortest road trip into a challenge. We stop counting the collisions and skidding incidents that land us in the ditch. I locate a shed with a stove near Sainte-Claire where I can keep Gurgler warm enough to start up. A Finnish refugee, who insists on playing a balalaika under our windows, agrees to tend the stove. As for us humans, we continue to freeze in the nuns' dormitory, which isn't heated, until the day when a V1 hits close enough to break our windows. We have a good reason, then, to move into a tiny room in the central building, which is heated. Our five cots fit together like the pieces in a puzzle and totally fill the space. No matter, we are deliciously warm.

The bad weather means that the DPs find it increasingly difficult to cross the battle lines, so the population in the camp remains stable at around eight hundred. As a result, we have leisure time that we spend talking and playing cards. We also make friends with several Belgian families who generously invite us into their homes. When we are not doing administrative work with Captain Ball, it's a real treat for

"The snow and black ice turn the shortest road trip into a challenge."

us to spend the long winter evenings in their beautiful, luxurious homes. We end up going often, individually or in groups, to the sumptuous property of the Peltzers, located outside of town. We are also invited by a Madame Jacqueline Zurstrasse, the young French widow of a Belgian killed several months earlier by German police. Svelte and pretty, always dressed in black, she manages, in spite of her own sadness, to create a relaxed and cheerful atmosphere. Whenever I go to her house I know that my hot bath awaits me! In her large, old-fashioned but comfortable bathroom, I find soap, perfumed oils, and thick towels from before the war. This unaccustomed luxury makes me forget the rigors of camp life. Later, we listen to music, chat, have dinner, and play bridge.

Hope of a rapid cessation of hostilities has long since been abandoned. Some say that the war will last months, even years. Those who are even more pessimistic talk about new German secret weapons that will totally wipe us out. Many reproach the Allied command for not immediately launching an all-out offensive and invading Germany while the weather was good instead of leaving the enemy time to regroup during the winter.

One day when the weather is good, driving on a snowy road through the countryside, I go to Maastricht with Captain Deloche and Captain Koldewey, who shows me around this corner of his country. With the exception of our generous hosts in Verviers, the Belgians are generally cold, even hostile, toward us. What a pleasant surprise, then, to find the Dutch warm and welcoming. They stop us in the street to thank us for being there and to invite us to their homes. The atmosphere reminds us of the happy days following the liberation of Paris.

Also in November, Captain Rothschild arrives unannounced at Sainte-Claire for an inspection tour. I go with her to Eupen, where we do some shopping, and then on to Aix-la-Chapelle. It is the first time in my life that I have set foot on German soil, and I feel the same tension I felt in 1940 when I crossed paths with Reich soldiers in Paris. We drive around the deserted streets among damaged and deserted houses. No one is here—no army, no civilians, not even a dog or a cat. The city is dead. The cathedral is a skeleton. The devastated city revolts and disgusts me just like Saint-Lô and Caen. My reaction surprises me; I tell myself without really believing it that the Germans deserved what they got. At the same time, I feel overwhelmed by the magnitude and uselessness of the material destruction and human suffering that never seem to end.

Thanks to Captain Rothschild, many problems are quickly resolved. I am to remain attached to Captain Ball's unit and am officially in charge of the teams at Namur, Huy, Jambe, and Marche, which are all under the jurisdiction of Major Litton with the ASCZ. Major Lewis doesn't get along with Major Litton and considers Namur a den of iniquity. He sulks every time I go there. I have fun teasing him, hinting that I'm going to request a transfer to the ASCZ and thus extort from him many advantages for my teams and myself. Even though it is unpleasant to be on the road, my trips to Namur feel like a real vacation. The war seems far away; there are no bombs or V1, and all the buildings are well heated. The dinners at the officers' mess are festive. While there, I meet all the bigwigs of the American Army. One evening, General Omar Bradley* himself asks me to dance. A jeep and a driver are put at my disposal to make the rounds of my teams. At Namur, life is beautiful!

The Ardennes Campaign or the Battle of the Bulge

After a particularly frustrating road trip that included getting stuck in a massive traffic jam and having to give up reaching my destination at Marche, I finally arrive back at Sainte-Claire to find the courtyard filled with DPs. The date is December 16, 1944. I am stunned to learn that the Germans have launched an offensive. Stavelot and Malmédy have already been taken, and Bastogne is threatened. They say that a German parachute troop has surrounded Marche, where I was headed just a few hours ago.

I decide to go to Spa to try to get news and, if possible, to bring my Spa team back to Verviers. I hardly dare think about what might be happening to the other teams at Stavelot, Eupen, and Malmédy. Halfway to Spa, and for the second time today, I am forced to turn back. The First Army high command with all its weapons and baggage is pulling back. An endless stream of trucks and jeeps loaded with tables, chairs, trunks, and all kind of other matériel is clogging the road. Even though I put on my headlights and keep honking, I keep getting forced into the ditch. Finally an aggressive MP orders me to turn around, yelling: "Can't you see we're retreating? What the f—— are you doing here?" I'm devastated to have to turn back once again and wonder what's going to happen. A look at the map reveals the danger of our being totally surrounded.

At Sainte-Claire, we spend the night sending the Russians and Poles to the rear so that we will have room for Belgian DPs from the Stavelot region, who are already pouring in on foot and in trucks. These miserable people had to flee their homes in a matter of minutes under a barrage of bombs and artillery. Many are wounded or suffering from frostbite. Our small infirmary is quickly overwhelmed. Some of the DPs are sobbing, others are in a state of shock. A few, who are terrified by the noise of artillery and aircraft, take the American officers aside and demand to be evacuated behind the lines in place of the Russians and Poles. It's hard work keeping everyone calm, but finally the warmth inside (in contrast to the intense cold outside) and their fatigue puts even the most pugnacious to sleep. Through the night we continue to move the DPs from Eastern Europe. Miserable to be sent away, the Russian women weep and cling to us as we help them into the trucks.

In the middle of all this confusion, I am relieved to learn that my teams are safe and have pulled back to various locations including Hombourg and Tongres, where Major Lewis is also headed with his staff. Our unit receives the order to be ready for a rapid evacuation. We're to send the new DPs across the river Meuse. Easier said than done, given our lack of vehicles! At Verviers we are apparently at the northernmost point of the German breakthrough. The city is a vital communications hub traversed by the troops and matériel being sent north to close the breach. Our camp, in the middle of a triangle of roads and rail lines, is not a good place to be.

The Allied forces in the Ardennes (between Aix-la-Chapelle and Luxembourg) include only four American divisions, who are supposed to hold a front of 120 kilometers. The command clearly did not expect any enemy movement during this exceptionally cold and snowy winter. But the Germans, commanded by General von Rundstedt,* took advantage of the situation and, in total secrecy, assembled ten armored divisions and fourteen divisions of infantry. With tanks out front and covered by what remains of the German Air Force, these powerful forces have cut through the vulnerable center of the American line between Malmédy and Bastogne. The German objective is to reach the Meuse between Liège and Namur, perhaps go all the way to Anvers.

At Sainte-Claire, around two o'clock in the morning, we are gathered in the unit office, a haven of calm. We note with satisfaction that, thanks to all our preparations, our system of dealing with DPs has stood the test, even though there are now more than five thousand people here, more than double what we had foreseen. Major Lewis is understandably concerned about the safety of the DPs since Verviers is being hit with an intense air and ground bombardment, plus V1 rockets. The almost incessant firing from our own aircraft only intensifies the deafening noise that engulfs us. After spending an hour on guard duty in the basement where we have herded the maximum number of people, I tumble into bed without undressing and fall into a deep sleep.

It seems to me that I have slept only a few minutes when Yvonne shakes me awake: "Everyone is looking for you! Captain Ball is frantic. He thinks you got hit by the V1 that landed a little while ago. How can you sleep with all this racket?" I get up, excusing myself: "I was so tired I forgot to set my alarm. But this is horrible! It's already morning!"

By the time I get to the office, the meeting has already begun. We organize a convoy in preparation for a retreat and discuss different possibilities for evacuating the camp. Throughout the day, we partially achieve our goal of finding transport by commandeering munitions trucks returning empty from the front.

With the permission I extract from Captain Ball, I leave for Hombourg. I'm extremely worried about the teams there, knowing they are so close to the German front lines, and I hope to be able to bring them back with me. The traffic is heavy, and the road, churned up by the tank treads, has turned into a mass of mud. All the intersecting roads are blocked by half-tracks. MPs stop me several times, but my orders are to go to Hombourg, so I get through. When I do, I discover that my teams have already left, and I have missed them by several hours. Another useless trip!

Later that day, we realize that the inhabitants of Verviers are leaving by the hundreds, mostly on foot or on bicycles. Those who remain nail planks over their windows and take refuge in their basements. Aside from a few small groups hurrying away loaded with suitcases and packages, all the streets, which yesterday were so lively, are totally deserted. Of all the various military installations, only the hospitals, the provost marshal and his ten MPs, and our camp remain.

When the bombardments stop, the city seems inordinately still. The only sounds are the wail of ambulance sirens and the rumble of vehicles passing on the main road. Our Belgian colleagues tell us that the remaining citizens of Verviers, expecting the imminent return of the Germans, hope that the Americans will leave so the bombardments will cease and Verviers will be declared an open city. It seems their wish is about to be granted because Captain Ball's unit receives the order to move out to Tongres. Captain Ball is livid and curses the "frightened old bags" of the high command. He finally manages to get through to the First Army on the telephone and tells them he is not going to budge. After a long and ultimately futile exchange, he is told that the order is formal: his unit is to leave, but the MMLA team and civilian volunteers are to remain in place with the DPs. Exasperated, he passes on to me all his instructions, coded messages, etc. When their convoy finally gets under way at the end of the afternoon, leaving us with one jeep, we feel like poor orphans, abandoned to our fate. Captain Ball swears he will return the following day, but as it turns out, it was three days later before his return. For my comrades and me those were three very long days.

To keep up our morale, we begin by drinking a whiskey and then move into the rooms left by the American officers. We meet with the heads of the various refugee groups to discuss the situation. On a material level, things risk deteriorating very quickly since our stock of coal and food is already dangerously low. In addition, after witnessing the departure of the Americans, the DPs are understandably anxious. We do our best to calm them by broadcasting reassuring messages over the loudspeakers, and the Dutch leaders go room to room trying to soothe fears. The evening meal goes on normally, but the news we manage to glean from the vague information on the radio is not encouraging: the Germans have penetrated thirty kilometers into Belgium and are only twenty kilometers from Liège. The Allies are pulling back across the Meuse (bad news for us since we're on the other side of the river!). Apparently, German parachute troops are being dropped everywhere so that they can cut communications and create confusion by turning road signs around. Dressed as civilians, they may even infiltrate groups of DPs. Others, dressed in American uniforms and speaking perfect English, circulate in captured jeeps to launch commando attacks.

A little later, the mother superior of the institute pays us a visit. Since our arrival in Verviers, she and the sisters have been models of efficiency and discretion. Quiet and quick, they are everywhere they are needed—taking care of the sick, comforting the wounded, and looking after the children. This evening, we go to their quarters for the first time. The mother superior welcomes us graciously and offers to hide us or to lend us habits from her order if we need a disguise. This proposal enchants us, and we devote the rest of the evening to a merry session of trying on nun's habits.

That same evening, I don't forget to set my alarm, but it turns out I don't need it; in spite of being exhausted, I can't go to sleep, imagining all the disasters that might occur. The following day that I had dreaded so much actually goes well. There is a full cloud cover so there are fewer bombardments, at least in our area. Yvonne, who left to look for a person with the impressive title "Steward of Food Supplies," comes back with good news: she has gotten the promise of a daily ten-liter delivery of milk for the children and the sick, which will supplement our dwindling stock of powdered milk. In addition, the large numbers of cattle killed in the raids are still in the fields, perfectly preserved by the cold and snow. Yvonne takes the truck with several men, plus a butcher, to cut up the meat and bring it back to camp. While Yvonne is doing this, Louise manages to send thirty or so of the oldest DPs to a home in Liège. Some resourceful young Dutchmen miraculously discover a storehouse of coal and bring back the precious commodity in two large wagons towed by tractors.

Things being what they are, the camp routine is greatly simplified. No more DPs coming in by the truckload; only a few on foot. The intake formalities are reduced to a minimum, and, since the American Intelligence officers are gone, there are no interrogations of incoming DPs. Reassured by our reserves of food and fuel, at last I feel more confident.

The following day, it is still cold and gray, but at least the snow has stopped. I'm in the office sorting out problems with the group heads when I see a short, little man in the courtyard wearing an American helmet that is much too big for him. He is clearly trying to get my attention. I go out and discover that it is Captain Blum, the French liaison officer attached to the First Army HQ. Although he is, in principle, my superior officer, I have seen him only once before; Major Lewis has always systematically bypassed him and dealt with me directly. Now, Captain Blum is getting all worked up, cursing the Americans. Thinking that he would do better to rail against the Germans, I nevertheless invite him into the office and offer him a cup of coffee in the hope of calming him down.

Having learned the day before that we were left at Verviers without our American Army unit, he is coming directly from Tongres—a difficult trek, given that the route was blocked by German parachute troops—with the intention of taking us back with him. I tell him that we are fine and suggest that I take him on a tour of the camp so that he can see for himself how things are. Back in my office after the inspection, the captain doesn't appear to be at all reassured. He orders me to assemble my team and our equipment for an evacuation. According to him, Verviers is about to be abandoned to the Germans. I answer rather sharply that you hear anything and everything at the command center, and that it would be completely idiotic to surrender Verviers, given that it is an Allied communications hub.

"In any case, I refuse to leave. Major Lewis and Captain Ball put me in charge of the camp, and I'm not leaving my post." To reassure him further, I add that I am expecting the return of the American detachment in the next few hours (of course, I know nothing of the sort, but I still hope!). Captain Blum continues to raise objections. I am trying to ease him out when an enormous explosion interrupts our conversation. A piece of plaster falls on the captain's head. With white powder all over him, he looks like a clown. I burst out laughing, grab a helmet, and, leaving hurriedly, shout over my shoulder: "Goodbye, Captain. Have a good trip back!"

Even though the courtyard is littered with debris, there is only slight damage to the building. All the newly repaired windowpanes are shattered, and the woodshed used as a welcome center is smashed in on one side. More seriously, our water pipes have been blasted. Three of the Dutch DPs are already on the spot, and I ask them to clear the courtyard and replace the windows (we have a good supply of new panes in the basement storeroom). They also get milk cans from nearby farms so that we can carry water from the nearest water supply, which is three hundred meters from the camp.

At that moment, an MP arrives from the unit that had been left at Verviers. He asks us to take in the families whose houses were destroyed in the raid. He also requests a vehicle to transport the wounded to the hospital. Since I'm the only member of the team available, I leave with the MP in our truck. When I return to camp, I'm surprised to see that Captain Blum is still there. He is livid because I left with his helmet on my head. I apologize and give it back to him. He reminds me that a lieutenant isn't authorized to wear a captain's helmet (!) and then announces that he is going back to Tongres to get official orders for our immediate evacuation. We finally find his driver, who is flirting with some pretty DPs, and it is with great relief that I watch his jeep disappear down the driveway.

That afternoon, an MP dispatched by the American provost marshal of Verviers turns up in our office. He hands me a message requesting the commander of the camp to come, armed, to police HQ accompanied by the French liaison officer. Since I am now both camp commander and liaison officer, I am the only one to leave with the MP. Their HQ is located in a small building in the middle of a square. To my astonishment, the square is filled with a big, noisy crowd shouting anti-American slogans. With some difficulty, we reach the steps of the HQ and end up on a small terrace surrounded by a balustrade. The provost marshal explains to me that the surprise German offensive with its incessant bombardments has created a wild panic in the population. False rumors added to the subversive action of an enemy fifth column have only fed the flames of fear. Delegations from the inhabitants have assembled in the square to demand the departure of the remaining Americans so Verviers can be declared an open city.

Someone brings a microphone. Armed MPs surround us. One of them warns me that we will probably be shot at, and, if this occurs, I am to drop to the floor and take cover behind the balustrade. The provost marshal begins to speak. Standing next to him on the top step, I realize that we are in a totally vulnerable position. Fortunately, the crowd quiets down while he addresses them in a calm, authoritative voice. He explains that the American Army has the situation in hand, that the offensive has been halted, and that everything will return to normal in a few days. He asks for calm and announces that the curfew will be extended for two hours, both morning and evening. He ends by asking everyone to return to their homes. I follow him to the microphone to translate his message into French. While I am speaking, I hear my voice, amplified by the loudspeakers, echoing around the square. It is a weird experience. People start asking questions, and we try to answer, but our responses are drowned out by the sound of the DCA and several small explosions. The crowd disperses quickly and, to our surprise, very calmly.

The provost marshal then admits to me that he gave the order for a false alert so that the crowd would clear the square! He also tells me that, in fact, he has no official information but that all the news he has heard is bad. The Allied line in the north is holding, but the center is soft. Saint-Vith and Saint-Hubert have been retaken by the Germans. The provost marshal drives me back to camp in a jeep after asking me to make a tour of the city to show that we are still here. He says our presence has a calming effect and that we should, therefore, circulate in town as often as possible. He complains about the order to evacuate the Civil Affairs units at exactly the time they had become indispensable.

On the cold morning of December 19, the sun is shining, and the sky is blue. It will be a good day from all points of view. The children in the camp throw snowballs and make a snowman. We hear at last the reassuring hum of our airplanes, the precursor of the biggest action yet since the German offensive began. As the day goes on, several visits occur. First, it's the surprise arrival from Paris of our commander, Captain Rothschild with her daughter Nicole. Pressured by our panicked families and because of her own concern, Captain Rothschild has been trying to reach us since the beginning of the offensive but was held back by the difficulty of obtaining an official order for her mission.

Next, our First Army unit returns, followed closely by Major Lewis, who is grumpier than ever. It is with total delight that I restore to him the reins of office. Captain Rothschild and I then leave the camp to try to check on our other teams. The team at Maastricht is fine, but another that we find totally by accident at Fraîture has been living in ghastly conditions for the last week. We send them to Verviers to rest and recuperate. The teams at Namur are overwhelmed by the huge number of Russian and Polish DPs pushed back from the combat zone. At HQ we get the good news that the German offensive has been essentially halted and that Stavelot and Bastogne have been retaken. The good weather continues, our planes are able to fly, the enemy bombardments are losing momentum, and artillery shelling continues only intermittently.

In spite of the intense cold, we have a joyous celebration of Christmas at Sainte-Claire. We prepare a good, hot meal for the DPs on an old wood stove. We set up a large Christmas tree decorated with garlands in the salon. We are able to give toys to the children, serve wine and beer to the adults, and sweets to everyone. People bring their guitars and harmonicas, and soon people are singing and dancing. Later the staff celebrates with a dinner of turkey and suckling pig. (Where does this feast come from? Better not ask!) We drink a delicious Krug champagne that Captain Deloche got in Reims on his way back from Paris.

The Battle of the Bulge is officially over on December 25, but, in fact, it is won decisively only after vigorous counterattacks by the British from the north and the Americans from the south. The armies finally link up at Houffalize in mid-January, cutting off a German retreat on one side and, on the other, pushing them back to their original positions behind the Belgian border.

Meanwhile, the air attacks continue, the thermometer swings between five degrees above zero and five below. Our electricity and gas are finally restored on December 29, but the water is not back on until January 10 of the new year. DPs continue to arrive at the rate of a hundred a day. Most of us with colds and flu are almost glad to have a fever since it keeps us warm! The DPs begin to suffer from a variety of illnesses: flu, pneumonia, measles, typhoid, and diphtheria. The infirmary personnel are sorely tried because we can no longer transfer patients to the municipal hospital, already filled beyond capacity.

The day after Christmas, Captain Ball and I are in the courtyard when an enormous shock wave followed by an unbelievably violent explosion knocks us to the ground. It feels as if a house has fallen on top of me, and I think I'm done for. But it turns out that the "house" is, in fact, Captain Ball who gallantly threw himself on top of me to protect me. I get away with some scratches on my face and some bruises, but there is serious damage to the camp. The pillars holding up the entryway collapsed at just the moment that one of our jeeps was driving in. The unfortunate driver was decapitated. DPs are wounded.

Of all our vehicles, mine is the only one that will start, so I load up the wounded and take them to the municipal hospital. Next, I set out for the military hospital hoping to get some drugs and medical supplies. Louise goes with me because she knows the head doctor and hopes that the connection will be helpful. The hospital is teeming with activity: to make our way, we have to step over the sick and wounded, who are lying on stretchers or even on the floor in the hallways. We don't succeed in catching up with any doctors or nurses, who are overwhelmed by the sudden influx of patients. Going from one floor to the next, we finally obtain, with much difficulty, some diphtheria serum, several other drugs, and some syringes and bandages. Holding tightly onto our precious booty, we have only one desire, and that is to get out of this nightmarish place as quickly as possible. The fact is, we feel safe only at Sainte-Claire.

We want to leave, but we can't, because our car is blocked by a large truck. While we are waiting impatiently for the driver of the truck, we watch an ambulance being loaded. One of the wounded—a smiling young soldier—asks me for a cigarette. We chat a while and then, as the ambulance gets ready to leave, he shouts to me: "I'll bet you'll be sorry that you can't come with me instead of staying in this death trap." Louise and I laugh and wave goodbye. I am getting really annoyed with the truck driver who has still not shown up to move his vehicle when we hear a V1 overhead. It is flying very low. The motor stops. Louise and I flatten ourselves against the hospital wall and begin to count. I watch the ambulance moving away, about a hundred meters from us. We hear the explosion, see the ball of fire and then the ambulance breaking apart. Pieces of sheet metal and fragments of all kinds burst upward and then arc down as if in a slow-motion film. Everything is engulfed in a cloud of dust. Stretcher-bearers come running, but we know there will be nothing left of the poor young man who was so happy to be heading to the rear. For the first time since I have known her, Louise's rosy cheeks turn white. The truck driver arrives and apologizes for keeping us waiting. As if from a distance, I hear my own voice saying: "You did well to take your time, otherwise we would have gotten the worst of the buzz bomb." My hands are sweating in spite of the cold. I'm shaking like a leaf and have trouble driving the car. After a few moments, I stop, open the door, and throw up.

Back at the camp, things are not much better. The nearest water supply is now three kilometers away. The gas and electricity are off again, and we are out of coal for the stoves and emergency furnace. We have latrines dug in the nuns' garden and organize teams to go for water, but the water freezes in the containers. Then there's more. One of the GIs comes down with diphtheria. A girl is hurt in a car accident. A Czech refugee commits suicide. Another is caught sending light signals from the roof. Our vehicles are frozen and won't start. We have no more straw and no more blankets. Our stocks of food are alarmingly low. DPs and victims from the city keep arriving. We deal with the problems as best we can and actually succeed in getting food supplies. But against the cold, there is nothing we can do.

Artillery shelling and the V1s terrorize the DPs and become harder and harder to endure. In a forty-eight-hour period, five large bombs fall near the camp. We have become an island in the midst of a sea of wreckage. Both the municipal and military hospitals are damaged. We can no longer evacuate any wounded or sick. We begin looking for coffins.

During the last days of December, the cloud cover returns, and bombardments diminish as a result. But the cold gets even worse. We succeed in sending three hundred Belgians on to Liège, but we still have eight hundred DPs at the camp. Too many for a place lacking water, electricity, and heat. On the last day of the year, there are several attacks by dive-bombers. The staff is relieved because dive-bombers are less dangerous than bombs. But the whine of the Stukas terrifies the DPs, who scream with terror. January 1, 1945, arrives with a flourish of new attacks. We are furious because everyone is saying that the battle is over but no one seems concerned about us. We feel as if we are being unfairly targeted. We amuse ourselves, somewhat bitterly, by composing letters of complaint "To whom it may concern." Perhaps someone heard our virtual complaints, because the attacks cease, and, little by little, life begins again.

A Day on the Slopes

On January 7, we celebrate the end of the Ardennes campaign with champagne. Our central heating is back on, and, even though there are many sick, everything seems easier now that the storm of battle is over. I decide to indulge myself by getting some fresh air over the weekend at an artillery installation, manned by young soldiers from the Second Division, not far from the German border. In periods of relative calm, the soldiers have become regular visitors to the camp, where they can drink, play cards, and decompress. Lately, Captain Ball, a movie lover, has even gotten hold of a projector and some films, which attract both civilians and military viewers, including the artillery crew.

They come to greet us for the first time since the offensive. We are particularly glad to see them since their unit in the front line suffered many losses. To our surprise, Lieutenants Christopher and Walters propose a ski weekend. My comrades are ill and can't go, but I decide to accept the invitation. Captain Ball does not approve of the excursion but promises to say I am in bed with a high fever if Major Lewis asks for me.

We leave the next morning at nine—the two lieutenants, the driver, and I. We go east through deep snow, which necessitates our putting chains on the tires. We continue on roads winding through a superb forest of pines and larches. The snow muffles all sounds, the sun is shining, the sky is blue, and life seems beautiful even though we are near the front line. The artillery installation is halfway up a hill bordered by spruce trees. The German forward units are only four kilometers away on the other side of the valley. We have lunch at the canteen. The officers, surprised to see me, nevertheless give me a warm welcome.

Before setting out to ski, we put on white camouflage suits. Lieutenant Walters, who comes from Colorado and is an excellent skier, leads the way through magnificent scenery to a spot where there are several good slopes. He stops behind a spruce tree, takes out his binoculars, and carefully scans the snowy hillsides. I don't see anything at first, but when he passes the binoculars to me, I see a German soldier hidden in a hole dug in the snow. Through the glasses, he looks very near. "No," says Walters in a whisper, "he's at least four hundred meters away. But don't make any noise. Voices carry in these conditions. Plus, he looks like he's alone. He must be a scout."

The lieutenant pretends to shoulder his rifle. "Don't shoot!" I beg. "He's eating and the poor thing must be freezing; his fingers are as red as his sausage."

"I guarantee that, given the chance, he would shoot at us. But it's the weekend, and I have no intention of alerting the whole sector, especially when you are doing us the honor of a visit."

We spend the afternoon skiing, and I haven't had so much fun in a long time. After dinner at the post, we go to an office in the blockhouse where I am to spend the night. We play bridge with two colonels (I win 250 francs). As a protection against arriving mortar shells, they place my cot against the wall. They also provide me with a loaded revolver in case Germans penetrate the enclosure under cover of darkness looking to take prisoners. There is a battery of 88s right under my window, but what I fear most is the ringing of the field telephone that is right near my feet. If it does ring, Walters instructs me to answer in a deep voice and then call him. Fortunately, the phone is quiet, and, tired by our day on the slopes, I sleep like a log, even though intermittent shelling startles me awake from time to time.

A meter of snow has fallen during the night, and I feel sorry for the poor GIs who have to sleep in trenches in the open air. It takes some doing to dig out the jeep that is to take me back to Verviers with three MPs. All the officers come to bid me goodbye and ask me to return whenever I can. But the occasion will never arise again because several days later, when a GI comes to return my skis, he tells me that Lieutenant Walters was killed the night before by a German patrol.

This unhappy incident leaves me profoundly depressed. I feel as if I bring bad luck. Whenever I get interested in someone, something horrible happens. I resolve from that time on to bury myself in my work, to ignore young officers, and to be less disagreeable to the older ones since, in general, they run fewer risks.

The Winter Continues

January, February, 1945: snow, cold, ice. New teams arrive, making a total of fifteen. As a result, I have to spend more time on the road and on administrative duties. We are visited by VIPs on inspection tours. Captain Ball tries to impress them with what he calls "eyewash for the brass." An American film crew spends two days with us working on a documentary.

A new liaison officer arrives: a Russian lieutenant named Konstantin. On the day he arrives in a jeep, Captain Ball says to me: "At last, here is our Russian liaison officer." "How can you say that?" I respond, dumbfounded. "He looks like a tramp. His clothes are in tatters, his hair is long, and it looks as if he hasn't shaved for a week!" But Captain Ball is right. The day after his arrival, Lieutenant Konstantin shows up in the mess clean-shaven, in a new uniform sporting a magnificent red star on the sleeve. His presence seems to calm the Russian DPs, and, even if they don't stop fighting, their conflicts are now quickly settled. Konstantin rapidly becomes indispensable. He speaks perfect German and soon is able to get along in English. If Captain Ball asks for something, always helpful, Konstantin manages to get it right away. His talent for scrounging will turn out to be particularly useful when we get to Germany.

Slowly, we learn Konstantin's story. He began his career as an engineer in Moscow. Mobilized in 1941, he was captured at Smolensk and spent time in a German prisoner-of-war camp. He escaped from the camp with the help of Olga, a young village girl. They were captured again and this time were sent to a forced labor camp. They managed to marry before being transferred to Aix-la-Chapelle. While they were there, Olga was killed in an air raid. Konstantin escaped again and made his way to an American forward post after spending ten days hiding in a forest in the cold and snow.

He often tearfully talks to us about Olga and, at the beginning, speaks of Russia with great pride. As time goes on, however, the tone of his remarks darkens, and he tells us that Russian officers captured by the enemy are now treated as deserters who are executed or exiled to Siberia.

Konstantin honors me with his loyalty and affection, calling me his "little sister." He decides he is my guardian angel and often accompanies me on my rounds. On a trip to Namur, I introduce him to Major Litton, who takes us to the mess. Konstantin and I make a big splash with our rendition of a Russian dance—but only after we down several glasses of vodka!

My usual inspection trips are not nearly so merry. I most often travel alone, and I frequently get blocked by snowdrifts or, slipping on the ice, end up in a ditch or colliding with other vehicles. I become a familiar figure in the district, known especially by the numberless GIs who tow and repair my car. Now accustomed to these "adventures," I no longer fear going out on the road by myself. But Major Lewis continues making scenes each time I go out and curses the "Frog Army" that refuses to provide me with a driver when Captain Blum has one. I try to explain to Captain Lewis that Blum is favored because he is a man, but that only enrages him more.

Around January 20, Major Lewis summons me to Spa and, handing me a telegram from SHAEF, says with fury in his voice: "Here! Read this!" The telegram contains an order prohibiting all MMLA teams from going into Germany. I am as outraged as Major Lewis at this news. We put our heads together to organize a response. The upshot is that I am to go to Paris to gather information about the situation.

In Paris, I go to see Captain Rothschild, who is especially indignant because she was neither consulted nor informed about the new order. We make the rounds of several offices, where we are often made to wait, once for three hours. We finally get in to see General Hamet of the PDR ministry, housed on the Avenue Foch. He is evasive and clearly knows very little about the work of the MMLA teams. I am frustrated and furious, but Captain Rothschild reassures me that everything will work out.

Fortunately, she is right. In February, General Hamet inspects the MMLA camps in our sector and is impressed with our work. After that, somehow the SHAEF telegram is forgotten. An MMLA team with the Third Army moves into Germany with their unit. I expect we will be next. The crisis is over.

At the end of February, the weather warms up. Now we have rain instead of snow, slush instead of ice. The roads are often flooded. The front line has not budged. Vehicles get stuck in the mud. Everything seems paralyzed.

An Excursion to the Front

Tom Leary, an English journalist, comes to our camp to report on the refugee situation. He invites us to the "Press Bar" in Verviers where the war correspondents—both men and women—gather. We discover another world with its own stories, jokes, and special language. The journalists drink a lot and that, added to the jargon of their profession, means that we comprehend only half of what they say. But, even if we don't understand everything, we are glad to be with them during these sad days of suspended action.

One evening, having drunk even more than usual, Leary invites me to come to the front with him, posing as a French journalist. It's absolutely forbidden, of course, but I decide to accept the invitation. He picks me up in a jeep with his inseparable collaborator, Miss Laxton, a British correspondent and field artist. Miss Laxton is a short, fortyish woman, plump, spirited, always smiling and often absent-minded. She carries her box of watercolors slung under her arm, looking as if she belongs in an English rose garden rather than in a battle zone.

We're looking for a command post called Jayhawk Forward. Leary wants to interview soldiers who participated in an attack the previous day. On the road to Aix-la-Chapelle, we come upon a seemingly endless convoy of trucks filled with German prisoners. We then speed toward Düren on a superb superhighway with pine forests interspersed here and there in the otherwise flat, deserted countryside. When we arrive in Düren, we find a totally demolished town. There is not a living soul to be seen. The only thing left standing among the ruins is a giant statue of Bismarck.

We wander from one village to another, from one military post to another before finally locating the CP of the 414th Artillery Regiment of the 104th Division in Buir, a deserted hamlet retaken from the Germans just hours before. Soldiers and vehicles move about in no apparent order. No one can answer our questions, not even an MP who has just arrived looking for his unit. I wonder how people manage to function in the midst of such chaos, but Leary tells me that it is always like this at the front. We see soldiers throwing a motley mix of objects from the windows of the few houses left standing. Apparently, they are trying to clear out a space to spend the night.

The GIs apparently think that all reporters are crazy, so they let us go where we want. Naturally, they are happy to see us women, and they whistle and call out as we pass. We pass several jeeps and ambulances lined up in front of a first aid station. We see four GIs sitting comfortably on a huge sofa on the side of the road. One of them is playing a saxophone. We ask them if they can spare a helmet for Miss Laxton, who has misplaced hers. They give us one. Artillery booms. The front line forms an arc along the road. Buir is the most forward point on the circle. To our left, we can both see and hear German artillery. The batteries must be some four kilometers away, judging from the interval between the sound of fire and the hit. From time to time, we hear the whistle of shells as they pass over our heads. Curiously, I don't feel any sense of danger. Nobody looks worried so why should I?

Entirely by chance, we finally come upon the command post Leary was looking for. We are welcomed by a charming Lieutenant Jones, who is surrounded by two dozen men. He doesn't seem at all surprised to see such a strange trio and allows us to interview the soldiers. Leary introduces me as a member of the United French Press, and I talk with a pleasant young Frenchman who is with the group. While we talk, Miss Laxton says she is going for a walk. Two MPs, who find her wandering around, think she is a spy and take her to another

CP. She talks her way out of it, however, and when we finally locate her, she is sitting in the courtyard of a farm, calmly sketching two emaciated goats. After finding Miss Laxton, we take off in our jeep and return to Verviers without incident. This day at the front leaves me with the impression of being in a crazy rally taking place in a chaotic, nightmarish landscape. There, soldiers fight seemingly at random, trying to survive amidst the mayhem and in complete ignorance of what is happening around them.

At the beginning of March, the First Army is on the offensive once again. Crowds of DPs arrive at our camp. We process and evacuate them, working day and night. Even though there is so much urgent work, everything goes smoothly. This time, there are more French among the DPs, up to a hundred a day, along with the usual Belgians, Dutch, Yugoslavs, Italians, and, of course, Russians and Poles. Around March 3, the population in the camp reaches twelve hundred. Alas, our "protégés" from the East, with whom we get along so well, have to move on. They leave in tears; some try to hide so they can stay.

On March 10, at eleven in the evening, we're still busy loading trucks when I get a phone call from Lewis, recently promoted to colonel. He announces that we are to leave the next morning at eight for a camp at Brand, several kilometers southwest of Aix-la-Chapelle. We spend the rest of the night getting ready to leave this place where we have spent the five cold months of winter and which has become so familiar to us. We know that nothing will ever be the same, but we don't have time for nostalgia. We have to pack up our personal belongings, along with the trunks of administrative gear, and all the matériel we use in our work. After feverishly doing all the paperwork pertaining to our departure, we finally have a little time to say goodbye to our Belgian friends before our morning deadline to leave Sainte-Claire.

Part 4

Germany. Buchenwald.

Vagliano and her team followed the Americans across the border into Germany in mid-March 1945. By then, everyone felt that the end of the war in Europe was near. Millions of DPs and POWs were on the move. Previously, the MMLA camps held a thousand or two. Now the teams were faced with housing, feeding, and caring for up to twenty thousand people at a time. Their task was made particularly difficult by the fact that they had no authorized source of food and no official doctors assigned to them. Vagliano provides ample details about the living conditions of the DPs, but hardly any about her own lodging. When she mentions in passing that her commanding officer at HQ arranged for her to have a hot shower, we understand that this was a rare treat.

The team first went to Brand, at the time a separate community, now absorbed into the city of Aachen (Aix-la-Chapelle). When Vagliano arrived, Brand was the largest DP camp in Germany. She describes the huge barracks where they set up camp, which we now know was the Lützow-Kaserne, formerly of the German Army, located on a campus of 103 acres. At the end of March, her team moved to Brauweiler, a small village, which a British Army soldier later described as "dismal, cold, and depressing." What Vagliano did not know while she was stationed there was that the monastery she mentions had been used by the Gestapo for the internment, torture, and murder of political and social "undesirables."

After welcome breaks to visit Cologne and Paris, and an adventure crossing the Rhine, Vagliano arrived in Wetzlar in mid-April. This industrial city had been heavily damaged by Allied bombs, but the MMLA team was fortunately able to occupy a large barracks with the amazing capacity of twenty to twenty-five thousand people.

Finally, on a visit to HQ at Marburg, Vagliano describes the dismal mood among the officers who, rather than being happy and relieved at the prospect of the end of the war in Europe, felt betrayed, especially by the recently deceased President Roosevelt and the concessions he had made to the Russians at Yalta. The officers rightly foresaw that the division of Europe would produce further problems and conflict.

❖

Brand

March 11–28, 1945

Captain Ball, the Dutch captain, and I arrive in Brand on a reconnaissance mission. *Colossal* is the first word that comes to mind as we look with some concern at the imposing barracks assigned to us. *Colossal* also, the immense Nazi eagles on the impressive façade. *Colossal*, the high vaulted entrance and the innumerable brick buildings that surround a vast courtyard. In the middle of the courtyard is a building that resembles an equestrian center or stables but that actually houses kitchens and a mess hall. The buildings are connected by paved roads bordered by gaslights. The whole ensemble resembles a prison or a fortified city. Colonel Lewis is waiting for us under the archway in a jeep that looks like a miniature toy in this setting.

To inspect the buildings and assign areas for lodging the various nationalities, offices, infirmary, kitchens, etc., we cover several kilometers and are exhausted by the time the whole detachment arrives toward ten o'clock in the evening. Almost one thousand DPs are already here. The liaison officers immediately go to work with their assigned groups, processing them and spraying them with DDT (the best protection against typhus, the disease most feared in the camps).

At first, the DPs arrive by dozens, then by hundreds, then by thousands. Our count rapidly reaches twenty thousand. Our orders are to keep the DPs from the East (mostly Russians and Poles) and to evacuate those from the West as quickly as possible, ideally within twenty-four hours. We have forty trucks of our own that pick up DPs at the front. In addition, other military vehicles going from the front to their bases often stop off to unload DPs that they have picked up on the way.

In Germany, we have to live entirely off the land since we can't obtain food supplies from the American Army. The day we arrive at

Brand, there are no stockpiles of food; in fact, there is no food at all. By nightfall, however, the heroic Lieutenant Konstantin arrives with three trucks loaded with dehydrated potatoes, flour, sugar, corned beef, and blankets. As time goes on, we get better and better at scrounging. Officially, this is the job of Yvonne and Lieutenant Schurr, but we all take our turn. Even Captain Ball takes a liking to going out on these unorthodox expeditions that quickly become our favorite sport. Konstantin is clearly the champion, and, thanks to him, our supply of provisions is quickly established.

Generally the food "commandos" go scouting in a jeep early in the morning. We start with the neighboring villages. The inhabitants are understandably reluctant to tell us about hidden food stores. But Konstantin doesn't buy into their stories, and they almost always end up telling us where we can find supplies. Our main source turns out to be stockpiles left by the Germans. We have to work fast to get to the depots before other military units lay claim to them. Once we find a storehouse, we put out signs saying "Danger of Death" or "Explosives" or "Deadly Gas." Konstantin then posts Russians from his personal guard, armed to the teeth, to keep watch. It happens that, in moments of dire need, we take supplies already claimed by other units that are guarded only by one or two unarmed locals. Our next move is to send out trucks. Sometimes it takes as much as several days to empty the larger storehouses. In this way, we obtain not only food but also straw, pharmaceutical products, blankets, tools, coal, wood, and even furniture.

Konstantin's biggest prize is an abandoned locomotive about ten kilometers away, hitched to three cars loaded with food. Somehow he manages to get the locomotive started and runs it on a rail line that ends only three hundred meters from our camp.

More successful at cadging supplies than the other units in the sector, we are soon on bad terms with them. In fact, they end up complaining to the command about our "gangster" tactics. Captain Ball is summoned to HQ. His reaction of injured innocence must have worked because there is no further fallout from the complaints.

As at Verviers, the kitchen at Brand is assigned to Yvonne and the infirmary to Louise. Yvonne organizes enough teams of cooks, aides, and servers to feed fifteen to twenty thousand people a day. The kitchens and mess hall are in an immense building at the center of the camp. Along the walls are several ranks of large metal vats about five feet tall. They are at work twenty-four hours a day, cooking a thick soup made of dehydrated potatoes, white beans, and canned or fresh meat when we have it. Dessert—either jam or a mix of the dehydrated potatoes, nuts, and dried fruits—is served with ersatz coffee and cookies. Children and the elderly are given milk and fresh fruit when they are available. Volunteer DPs make bread in the bakery next to the kitchens. The DPs get only one meal a day. They are required to show color-coded cards that are stamped and dated. From six in the morning until seven at night a long line forms on the one side of the mess and snakes through, emerging on the other side.

Louise is responsible for the infirmary. Unfortunately, no doctors are assigned to the Civil Affairs units. We are lucky, however, to have with us two volunteer doctors from Verviers, who will remain with us until the end of the war. For an infirmary, we have a small room with a dozen beds where we isolate those with contagious diseases. The seriously ill are transported to the nearest civilian hospital. Typhoid, diphtheria, measles, and several cases of typhus all occur, but we are lucky enough to avoid a real epidemic (other camps are not so fortunate).

Our basic medical staff is assisted by volunteer nurses who work all day looking after cuts and bruises, skin disorders, chilblains, and, especially, scabies, which we on the staff also get. Louise is also responsible for all the medical and surgical equipment. She gets her supplies either by "liberating" German Army stocks with the help of Konstantin or by charming the military doctors in nearby units. It's a weighty task for a nineteen-year-old whose only preparation is one year of nursing studies.

Contrary to what we anticipated, language problems are easily resolved. The liaison officers look after the DPs of their respective nationalities and serve as interpreters when needed. The team is fine with French, gets along well in English, and somewhat less well in German. When the need arises we call on DPs to help out with other languages. Captain Ball outfits a truck with powerful loudspeakers, and this sound truck circulates from morning until evening making announcements in all the relevant camp languages. Sometimes it plays music. The sound truck serves its purpose, but the incessant noise soon becomes hard to bear.

On the second night, the loudspeakers provoke a tragicomic incident. Several trucks carrying DPs arrive at the camp around two o'clock in the morning. A guttural voice can be heard giving instructions in German. Just a few kilometers away, some GIs at a forward camp are wakened by the noise. Thinking the Germans are attacking, they sound the alert and open fire. The other soldiers at the post join them. A general fusillade ensues. After that, use of the loudspeakers at night is strictly forbidden.

The Nazi eagle at the camp entrance is camouflaged by a large American shield with the eagles' wings painted red, white, and blue. We put up an immense sign signaling that the camp belongs to the D3F1 of the First US Army. The offices are furnished and given a new coat of paint. The redecorating gives our lugubrious quarters the look of a spruce, well-organized space. Most importantly, it meets Captain Ball's taste for correctness and a good presentation.

We receive numerous visits from superior officers on inspection tours as well as groups of liaison and Civil Affairs officers. We organize tours for twenty or thirty military at a time and, once, for the same number of war correspondents. Our routine is to welcome them, give them something to drink or, sometimes, lunch, give a presentation about the functioning of the camp, and, after the tour, answer questions. Captain Ball most often takes charge of our "tourists," but he occasionally calls on me to replace him. It appears that he does this with some hesitation because he worries about my hasty remarks and my notorious inability to recognize the different services and ranks.

The DPs

Brand is a forward camp. Our job is to receive the DPs who have just been freed. Due to their recent liberation, they have not been processed by the CIC. As a result, some undesirables—traitors, spies, criminals,

German soldiers, etc.—are among them. The liaison officers, who have black lists, are on the lookout for those who are wanted by their national security. At the same time, the American CIC carries out many detailed interrogations. All this monitoring turns the intake process into a seemingly interminable affair that often keeps us up until the early hours of the morning. We also keep an eye open for those who have been deported or released from prison; their evacuation is a high priority, and we keep them in a special building next to ours. We also have a VIP barracks where we house, among others, a government minister and his family from Luxembourg and several Dutch and Belgian political figures.

Thousands of POWs, including ten thousand French, transit our camp. We are somewhat surprised, however, to see several hundred Italian POWs arriving at Brand. They cheer everyone up with their singing until a visiting American commander exclaims: "The last time I saw these bastards, they were shooting at me in the desert." He protests to our command, and, after that, the Italian POWs are sent back to camps housing German POWs. Alsatians pose a particular problem since they are wearing German uniforms. We decide on our own to give them civilian clothes as soon as they are processed so they can be sent home directly.

It seems strange to say, but we especially welcome the POWs because they arrive in organized groups with a leader. They have no baggage and are highly disciplined. When it is time to leave, they are only too glad to jump in the trucks. Remarkably, even after four years of prison, they are good-humored and grateful for our efforts.

Russians are by far the most numerous among our "clients." Thanks to Konstantin, they cause us few problems by comparison with other camps, at least judging by the terrifying stories that reach us. Konstantin has blossomed since joining us. He has formed a personal guard of twenty or so toughs and imposes tight discipline on them. Impeccably dressed, he somehow has gotten hold of a pair of magnificent cavalry boots that everyone envies. One day he organizes a soccer match between the Russians and Poles. It starts out well but quickly turns into a general brawl that sends several players to the infirmary.

The number of volunteer aides continues to grow until there are three hundred who act as drivers, guards, interpreters, cooks, and nurses. We also have teams of painters, carpenters, electricians, and plumbers.

The POWs from the West are mostly French, but there are also Belgians, Dutch, and Luxembourgers. We transport them in trucks to the rail stations at Aix-la-Chapelle and Verviers, where our camp is now run by one of my ASCZ teams. Usually Captain Deloche accompanies the French, but on March 17, I accompany a convoy of thirty trucks to Verviers. As we go through the town, passers-by gather and give us an ovation.

Colonel Lewis and I

The mission to Verviers is a godsend for me because, for the first time, I have had a serious falling out with my boss, Colonel Lewis, who refuses me authorization to go into the Namur region controlled by Colonel Litton. As soon as the POW train leaves the Verviers station on March 17, I set out for ... Namur. Since I am officially AWOL, I think it preferable not to draw any attention to myself, but Colonel Litton insists on taking me to an evening affair. I'm in combat uniform with a very dirty field jacket, pants, and boots. In the midst of the clean, well-dressed company at the soirée, I stick out like a sore thumb. It's a sure thing that Colonel Lewis will soon find out about my escapade! During the evening, I have the great good luck of meeting General Bradley again. He gives me the order for an unlimited mission, authorizing me to circulate in the entire zone he commands, that is, the sector occupied by the First, Third, Seventh, and Ninth Armies. I would never have requested so much, but General Bradley's orders end up being of enormous help to me.

When I return to Brand on March 19, Captain Ball sternly urges me to reconcile with Colonel Lewis, who is expecting my—preferably public—apology. It all started a week ago, the day after our arrival in Brand. Colonel Lewis was razzing me with preposterous comments about his loathed counterpart, Colonel Litton. With acid sarcasm, Colonel Lewis claimed that I was going too often to Namur, insinuating that there was "something" going on between Litton and me. Even though it felt as if there was real jealousy behind his remarks, accustomed to this kind of provocation from him, I didn't respond. He described me as a nasty piece of work and expressed pity—rather humorously, I have to admit—for my future husband. I laughed and still didn't respond. But his third attack went over the line. Apropos of nothing, he declared: "All Frogs are impossible. You can't trust them or work with them. I understand why General Eisenhower can't stand de Gaulle."

With that, I got up and said, "Thanks for the compliment." I should have sat back down and shut up, which would have put me in the winner's column, but instead, I lost it and aimed major insults at him, his American Army that abandoned us at Verviers, and, especially, his President Roosevelt who supported Giraud over de Gaulle, refused to recognize the French Provisional Government, and tried to impose AMGOT on us. Dinner ended in an embarrassed silence.

Eight days have gone by without our speaking, a situation that vastly complicates our work. Following Captain Ball's urgent request, Colonel Lewis and I make peace the day after my "incognito" trip to Namur. He immediately accepts my apology for the remarks about the "abandonment" at Verviers, knowing full well that I will not retract the rest. So we are reconciled . . . until the next time.

Several days later, I go to First Army HQ at Euskirchen to consult with Colonel Lewis. Ever since our reconciliation, he has been extremely pleasant and helpful, though he tells me yet again—without animosity—that he doesn't like me going out on the roads alone. He arranges for me to take a hot shower and invites me to the mess. We talk amicably about the problems we are facing and the urgent need for more MMLA teams.

The advance of the Allied armies liberates millions of POWs, and the crowd of DPs clogs the roads, slowing military operations. The German Army uses DPs as a human shield, putting them out in front of their army. They also mix them in with their combat units, hoping to discourage the Americans from opening fire on them. This tactic doesn't stall the offensive, but it does produce great confusion and many tragic situations. We do our best to receive, classify, and evacuate the multitude of victims who have been abandoned in a catastrophic situation.

The Civil Affairs detachments of the US military government were established precisely to deal with security, administration, and provisioning of liberated cities. Their mission is to restore "normal" conditions as quickly as possible so that the DPs can return to their homes. But there are many more DPs than predicted, and, what makes the situation even more urgent and difficult, the Germans free them en masse, all at once. To deal with the emergency, numerous army units are shifted from combat to guard duty, protecting DPs. In this context, our army unit and MMLA team are looked on as specialists, and as a result, we are assigned the toughest missions.

Brauweiler

March 28–April 13, 1945

The Allied armies are advancing rapidly. Patton's Seventh Army is already marching on Frankfurt. We receive orders to move to Brauweiler, a small village near Cologne. Yvonne, Louise, and I leave Brand on March 28. It is a rare chance for us to be together with time to chat. Like old geezers we talk about the "good old days" in Normandy when our difficulties were small-scale compared to now when the problems are so huge and complex that we feel like grains of sand blown before a hurricane wind.

    We have the wonderful luxury of a driver. Although Charles has a soft spot for Yvonne, he adopts us all and calls us "my lieutenants" or "my girls." In addition to being our driver, he becomes our bodyguard and baggage handler. He also maintains our cars and helps us move into our new quarters, setting up our camp beds. He quickly becomes indispensable and, looking back, we wonder how we ever got along without him. When we are alone, we call him our "nanny."

    Brauweiler is a strange and somehow distressing place. Undamaged by the war, this fortified medieval village is dominated by a monastery. The narrow, winding streets are lined with houses built of dark gray stone with paved courtyards or small gardens in back. There are also several churches, chapels, a vast and forbidding abandoned prison, and an old factory. It is not an ideal place for a camp since there is room to house only five hundred DPs. In addition to the camp at Brauweiler, we are tasked with setting up new military government detachments and overseeing several camps in the suburbs of Cologne. Our team is quartered in a small house on the edge of the village with a view of the countryside.

    Brauweiler is the only locality where we meet hostile German civilians. We are accustomed to being welcomed with smiles and flowers and offers to denounce local Nazis. Here, however, the villagers walk with their heads down, looking up now and then with eyes full of hatred. The only food they provide is frozen potatoes, sour milk, and rotten eggs. At night, we hear gunshots and venture out only to go next door where our American Army unit is lodged. One night, just after our arrival, a large paving stone shatters the window and knocks over the kerosene lamp we use for light. Luckily we are able quickly to douse the fire ignited by the overturned lamp. From that night on, in spite of our protests, Charles sleeps on the floor by our door.

The day after our arrival, I accompany Captain Deloche and the American Lieutenant Helm to Cologne. After completing our mission of acquiring a new engine for one of our trucks, we visit the ravaged city. Even though the cathedral took several hits, its two immense towers remain intact and appear even higher than ever in the midst of the flattened buildings surrounding it. Even though we're not supposed to, we go inside and are overwhelmed by the beauty of the place, enhanced by a curious greenish cast to the light. Every now and then, the birds that have moved in knock down a stone that falls in a cloud of dust. The artillery post on the other side of the river continues to bombard the city even though it is deserted. Through a hole in a fence by the river, we can see the enemy positions.

Next we go to Duisdorf via Bonn. At the First Army HQ, we meet Captain Ball, who tells us that we are to leave immediately for Wetzlar on the other side of the Rhine. But before we leave HQ, the order is countermanded. We are to remain at Brauweiler to greet a group of new military government officers. Our job is to train them and move them into various centers in the region. We are not happy about our new role as instructors behind the lines instead of following our combat units.

On our way back to camp, we have the great good fortune of finding a delightful road along the banks of the Rhine. For a moment, we feel like carefree tourists. Back at Brauweiler, Captain Rothschild has arrived, and we set out immediately on an inspection tour of the MMLA camps. On the road, we pass thousands of miserable DPs and prisoners. Our camps are overwhelmed by masses of DPs. To keep up with the influx, the team members have to work day and night and are thoroughly exhausted.

Captain Rothschild orders me to go to Paris to get five new teams. The night of my departure on April 4, three thousand French plus ninety Hindus (how did they get here?) arrive at Brauweiler. Our buildings are already filled to capacity, so we settle them in basements, attics, and even one of the chapels. We barely get them moved in when thirty-three trucks arrive with Russians, Poles, and two hundred more French. We pile them in as best we can.

Arriving in Paris on April 5, I am delighted to learn that I have been assigned a 15CV Citroën with a driver. I can finally return the beloved Gurgler to my father. Unfortunately, I am able to assemble only three new teams instead of the five requested. On top of that, my driver gets sick and has to stay at Verdun. My colleague, Renée Henchoz, and I leave empty-handed for Bonn via Luxembourg. It is a long journey. I try to take a short cut, get lost, end up on damaged roads, and five times have flat tires. At nightfall, we find ourselves definitively stuck in empty country and are forced to take refuge in an abandoned house. At dawn, I take off on foot, leaving Renée with the car and my tommy gun. After walking about two kilometers, I come to Mechlenheim, a small village. The gracious burgomaster serves me a copious breakfast and takes me in a cart to the nearest busy road. Luckily, Bonn is only twenty kilometers away. I hitch a ride to an American Army depot, where I get three new tires. A jeep takes me back to the car, where Renée is beginning to wonder whether I was ever coming back.

Crossing the Rhine

Renée and I spend the night at Duisdorf, where I learn that my team and Captain Ball's unit have already left Brauweiler for Wetzlar. The next morning, April 13, I leave immediately to join them, driving my car all alone to cross the Rhine.

The pontoon bridge that spans the river, driven by a strong current, is now in the shape of an arc rather than a straight line. The

Pontoon bridge across the Rhine. (Courtesy of the Naval History and Heritage Command)

treadway bridge has lips on the edges to create a track for the long line of vehicles waiting to cross. The traffic control officer is reluctant to give me the green light to proceed across the bridge because the span of the tracks is designed for American jeeps and trucks and not for a light Citroën. After an intense discussion, the officer agrees to let me give it a try.

The weather is bad, and the bridge, buffeted by waves and wind, pitches and rolls. Trying to drive across it is like riding on the back of a heaving sea serpent. I cling to the steering wheel for dear life. After going about halfway, I'm between two pontoons when a particularly strong jolt pitches the car over the lip. The truck in back of me tries to push me but succeeds only in shoving the car completely sideways with the front hanging out over the roiling water, which is a nasty greenish-brown color. I don't dare get out of the car because that might upset the balance and pitch it into the river.

While in this impossible position, I have the leisure of contemplating, on my right, the famous Remagen bridge. This railroad bridge, miraculously left intact by the retreating Germans, made it possible for the American Army to cross the Rhine between March 7 and 17, when it suddenly collapsed. Between then and now, the Americans established a bridgehead on the eastern banks of the Rhine and built pontoon bridges, like the one I am on now.

My car, lurching sideways over the water, is creating a huge backup of vehicles. There are so many that the western bank now looks like a vast parking lot, while the road in front of me is totally empty. I hear honking and loudspeakers. I'm increasingly afraid that I'm going to end my days in the Rhine. In anticipation of bad luck, I take off my jacket and boots and prepare myself mentally to open the door if I go into the water.

Finally, a tow truck backs up to my car from the east side of the river. When it gets close enough, two GIs succeed, with great difficulty, in attaching a large hook under my bumper. They crank up the front of the car (please let the bumper hold!) and tow me to the far bank of the river. I am so relieved to be on solid ground that the shouts of the red-faced sergeant, who is justifiably furious, don't faze me.

"Jesus Christ! It's a damn woman! If you want traffic blocked for an hour, you can be sure it's a damn woman!"

"I'm sorry, Sergeant. My car is too low . . ."

He interrupts me, yelling, "Get the hell out of here and fast!"

I rapidly cover the hundred thirty kilometers to Wetzlar because, thanks to me, the road is empty.

Wetzlar

April 13–19, 1945

Wetzlar, home of the Leica factories, is the German capital of optics and photography. We occupy the large, modern barracks that once housed the German cavalry. There is room for twenty to twenty-five thousand people. One of the buildings is reserved exclusively for Russians; the others house DPs and POWs from the West. The French are the most numerous, with between seven and eight thousand people.

The DPs arrive by the thousands; some in American Army trucks, others find their own way. Hundreds arrive on foot or piled into all kinds of vehicles that we keep in a huge parking lot. There are landaus, wheelbarrows, carts, sulkies, station wagons, bicycles, motorcycles, hearses, ambulances, and cars of all ages and types, from a Model T Ford to the latest sport Mercedes. We also create an area for the animals that were hitched to anything that could roll: emaciated nags, farm horses, purebreds, mules, donkeys, goats, and dogs. The most unusual contraption brought in by three POWs, who must have liberated it from a circus, is a covered wagon—Wild West style—pulled by a camel.

The war in Europe is effectively over. Since the risk of bombardments or counteroffensives is nonexistent, the atmosphere at Wetzlar is very different from that of our previous camps. In contrast to the usual austerity, Wetzlar feels like a permanent party. The DPs who are being repatriated are so happy to be going home that they put flowers around the windows and doors and set up little triumphal arches trimmed with branches and multicolored paper flowers. The repatriation goes more quickly than we expected. Instead of taking several months, it takes only two or three weeks, due to the mobilization by the Americans of trucks, trains, and airplanes that are not needed by combat units. While the DPs are waiting to leave, they play games, dance, and sing.

In the Russian camp, the mood is quite different. Lieutenant Konstantin tells me that the DPs are very worried, terrified even, by the idea of returning to the USSR. There is a rumor going around that they will not be sent home but rather be deported to Siberia, and the soldiers who were in German POW camps will be court-martialed for desertion. They flood the American detachment with requests for immigration status for the USA or for Western Europe. Their pleas for help receive no response. For my part, I am convinced that the rumors are false or exaggerated. When I express this opinion to Konstantin, he just shakes his head sadly and says, "Little sister, you don't know Stalin."

When I go to First Army HQ at Marburg to meet with Colonel Lewis, I am astonished by the gloomy, pessimistic mood there. I have dinner with Colonel Lewis, Colonel Gunn, commander of the G5, and several other high-ranking officers. They are outraged by the Yalta agreements, reached in February, and by the actions of President Roosevelt, who had just died a few days before. In spite of Churchill's objections, Roosevelt had yielded to Stalin and effectively ceded Eastern Europe to the Russians. Some of the particularly bellicose officers want to forge ahead and attack the Russians; if not, they say, everything will begin again in a few years. A young captain actually sheds tears of indignation because his unit had to stand down to allow the Russians to be the first to enter Berlin. Only one of the officers defends the president's political decisions, pointing out that, if the war in Europe is over, it is still going on in the Pacific. He says that in return for the advantages given to the Russians in Europe, they will join the Americans in fighting the Japanese. Finally, Colonel Gunn gets up and ends the discussion: "We have won the war, but the politicians are going to lose the peace." This conversation, which I listened to with the greatest interest, would often come back to haunt me in later days.

For the moment, however, my daily concerns are of an entirely different nature: I am very worried by an announcement coming from the PDR minister to the effect that all the female MMLA teams in Germany will, beginning in April, be administered by the UNRRA (United Nations Relief and Rehabilitation Administration). I confront Colonel Lewis about the announcement and beg him to send me immediately temporary facility and water had been restored to the camp. Journalists, including Edward R. Murrow, Margaret Bourke-White, and Marguerite Higgins, had visited the camp and documented the appalling conditions discovered there. The arrival of Lewis, Ball, and Vagliano marked the transfer of responsibility for the camp from the Third to the First Army.

Vagliano's personal observations of this transition period provide an insider's account of the organization of the camp and the steps that were taken to protect, rehabilitate, and repatriate the remaining internees. Her reaction to being housed in the commandant's villa—throwing out all the furniture—reveals the helpless fury many felt at having to witness the callous cruelty of the SS who ran the camp, described by Colonel F. M. S. Miller as "a sadist's paradise." Her account of the discovery of a group of wild children at Buchenwald is unique to the history of the camp. The reported number of children discovered at Buchenwald varies from 877 to 1,400. The children that Vagliano and her team cared for, however, seem to have been unidentified; they may have been deportees from the Auschwitz Camp in Poland who panicked and hid, but no one seems to know for sure where they came from or how they ended up living shut up like animals in a shed.

Her description of the disruptions caused by VIP visits to the camp (halted by General Bradley on May 9) sheds a new light on both the humanitarian and political aspects of these visits. And her description of the thieves and confidence men who tried to take advantage of the chaotic conditions during this period uncovers the corrupt underbelly of wartime mentalities.

After the departure of the First Army G5 unit, Vagliano and the MMLA teams worked with the UNRRA on their last heartbreaking assignment: the repatriation of Eastern Bloc nationals who knew they faced execution or the Gulag. Her reaction to VE Day, which she expected to be jubilant, reveals the resentment of many combatants over the partition of Europe agreed on at Yalta. After witnessing the division of Germany and overseeing the vast refugee and DP camp network in the American zone, Vagliano was at last free to return home in October 1945. She was just twenty-three years old.

❖

Weimar. The Elefant Haus Hotel

The autobahn to Weimar, lined with lovely trees, is relatively free of traffic. It's a beautiful day; spring is coming, and the forest is radiant with the whole gamut of greens. After the endless winter with its wreckage and destruction, we feel reborn. Since it's clear that the war in Europe will soon be over, we are delighted with our new assignment, believing it will be the last.

We arrive at our destination. Weimar is associated for me only with vague memories from school of Goethe and the short-lived republic of 1919. The town is surrounded by gentle, rolling hills. We have no trouble finding the Elefant Haus Hotel, located on the town square. It is as luxurious as it was under the Nazi regime when it was a plush party meeting place. I can't help thinking that the imposing concierge who addresses me obsequiously first in English, then in French, also must have welcomed Goering, Himmler, and probably even Hitler.

I am amazed to find out that, for once, I am actually expected and that a room has been reserved for me. A bellboy takes my battered US Army duffle bag and backpack and leads me to my room. In the corridors, the walls are lined with a soft gray silk, and the carpeting is so thick it muffles even the sound of my boots. Even though the hotel is brimming with activity, the sound- and bulletproofing make it seem calm and quiet. My room is a subtle symphony in gray and rose. Amazed, I walk around and admire every detail: the soft bed, the comfortable armchairs, the rosewood desk and bureau, the crystal chandelier whose drops jingle happily. Most wonderful of all is being alone and having a bathroom all to myself. Without waiting one more minute, I run a hot bath in the pink tub and am lolling about when the telephone brings me back to reality. Colonel Lewis is waiting for me in the hotel bar and is growing impatient.

Sitting stiffly, pipe in his mouth, he is already at a small corner table. All chrome and glass, the bar is modern and elegant. The tinted mirrors color the colonel's face an unaccustomed rosy color. He seems, however, ill at ease. To the rigid Protestant pastor, this unaccustomed setting must seem like the gates of hell (I wouldn't know until later how accurate this impression was). I greet him with a cheery "Hello, Colonel. This is really a terrific place. Much nicer than a refugee camp!"

The colonel doesn't seem to be in the mood to kid around. "We have to talk seriously, Lieutenant. But first, how was your trip?"

"Very good. No problems. Now that the war is almost over, I'm getting used to finding my way."

"Fine. What do you want to drink? They have everything here—whiskey, champagne, vermouth, vodka . . ."

I am stunned by the offer of a drink because the colonel is, you might say, a teetotaler by profession. It is certainly the first time he has offered me anything but tea, coffee, or fruit juice. When I don't answer, he goes on: "I'm having a whiskey and soda. How about you?"

"The same for me, Colonel. Thank you."

The waiter brings our drinks. The colonel takes a sip and says: "I haven't had a drop of alcohol for thirty years. I'm not enjoying it, but maybe it will do me good."

We talk about this and that, but it is clear that the colonel's mind is not on the conversation. Finally, he turns to me with a grave look: "I have a tough assignment for you."

"What is it? Are you sending us into the Russian zone?"

"No. To Buchenwald."

"Buchenwald? But that's a concentration camp!"

"Exactly. I have just come from there. That's why I needed a drink. Not only to get over what I saw, but also to work up the courage to send you there. Believe me, if I could do otherwise I would. But there's only Captain Ball's unit and your team that can deal with the situation. I don't like the idea of sending you girls in there. You're entirely free to accept or refuse the assignment, and believe me, if you refuse, I won't hold it against you."

"Of course, we'll go since you ask us to. But I don't know anything about the camps except that the internees are very badly treated and die by the dozens."

"No, by the thousands."

Alarmed by this revelation, I go on: "Up until now, we've been dealing with refugees and DPs in relatively good health, but in these circumstances doctors and nurses will be needed. We don't have the necessary skills, and I'm afraid that, with all the goodwill in the world, we may not do much good."

"Don't worry about that. You'll have more than enough to keep you busy. But let me explain the situation."

I interrupt him: "But where is Buchenwald?"

"It's here. Just a few kilometers from Weimar. Due to ignorance or bad planning, we're just not prepared to take charge of the camps and to evacuate them. Of course, we knew that they existed and where they were, but no one could imagine how big they were or the abominations that were taking place. More than fifty thousand people have died at Buchenwald, and the prisoners are still dying like flies of starvation, exhaustion, typhus, and other diseases. During the first days, those who seemed more or less all right were evacuated pell-mell. Proper precautions weren't taken, and many died. Beginning today, the camp is my responsibility. We have to act quickly, and I need you. One more thing, there are a lot of politics involved."

"Politics?" I reply dumbfounded. "What have politics got to do with it?"

"Plenty. Every government in Western Europe has its eye on the camps. It is absolutely essential that we do the right thing, and the right thing for us means sending home alive the greatest number of internees possible, and as fast as we can. We're going to have any number of government delegations on our case, and it's not going to be good enough to tell them we're doing our best. We'll have to talk to them, show them around, explain what's being done and why. We'll have to answer all kinds of questions, some of them stupid. So we have to establish priorities, take a census, organize the evacuation, I don't know what else. Believe me, you'll have plenty to do."

"How many are there?" I ask weakly.

"We don't know exactly. Between fifteen and twenty thousand. One thing, the camp records have been well maintained. Depend on the Germans to be efficient," he concludes bitterly.

We remain silent for a few minutes. Everything has changed in an instant and seems unreal.

"Colonel, since you went there this afternoon, tell me what it's like."

"I can't," he says. "It's horrifying. Worse than anything you could imagine. The camp was liberated just a few days ago by a division of the Third Army, and they have now handed it over to me. What else do you want to know?"

"When are we going?"

"Tomorrow morning with Captain Ball. His detachment and your team will follow in the afternoon. I'd like to get you settled as quickly as possible so you can begin work right away. There's not a moment to lose."

"Do you mean to say that we have to live there?"

"Yes. But don't worry, there's a comfortable place for you to stay. You'll see tomorrow."

Now that the colonel has broken the news about Buchenwald to me, he doesn't bring it up again. Later I observed that this was common: people who had been to Buchenwald didn't want to talk about it.

That night, I don't sleep much, suffocated and revolted by the luxury that pleased me only a few hours before. The room is too hot. The bed is too soft. I'm afraid of tomorrow . . .

Arrival at Buchenwald

It is a warm, sunny day when Colonel Lewis, Captain Ball, and I leave Weimar in an open jeep. Buchenwald is a short twenty-minute drive from town. We go up a perfectly straight road that cuts through a thick forest of pine and silver birches. The same forest where Goethe and

Entrance to Buchenwald, April 22, 1945.

Eckermann strolled. The same forest that gave its beautiful name to this horrifying camp.

The trees don't thin out: they just stop abruptly as we come to a double barbed-wire fence. We drive through an open swing gate guarded by a GI and follow a dusty track bordered on one side by trees and on the other by barbed wire interspersed with deserted watchtowers. We see numerous large, two-storied wooden barracks, the stories connected by exterior staircases. A small white stone building topped by a high chimney stands out among the gray buildings.

"That's the crematorium," the Colonel explains.

A number of prisoners—some singly, some in groups—dressed in their striped uniforms are sitting propped against the walls or walking slowly in the sun. Since we left the forest, we have been smelling a ghastly odor of death and decay.

We go directly to the administration building—a large, ramshackle, concrete construction partially hidden by trees. We meet Major Schmuhl,* who has been responsible for the camp since its liberation. He talks nervously and seems almost dazed as he tells us he is leaving that very day, the sooner the better. The first thing he does is show us several large lampshades decorated with fine black designs. What appears to be parchment paper, he explains, is really human skin, and the designs are tattoos. One of them I remember shows a ship in full sail. Schmuhl tells us that Ilse Koch,* the wife of a former commandant of the camp, liked to walk among the prisoners, whom she forced to strip to the waist so she could select the best tattoo specimens. She would then watch her victim be tortured, killed, and flayed. She liked to make the lampshades herself. This notorious behavior earned her the reputation as "the Bitch of Buchenwald."

The major leads us to his office to give us our orders and to pass on information about the organization of the camp. He then turns us over to an internee escorted by a GI who is to give us a tour of the camp. Our guide is so thin that his striped shirt and trousers flutter in the breeze as though they were hung on a scarecrow made of sticks. His head is shaved; he has burning eyes, a great bony nose, and a wide slit of a mouth that reveals a few blackened stumps of teeth. He proudly explains that the Americans have selected him as official guide because he speaks five languages and has spent two years in the camp. He gives us a big smile and seems delighted with his role. He speaks with a middle-European accent, maybe Hungarian, and cringes and fawns with a sickening obsequiousness before the Americans, whom he calls "our great liberators." During the tour, he spares us none of the monstrous details about the camp, in fact, he seems to gloat over them. His voice rises high with excitement, even pride, when displaying the more gruesome highlights of the tour. Even though I know that he must have endured these torments himself, his manner repulses me and, instinctively, I affect a great calm in order to foil his evident satisfaction in shocking me.

Near the entrance to the camp, the guide shows us a dog kennel where a prisoner was always chained. The prisoner's job was to bark like a dog whenever one of the "masters" walked by. In return, he would get a kick in the face. The kennel is empty, but our guide signals to a poor, frail being and, by way of demonstration, makes him get down on all fours and pretends to kick him. After this heartbreaking scene, the guide takes us into one of the barracks. The smell is so foul that the air is unbreathable. In the dim light we can see bunk upon bunk occupied by human bodies—some still alive, some dying, some almost certainly already dead.

Outside the barracks a few prisoners are walking around. Others drag themselves to the latrines or wait for the mobile field kitchen to distribute food, but in small quantities since anything more might prove fatal. One by one, we go into all the barracks, unable to tell the living from the dead.

Meanwhile, our tireless guide describes daily life at Buchenwald. He tells us that each day, convoys of prisoners were loaded like livestock onto trucks and taken to underground factories at Dora, Ohrdruf, and others, where the V1s and V2s were manufactured. Those who left rarely returned for the simple reason that they were not fed enough to keep them alive.

He also describes the daily roll calls that—regardless of the season or the weather—began in the morning at four o'clock and were held again in the evening at the end of the workday. Dressed only in their striped pajamas, the prisoners were made to keep absolutely still for hours at a time, sometimes at attention, sometimes kneeling. If someone moved or fainted or became ill, he was either clubbed to death by a guard or hanged for all to see.

We learn from the guide to what extremes the human imagination can go in its search for the most cruel methods of torture and are dumbfounded by the truly demonic sadism of the men and women, guests of the commandant, who took pleasure in watching unimaginable scenes of torture while listening to the screams of the victims.

Besides the standard techniques of torture like freezing or boiling baths or death by slow electrocution or burning, they invented other methods of inflicting pain and death: victims were tied naked to stakes, covered in jam, and left to be stung to death by bees; or they were immersed in mud-filled tanks, having to stand on tiptoe to keep their head clear, until they tired and drowned in the filth. After visiting the torture block and seeing all the instruments devised to make death as slow and painful as possible, we come to the white building with the tall chimney—the crematorium.

Our guide explains, his voice mounting in a crescendo, that the prisoners who were condemned for any infraction, however small—stealing a piece of bread, smiling at an SS officer, moving during roll call, etc.—were lined up in front of a trapdoor and then pushed one by one through a chute into the basement. They fell from a height of thirteen feet or so onto a cement floor. The lucky ones died from the fall; others broke their brittle bones. The survivors were hung up on large meat hooks embedded high up in the walls. If it took them too long to choke to death, a guard would smash their skull with a mallet. A miniature train would then transport the bodies to six ovens large enough to handle human bodies. Even though the ovens worked day and night, the bodies waiting to be burned still piled up outside the door of the crematorium. Indeed, in the courtyard, we now see hundreds of corpses, still neatly stacked, forming a mound several meters high. So white, so fragile, they look more dead than the dead. Hundreds of buzzing black flies circle above the poor abandoned bodies.

We leave the crematorium silently, not daring even to look at each other. At the gate, the guide is waiting for us, twisting his prisoner's cap nervously in his hands. With a smile, he says to us in French: "Merci, messieurs, dames."

"What the hell does he want now?" asks Captain Ball in a weary voice.

"He wants a tip," I tell him, blindly holding out a bill.

I must have given him a large bill because the guide thanks me effusively. He bows and says pompously: "It's a great honor for me to have received our first lady visitor. If Madam wishes, I would be most glad to show her many other things." I say, "Thank you," and hurry away to join Captain Ball and Colonel Lewis, who are slowly and silently making their way back to the administration building.

My body aches all over as if I'd been beaten. My knees are buckling, and my jaws are sore from clenching my teeth. Both hands are bloody from digging my nails into my palms. Captain Ball offers me his arm and says: "General Patton was sick after his tour and he's no softie, so don't be ashamed if you do the same."

"I'm all right, thanks, but I never thought the day would come when I wished to be back at Verviers in the cold with bombs dropping around us. At least it was human ... here, we're in a nightmare. It's like Bosch's paintings of hell. We have to get these people out of the barracks right away or they will *all* be dead."

"You're right," Captain Ball responds calmly. "But we mustn't rush into things or we'll do more harm than good. We have to make plans first and wait for the military field hospital to arrive. Colonel Lewis is working on it and has just gone to get news. Meanwhile," he says with a grin, "let's get cracking."

We never work so hard as during our first day and night at Buchenwald. The same desperate rage and sense of shame unites us. We work without stopping, speaking only when necessary, too busy and too outraged to think.

Just outside the compound are large stone barracks where the SS units were housed. Our American detachment and the MMLA team arrive and immediately begin to clear and clean the barracks. We send several trucks to Weimar to requisition beds, blankets, and provisions. Others go to Eisenach to get our workers. We are relieved to learn that the American hospital units are on the way. By early afternoon we start moving the prisoners out of their barracks.

We use all our vehicles, including the old Peugeot, to move them to the old SS barracks. The healthier ones go on foot. Sorting out the dead from the living in the prisoners' barracks is a slow and gruesome business. There are many dead still lying on the filthy shelves that served as beds, and we can't tell the difference until we touch their skin. The GIs work in silence, their faces taut and grim. The prisoners weigh so little that the GIs take them up in their arms and carry them like children to the waiting vehicles, which we have lined with mattresses. One of the GIs stumbles and falls with his precious burden. He curses and, in tears, picks up the prisoner again. The quiet is made more oppressive by the incessant buzzing of the flies. We talk only when necessary and never above a whisper. As each barracks empties, a neat pile of bodies grows by the door. Never afterwards do we mention that first afternoon. We are too shocked and ashamed to voice our thoughts out loud.

The Chalets

Much later in the day, after the army ambulances arrive, we go to inspect our living quarters. We walk through some woods where the air is fresh and clean, breathing deeply, as though the refreshing air could clear out our lungs and minds. The beech and birch trees are pleasantly spaced. Spring flowers bloom in the grass. We reach a dirt road and follow it up a steep slope. At the top, a heavenly view of the Ilm valley unfolds below us. The rays of the setting sun cast a silvery red glow on the river. The rolling green hills are shrouded in the evening mist.

I don't know what we were expecting for housing, but certainly not the idyllic setting now before us. A half dozen chalets, surrounded by rock gardens and flowers, are nestled by the road. It looks like a Swiss mountain resort. Here, only a three-minute walk from the camp, are the charming homes of the master torturers and executioners.

The chalet where we are to live for the next month is the same one previously inhabited by Kommandant Koch* and his ghastly wife, followed by the last camp director, Hermann Pister.* He obviously left in a hurry for we find food and drink in the kitchen, flowers in the vases, an open book in the library, fur coats and clothes in the closets, and fine French lingerie in the drawers. The team members, who have not yet seen the camp, are understandably delighted with the comforts of our new lodging.

As for me, I walk through the chalet in a daze. Although in bad taste with too much pink and green, everything is new and clean, even luxurious. On the second floor, I discover a little girl's room, all in pink, with dotted-Swiss curtains and reproductions of English nursery rhymes on the wall. It's all too gemütlich for words. The living room is painted bright green and furnished with a large sofa and chairs covered in chintz. Pots of geraniums hang from the walls. Next to the living room is a study. On the massive mahogany desk is a beautiful Chinese porcelain lamp, topped with one of the human-skin shades.

This charming little pastel dated Christmas, 1943, sat on the commandant's bedside table.

From the cushioned window seats in the bow windows, you can sit and admire a magnificent view of the valley below.

Sickened by what I see, I tell the members of my team to choose any room they want. I settle into a small room on the top floor, probably a maid's room. After letting off steam by throwing all the furniture out the window, I ask the faithful Charles to bring up my camp bed and gear. For once, he grumbles, pointing out that I would be much better off sleeping on a real bed with a mattress and linen sheets. Not in a mood to get into a discussion, I tell him to do as I ask. I would gladly have wrecked and burned the whole place but instead I give him an order: "Change out the furniture for the whole house. All the furniture for the whole house, you hear me!" Stunned, he just nods and replies: "Yes, Lieutenant."

Leaving the team to settle in, I return to the camp with Captain Ball. The dismal to-and-fro of the stretcher-bearers continues through the night in the pitiless glare of headlights, interrupted only when the exhausted GIs stop for a breather.

Back at the chalet, my team and I talk late into the night. I feel I have to tell them what I saw and heard at the camp in order to prepare them for their arrival the next day. We go to bed reassuring each other with the motto from *Gone with the Wind* that we have used since Normandy: Tomorrow is another day.

In the morning, before entering the camp, we go to the military hospital in Weimar for the typhus booster shots that we have to have every month. We fall into line behind some GIs who are there for the same reason. The doctor administering the shots is the same one who took care of us in Aix-la-Chapelle. He greets us with a cheerful "Ah, here come my Typhus Girls!" Everyone turns around and glares at us while we try to look as dignified as possible. When the doctor learns that we are to be stationed at Buchenwald, he gives us a cocktail of injections to protect us against typhoid, diphtheria, and tetanus. Even though this combination is apparently quite strong, nobody faints, and we are glad we are able to hold up in front of the GIs. As we leave, the doctor tells me that we must now come in once a week for the typhus boosters.

I hate getting these shots and reply: "Is that really necessary?"

"No, of course not," replies the doctor who likes kidding around. "I just can't get along without you girls."

"In that case, come have a drink with us. It would be much nicer."

"I won't say no, Lieutenant, but you won't get away with that. I'm giving you an order to come back here with your team every week for your shots. It's extremely important."

"OK, Captain. In that case, we'll be seeing you soon."

The Second Day

Back at Buchenwald, the process of moving the prisoners continues, the stretchers and ambulances going back and forth between the camp and the SS barracks, which, it soon becomes clear, are not large enough to accommodate everyone. We organize cleaning details to clear out and disinfect the camp barracks. I suggest that we bring in locals from Weimar to help with the task, but this idea is quickly rejected because there aren't enough MPs to protect them as they work. During the night, the prisoners had gotten hold of two of the former guards, killed them, cut them in pieces, and stuffed them down a drain. Instead of getting locals to come work, then, we send more trucks to Weimar to requisition mattresses and blankets.

Midafternoon, the army field hospital arrives. It is comforting to see their dark green tents sprouting up like mushrooms among the pine trees because the camp hospital is totally overwhelmed. Captain Ball goes immediately to check in with the commanding officer, who is tall and bald. The health officer, Colonel William E. Williams, is someone we have met before and don't especially like because when he inspected a few of our refugee camps he had expressed strong disapproval of our unorthodox procedures.

The two officers very quickly get into an argument. Captain Ball, scarlet with rage, declares: "Maybe it's not my business to tell you how to run your hospital, but my orders are to get the prisoners out of this camp alive and repatriate them as quickly as possible. I don't think sending your nurses away for R&R is going to help."

I put in my two cents: "What, no nurses? We need nurses even more than doctors!"

The major turns toward me, and the dark look he gives me clearly means, "This is none of your business."

Then to Captain Ball, in a pompous tone: "You don't seem to realize, Captain, that we are making a great exception, indeed a unique exception, turning over a military hospital for the care of civilians. In these circumstances, the command doesn't think it right or wise to impose such an assignment on our female personnel. Our nurses will be replaced by male German aides."

And with that, the major turns on his heels and leaves.

"Of all the shits!" Captain Ball explodes. "Guess where he sent the nurses."

"I don't know. Paris, maybe?"

"No, they're sunbathing on the Riviera!"

The Organization of the Camp

We realize very soon that Buchenwald is a larger and more complex place than we had at first thought. The camp is divided into two parts: the main camp, which is bad, and the little camp, which is appalling. Outside of the main compound stand several constructions: SS barracks and, hidden among the trees, several large cement buildings painted with the familiar German gray-and-green camouflage. Apparently these buildings were occupied by the guards and SS officers. Then in the chalets scattered around the commandant's house, where we live, VIP prisoners were housed. These included well-known political figures like Georges Mandel* and Léon Blum* and his wife. These VIPs were not allowed out of their quarters but otherwise were well treated.

In the administration building, in addition to numerous offices, are a library, a movie theater, lecture halls, supply rooms, kitchens, and a recreation center with ping pong tables, billiards, and baby-foot games. There is also space that was used as a bordello and a canteen where prison script could buy cigarettes, soap, toilet water, silk stockings, foie gras, and caviar. All these facilities were in principle open to the internees, but we speculate that they were created to bluff the Red Cross and were probably reserved for privileged categories like the SS, the kapos, and their protégés.

The Buchenwald hospital is in stark contrast to the rest of the camp: a large building, it is impeccably maintained and equipped with the latest medical apparatus. The sick prisoners who were lucky enough to be hospitalized received care from a first-class team of physicians, including the head surgeon, a well-known Austrian doctor.

There is also a "research" department that carried out experiments on the prisoners. The research physicians used the internees as guinea pigs, testing vaccines for typhus, cholera, and diphtheria. The vaccines were not effective, and hundreds, if not thousands, of the prisoners were allowed to die in agony. Also in the research area, experiments with hormone transplants to cure homosexuals were carried out. It is impossible for us to understand how, on the one hand, men were mercilessly slaughtered while, on the other, the most sophisticated scientific equipment kept others alive.

The prisoners in Buchenwald come from every country in Europe and elsewhere. In all, there are thirty different nationalities represented. The majority are political internees, resistance fighters, and partisans. Others include POWs captured while trying to escape, common criminals, black marketeers, Jews, Gypsies, homosexuals, and even children.

The Russians, the largest national group (around eight thousand when we enter the camp), were kept apart from the other prisoners. Perhaps hardier and more accustomed to harsh living conditions, the ones who survive appear stronger and healthier than the other prisoners even though we learn that they had been treated as savagely as the others. Ironically, the Russians who remain are resisting being repatriated because they are afraid of reprisals at home. Many of them are recaptured POW escapees and, according to the Soviet code, they should have either died fighting or made it back to their own lines. Those who did not are considered deserters, and the firing squad or the Gulag awaits them in their native land.

Most of the camp guards were Ukrainians and Poles. Hated by everyone, by the time we arrive, they have already disappeared from the camp.

The deportees from the Western democracies suffered the most. The French are the largest group among these. Out of twenty-eight thousand French prisoners, more than twenty thousand died, perhaps because of their lack of organization. Since the liberation of the camp, five thousand Frenchmen have been repatriated, leaving only two thousand or so, who are in a pitiful state. In addition, during the last days of fighting, in a last-ditch effort by the SS to empty the camp, several thousand of the

Western prisoners were sent out on forced marches or were crammed onto trains. Most of them died of exhaustion or were executed.

The prisoners were subdivided into groups, "blocks" and work details, called Kommandos, according to a system that at first is an enigma to us. We try to figure out how one got into the right group, where you had a chance of survival, or the wrong group, where you had hardly any, and we hear many conflicting, contradictory, and hair-raising tales. Actually, the basic organization followed a rigorous logic based on nationality and political allegiance, that is, communist or noncommunist. But religion, race, social class, cunning, bribery, friendship, and sometimes pure luck could also determine life or death.

The SS officers in charge of Buchenwald had essentially turned the management of the camp over to the German communists, many of them interned in the mid-thirties. These leaders of the German Communist Party held all the key posts in the camp. To help them in their administrative tasks, they chose national delegates among the foreign communists—mainly French, Czech, and Spanish—and formed the Committee, which ran the camp from Block 40. The members of the Committee were the lords of Buchenwald, and, in many cases, the death or survival of the prisoners depended on them. They not only supervised distribution of the meager rations allotted by the Nazis, they also made up the infamous "transport" lists of the men who were sent out to work in the underground plants (Dora, Ohrdruf) or in the less barbarous factories in various other locations. In addition, they selected the men who stayed in the compound to clean and carry out administrative details, and those who were sent to the infirmary. The Committee ran the camp with great efficiency and, often, with great brutality.

Some people tell us that the SS set up this barbarous system in order to justify themselves in the future with the excuse that the camp was the way it was because it was run by the communists. Later we learn that the SS officers in charge were above all fearful of giving up their cushy job and being sent to the Russian front. To stay on good terms with the top Nazi hierarchy, they had to maintain peace and quiet in the camp, and the best way to discourage an uprising was to put the communist prisoners in charge. Whatever the reason, if you were unfortunate enough to be sent to Buchenwald, you had an infinitely better chance of surviving if you were a communist.

The Children of Buchenwald

Since the liberation of the camp, close to two hundred prisoners are dying every day. Our one and only concern is to put a stop to this ghastly loss of human life. We now have three hospitals: the camp hospital, the army field hospital set up in tents, and the 45th Evacuation Hospital, which administers the two SS barracks. In all, there are more than four thousand sick prisoners that need to be saved.

I enter one of the tents where the sick lie silently side by side—dozens of emaciated skeleton-like bodies. The only parts of them that seem alive are their great dark eyes burning with fever. Their skin, so brown and thin it looks like parchment, hangs on their bones and is pocked by festering sores. The doctor looks exhausted and seems somewhat bewildered, stunned no doubt by the catastrophic and unprecedented situation confronting him. He explains that he has to feed the patients intravenously; solid food or even liquids would kill them outright.

I stop by a bed and am astonished to discover a small child lying there. "Yes," says the doctor, "we even have children here." But there is nothing childlike about the figure I see in the bed except his size. His dark brown skin is literally stuck to the bones of his emaciated face, and his body is so small and thin that it makes his head look enormous. His enormous dark eyes focus on me, and a faint smile ripples across his face like a light breeze.

The doctor remarks, "Good, he likes you. He has never smiled before. It's probably the first time he's seen a woman. Stay with him, it won't be long." I stand by his bed and hold his small, fevered hand. It is so hard and brittle, it feels like a bunch of twigs. He smiles again once or twice in the fleeting way a baby does and then seems to go to sleep. But his hand begins to grow cold and his breathing slows and then stops. An attendant carries his little body away to make room for another patient.

The doctor comes back and asks me to visit the other children. "When we arrived," he explains, "there were around 850 children here.

Many of them died, and we transported most of the others to the American Red Cross hospital in Weimar. But around forty of the children are still here and, up until now, we haven't been able to do anything for them except continue to feed them. Please see what your team can do. I think they will be less afraid of you women than they are of us. It's not a pretty sight that you're going to see. Good luck!"

A doctor leads Louise and me behind the administration building to a shed-like structure with a sloping roof. We follow the doctor down a dimly lit corridor and come to a steel door with a lock on it. As he opens the door, we hear a rustling sound as if animals, grunting and panting, were pushing into the far corner of the room. At first, we can't see anything clearly because the only light is coming through barred slits high up in the walls. A horrible, acrid smell overwhelms us. As our eyes grow used to the dark, we are able to discern a mass of naked, whimpering children. They are huddled in the darkest corner of the room, watching us in terror. The doctor stays behind on the doorsill while we go forward, speaking softly and cooing the way we would to a baby. We hold out some sweets that we had brought with us. Petrified, they remain plastered against the wall, unmoving. Finally, one of them approaches us on all fours and snatches a piece of candy. The others follow, grab the sweets and then begin to fight over them. We stay where we are, continuing to speak in a low voice. Gradually they crawl toward us, curious, and touch our skirts and legs. We reach down and pat them as if they were a pack of puppies. Grunting and making sharp little cries, they jostle each other to get closer to us. When they tug at our clothes and scratch our legs, we begin to feel afraid and hurry to leave.

Of the 850 or so children at Buchenwald, why these forty were left behind, we don't know. Maybe they are the youngest and wildest, or maybe they were just overlooked in the general confusion of the liberation since the place where they were kept looks like a storage shed. All of them are boys and appear to range in age from three to eight years old. Most likely Jews or Gypsies, they are almost certainly from Central Europe and Poland. The youngest must have been born in the camp; the older ones were probably taken from their interned mothers. The conditions in which they lived have turned them into animals. They were locked up night and day. The ridged cement floor is sloped slightly toward a hole that carries off their excrement. Their bed is a kind of litter filled with straw. Their food was thrown in to them once a day. The children and the room were apparently cleaned at the same time by means of a powerful water hose attached to the wall. Their heads are shaved—the only sign of human attention. These wretched children may have served as fodder for medical experiments. Nobody in the camp wants to talk about them. Even the other prisoners do not seem to be aware that they existed.

Our team, along with refugee female personnel, is assigned to take care of the children because they are terrified of men. With some difficulty—because they wriggle like eels—we transfer them to a brighter room, furnished with children's beds requisitioned from Weimar. We have to teach them everything: how to stand up and walk, to use the toilet, to wash, eat, play, and sleep in a bed. Even so, for quite a while, we often find them sleeping on the floor under their beds. Gradually their eyes become accustomed to the light. It thrills us to note each small improvement—the first smile, the first laughter, the first words. We choose names for them and repeat them over and over until they understand what a name is and respond to us. The first time we take them outside is a great event. They stand in awe, gazing at the sky, the trees, and the grass. Timidly they pick up stones, pinecones, flowers, and even dirt that they then carry back and put in their beds, where they keep them like precious treasures.

At first, all the children are alike: skeletal arms and legs; swollen stomachs; pinched faces; pointed chins; huge, frightened eyes; dark yellow-brown skin covered with sores and scars. As the days go by and they take on both flesh and confidence, their individuality begins to emerge. We divide them into small groups according to size. They immediately become attached to the women who take care of their group. They especially adore Louise because she sings to them and teaches them games. Every new smile on their faces is a joy to us.

Strangers, especially men, continue to frighten them. When the occasional visitor from the American Army arrives, they run to us for protection. One day, a soldier from our detachment, wanting to give them a gift, throws a big, red rubber ball in the middle of the circle they had formed around us. The poor things had never seen a ball, of course, and they scatter in terror like frightened little birds as the strange orb bounces up and down. Several days later, however, they are playing with the ball for all they're worth.

These minor successes with the children renew our zeal for our work. We are astonished by the rapidity of their adaptation to their new life, and each step warms our hearts. Personally, after the first day, I am not able to spend much time with them since I have many other jobs to do, but not a day goes by without my stopping by to see "my children." Even if the only time I have is in the middle of the night, I go to watch them sleep, check on the ones who have fallen out of bed, and comfort those who are crying.

The MMLA Team

Our tasks at Buchenwald are assigned as follows: Yvonne, as usual, takes care of administration; Louise is responsible for the children and for keeping a count of the internees hospitalized at Weimar, Erfurt, and Jena as well as the sick in the nearby refugee camps. Anne Levert and Anne Dufraysseix keep track of the records of the French political prisoners as well as the lists of personal effects and documents that were taken from them when they arrived at Buchenwald. The building where the records, documents, and personal property are kept is a curious wooden tower, several stories tall, in the middle of the camp. Everything stored there has been scrupulously classified and catalogued. We find file drawers filled with carefully arranged rings, pieces of gold, cuff links, coins, etc., each object labeled with the name, nationality, and matriculation number of the owner, with the date of his arrival at the camp and, in the majority of cases, the date of his death, or according to the term used by the Germans—*Entlassen*—his "liberation."

Working with two officers of our American Army unit, I am in charge of organizing the repatriation of the prisoners, including air transport, when needed. I also look after French-speaking visitors to the camp. In addition, during the course of the five weeks we spend at Buchenwald, the other MMLA teams that I need to visit regularly arrive at Erfurt, Leipzig, and Eisenach. My workdays become increasingly long, and often I don't get on the road to check on my teams until evening, which means a late-night return.

At Eisenach, which is eighty kilometers from Weimar, Colette Fustier's team with their American unit is installed in a huge barracks where they oversee a transit camp for fifteen to twenty thousand DPs principally from Western Europe. In this case, the DPs are repatriated by rail or land route. Another French group oversees two hospitals and several hotels that shelter more than three thousand French prisoners from Buchenwald. We try—not always successfully—to put pressure on the Americans to facilitate and expedite the repatriation process. For their part, the Americans reproach us with not using authorized routes and with evacuating the French prisoners too quickly. As a result of these bureaucratic tangles, many prisoners are stuck here, some for months.

Administration and Evacuation

The internal administration of Buchenwald turns out to be simpler than expected because we are able to maintain the previous arrangements for the running of the camp. Captain Ball summons the twenty-seven Communist representatives of different nationalities from Block 40 and tells them they should continue operating as before, but now, of course, under the supervision of the Americans. This will continue as long as there is no political agitation or discrimination. Food distribution, lodging, sanitation, record keeping, and surveillance all fall under their responsibility. Taking over a camp already efficiently organized saves us many headaches—but we acquire many others.

Our main concern is the evacuation of the eight thousand or so prisoners who are well enough to return to their home countries in Western Europe. Transport is generously provided by the American Army, which furnishes a substantial number of military planes, equipped as flying hospitals and staffed by medical personnel. The

Americans also provide trucks and ambulances to shuttle the evacuees from the camp to the airfield at Weimar. Thus equipped, we are able to order six, eight, even ten planes a day.

Before they leave, the evacuees have to be checked by a doctor, inoculated against typhus, and provided with clothes and necessities. They also have to be screened by the American CIC and the intelligence officers of their nationality. Despite the delay caused by these procedures, thanks to the enormous transport facilities at our disposal, everyone who can be moved is repatriated within two weeks, and in the great majority of cases, in the first week.

Repatriation

The repatriation process does not continue without problems, however, some very serious. As Colonel Lewis warned me that evening at the Elefant Haus Hotel, the eyes of Europe are trained on Buchenwald, the first large concentration camp to be liberated by the Allies. From the very beginning, the American military authorities absolutely prohibit any evacuation other than by official American military transport. This rule makes sense from the point of view of those responsible for the liberated camp, but it is not greeted favorably by the countries concerned. We are soundly criticized by their highest government officials as well as by individuals and private organizations. Emissaries from Western Europe descend on Buchenwald. Government ministers, senators, bishops, generals all want, no, demand that their nationals be sent back immediately without taking into account their physical condition.

On April 27, the first national delegation arrives from Belgium. The mission is led by Premier Van Zeeland,* a charming man who invites us to the Elefant Haus for drinks. He thanks us for what we are doing—a rare occurrence—but insists that we make every effort to get the internees back to Belgium by May 1, so that they can participate in the May Day parade. His motivation is clear: to strengthen the position of his government with respect to the parties of the Left, especially the Communists. We respond that we are perfectly aware of the importance of May 1 and that we will do our best to repatriate on time the Belgians who have been released by the medical authorities. He agrees to this and simply asks us to do everything we can. Captain Ball assigns me the task of overseeing the repatriation of the Belgians with the help of a First Army liaison officer. It turns out to be a total fiasco.

Everything begins well enough. On April 30, we drive three hundred people in a convoy to the Weimar airport. No problems. We have trucks and a dozen ambulances. When we arrive at the airport and see the planes lined up ready to take off, I congratulate myself on how smoothly things are going. But when I go to the Air Force office to turn over our lists, the officer on duty informs me that there is significant turbulence over the Rhine and that the planes are grounded. After much arguing, he advises me to return to Buchenwald. Instead, we decide to unload the trucks and wait until the skies have cleared. The Belgians are furious. They sit on the ground and refuse to budge. We try to calm them and finally get them settled as best we can in an empty hangar. We set up a kitchen and an infirmary and wait for good weather. We think the wait will be for a few hours. In fact, the planes are grounded for three days!

We procure beds and stretchers, two ovens, and food. We get a doctor and nurses to staff a first-aid station. The Belgians think we are making up the whole story of bad weather for political reasons so that they will be kept from participating in the workers' parade on May 1. After the first day of waiting, there is so much bad feeling that we get permission from the Americans for one plane to take off with leaders of the group. They return after three hours at the request of the Belgians themselves; airsick and frightened by the turbulence, all they want is to get their feet back on solid ground. This fruitless attempt has the effect, however, of calming tempers. Finally, after two days of waiting at the airport, the Belgians take off and finally arrive in Brussels—on May 2.

Quite apart from official delegations, countless other charitable and health associations plus many individuals begin to arrive at Weimar looking for compatriots, relatives, and friends. Dozens of vehicles, many of them antiquated and run-down, line the road leading to the camp. We welcome those who have come to look for lost ones and help them look through the camp records. If possible, we take them to meet those of their nationality still in the camp. Trying to trace a husband, father, brother, or friend is an agonizing experience. Once in a while, a happy reunion compensates for these desperate searches. But for every positive outcome there are a hundred that end badly.

It is heartbreaking to see these poor people who have driven hundreds of kilometers across Europe, often in very difficult conditions, only to find out that they can't take their prisoners home. They can't understand why we would keep people in this camp where they had suffered so much, especially since the internees want nothing more than to leave as soon as possible. Usually the encounters don't go too badly, but sometimes these well-intentioned people think that proper nutrition, medical care, and comfortable transportation are just excuses that we use to hide some political aim.

Very sadly, one night our concerns prove to be amply justified by a terrible incident. In the middle of the night, one of the charitable organizations literally kidnaps sixty or so French internees. The roads are so bad and the suspension on their vehicles so defective that several of their passengers die within hours. Those who survive are in such bad shape that the convoy has to halt at Eisenach, only eighty kilometers from Weimar. It takes several months of care and rest before the kidnapped prisoners can be returned home.

I am particularly distressed by this catastrophe because I am the one who failed to convince the people responsible for the convoy to desist from their action. Their aggressiveness in our discussion plus certain remarks I overheard made me suspect what they were planning. Even Captain Ball, who had met with them at my request, was not able to put them off with the sternest warnings. I feel guilty for my weakness and resolve to be firmer and more assertive from here on out, especially since Captain Ball accuses me of favoring the French. After this tragic episode, the MP guard around the camp is reinforced, and nobody is admitted without first checking in at First Army HQ. A similar incident will not happen again.

The multiple regulations and prohibitions established by the First Army still do not prevent some imposters and crooks from reaching us. As in all periods of upheaval, disreputable people come out of the woodwork, looking to profit from the situation. In this case, some of them volunteer for a repatriation mission and, once inside Germany, disappear into the countryside to steal cars or loot bombed-out houses. Others contact families of POWs and deportees and extort money from them under the false pretense of searching for their friends or relatives. After getting our fingers burnt several times, we are on the alert and have learned to identify the imposters and crooks, who are then thrown out by the MPs. As time goes by, we begin to suspect everyone and, unfortunately, we occasionally treat very badly some perfectly legitimate visitors who must think we are totally odious.

One afternoon, as we are finishing a late lunch at the chalet, an elegant young man in a French uniform with three stripes on the sleeve bursts into the dining room. He is tall and handsome, but his arrogant demeanor and the abundance of military decorations lined up on his chest begin to make me doubt his authenticity. He sits down next to Captain Ball and begins to speak to him in English.

He declares that he has orders from the French government to find and repatriate the personal belongings of French prisoners and deportees. In the course of the conversation, he drops some important names, both French and American. Captain Ball is visibly impressed. The meal over, I get up, ready to return to my duties, when Captain Ball asks me to stop by his office. He gives me the key to the registration building where the camp files are located. He asks me to give the French captain the audit of valuables belonging to French internees. I raise objections, but he tells me that the officer's papers are in order and that he has a pass issued by the First Army. I obey and take our visitor to the camp. Once in the registration building, however, I find excuses to put off opening the safe. Furious, the captain treats me with contempt (which is surprising on the part of a supposed member of the FFL, whose officers always treat female uniformed personnel with respect). I claim to have joined the MMLA after the liberation of Paris and pretend to speak English badly. I ask him if he knows so-and-so (a name I make up on the spot) and he answers in the affirmative. My method is a little primitive, but the results confirm my suspicions.

Since the two members of my team who look after the files are not there, I myself turn them over to him. But the files are not what interest him. He asks me to open the safe. To gain time, I respond that I have lost the key. He turns angry and nasty. I tell him there is no reason to get upset; I must have left the key at the chalet.

"Of all the stupid idiots!" he shouts. When he eventually runs out of insults, I say, "We'd better go back and get the key."

"You go," orders the captain. "I'm staying here."

"No. It's not allowed. Nobody is authorized to be here unaccompanied."

"You do what I say, or . . ."

"I won't go without you. Those are my orders, and you'll never get the key if we both stay here."

We leave and, fortunately, run into Captain Ball. The supposed captain calms down, and we go to look for the key. Taking advantage of a short absence of the captain, I am able to tell Captain Ball about my suspicions. He laughs and reminds me of an unfortunate incident at Brand when I mistook a perfectly innocent priest for a spy. Nevertheless, Captain Ball tells me that he has decided, in any case, not to turn over any valuable objects to our visitor for fear of his being robbed while on the roads. Finally, he summons an American Intelligence officer and a liaison officer from First Army HQ to question the supposed captain and to verify his papers. A quarter of an hour later, he emerges from the office, free of all suspicion. I make myself scarce before he can unleash his fury on me.

Much later that evening, however, I learn with gleeful satisfaction that the handsome captain really is a crook. The Intelligence officer had his car searched and also called the authorities in Paris. It turns out that the captain had been operating successfully in the British sector and had already collected millions in cash and jewelry. Now, I am glad to say, he is in an MP cell at Weimar, waiting to be transferred to the French authorities at the border.

Visitors

While we are busy repatriating the Western European internees, the camp is visited by hundreds of military and civilian visitors, or "tourists," as we call them. Buchenwald begins to resemble a macabre human zoo. We accept the situation, realizing that it is important for the greatest number of people possible to see with their own eyes the degree to which the Nazis succeeded in their monstrous campaign to dehumanize and exterminate their victims. Still, the sideshow aspect of it is hard to swallow.

General Patton, commander of the Third Army, has ordered all his troops to come to Buchenwald. Known for his plain talk, he announced, "If the GIs don't know why they are fighting, after they visit Buchenwald, they'll know." And they arrive, thousands every day—in jeeps, cars, trucks, and buses, turning the area around the camp into a giant parking lot. They begin arriving at nine in the morning and keep coming until nightfall. A continuous line of khaki figures weaves around the barracks and the four crematoriums. With the help of the camp committee, Captain Ball organizes a team of guides and, all through the day, you can hear high-pitched foreign accents ghoulishly describing in English the high spots of the camp. When the crowds become overwhelming for the individual guides, we use sound trucks, audible at five kilometers, for what we call the "Horror Show."

In addition to the group tours, there are also private tours for VIPs. In the early morning Captain Ball and I are usually both in the chalet office organizing the work of the day. The office, which belonged to the German camp commandant, is filled with sunshine. The windows open onto a lovely view of the valley. One of the lampshades made out of human skin somehow got left here, but it has become part of the landscape, and we don't even notice it anymore.

Inevitably the phone rings. With a "Damn, here we go again!" Captain Ball answers and, immediately changing tone, says, "Buchenwald Camp. Captain Ball speaking."

Pause. "Good morning, Colonel W." I understand right away that it is the colonel at the First Army HQ calling to announce another official visit, and I tune into Captain Ball's end of the conversation.

"Of course, Sir. We'll be glad to show them around the camp." Pause. "No Colonel. No trouble at all." Pause. "A party of six, you say. I'll note the names." Pause. "As you say, Sir. The grand tour." Pause. "With the skin lampshades. Of course, Colonel." Pause. "Thank you, Colonel. Good-bye, Colonel."

Captain Ball slams down the receiver, leans back in his chair, and announces with disgust: "Tomorrow at ten hundred hours, a bishop, two generals, and three labor leaders. And they want to see EVERYTHING."

"If they keep on showing the skins and passing them around," I observe, "there won't be any left. The last time when we counted them up after the tour, there were two missing."

"I'm sure the Senator pinched one of them," Captain Ball answers. "He was in a hell of a hurry to leave."

The next day, after spending the night at the Elefant Haus, the group arrives at exactly ten o'clock. Captain Ball greets them in his office and delivers his "background" speech about the camp, enlivening it here and there with human interest anecdotes and a pinch or two of black humor. Then the same guide who showed us around the first day comes in, grinning and dressed in his stripes. With one of the American officers, he shows the group around. Two hours later they return, worn out and shaken. They are revived by cocktails and an excellent lunch at our mess. When coffee is served, it is time to pass the skins around. You can get used to anything.

Patton insists as well that Buchenwald should be visited by the civilian population of Weimar. The camp is put off-limits for a day while American soldiers go house-to-house in Weimar, leading the population to the camp on foot. From a distance the line looks like a long, dreary funeral procession. At the end of the visit, like it or not, they are shown a film made during the first days after the liberation of the camp.

The Weimar population—young, old, women, and even children— appear to endure the dreadful experience stoically and show no apparent reaction to the scenes of horror they are witnessing. No one speaks, children's cries are soon quieted. A few people collapse. And then, when evening comes, they return to town on foot or in trucks.

Apparently, the inhabitants of the town knew of the existence of the camp but nothing more—and probably didn't want to know. What's more, the area around the camp was off-limits and guarded by SS with dogs. We are told that the civilians who got too close were arrested and imprisoned. Judging from people's reactions on the spot, we come to believe that the horrific revelation of the concentration camps was as shocking for the Germans as it was for the rest of the world.

May 8, 1945

Germany's unconditional surrender is signed at Soviet Headquarters near Berlin by Field Marshal Keitel* in the presence of Marshal Zhukov,* representing the Soviet Union, Air Marshal Tedder* for Great Britain, General Spaatz* for the United States, and Marshal de Lattre de Tassigny* for France.

The war in Europe is over. Over the past two years, how often we talked about this glorious day, anticipating our joy and happiness! But when VE Day came, I didn't even know about it. I was completely out of it in the Weimar military hospital.

My left arm had been bothering me for several days, swollen with red welts that made it look like a colored chart of blood vessels in an anatomy book. Then I develop a high fever. Over my protests, Captain Ball takes me to the hospital. The head doctor diagnoses blood poisoning probably caused by an insect bite or a scratch that has become infected. Fearful, I ask if they're going to amputate. The doctor laughs and reassures me: "It's not that serious, Lieutenant, but you're going to have to spend several days with us." He prescribes penicillin and sulfa shots every three hours and turns me over to a smiling, motherly nurse.

When I wake up after sleeping for twenty hours, I find myself lying in a small, square, white room. There are two other beds in the room— one occupied by a woman with short, dark, curly hair and the other by a redhead who is doing her nails. The redhead speaks to me in a shrill, nasal voice: "Jeez, I have to hand it to you. I didn't know anyone could sleep through all the shots, doctors' visits, and fuss. Tell me, Girl, how do you do it?" Her voice annoys me so much that I turn over and close my eyes again. The dark-haired woman takes my side and says in a soft Southern accent: "Leave her alone. Can't you see she's knocked out?"

Not content, the redhead keeps on hassling me. I don't respond. The truth is, I'm still in a fog and don't entirely understand where I am. I suddenly find myself thinking about Timmy, killed in the blue sky over Normandy, and about so many others, about the V1 at Verviers, and then about the barracks at Buchenwald and the children. What makes it so awful is that these nightmares are all real.

The shrill voice of the redhead cuts through my dark musings: "Tell me about your boyfriends, Frenchie. While you've been snoozing away, colonels, commanders, and captains have been trooping through here. Tell me how you do it. What do you foreign girls have that we don't?"

"They're not my boyfriends, just the officers I work with. It was nice of them to come see me."

"Well la-di-dah. Isn't she a prim and proper miss and with an English accent to boot. Where do you work?"

"Buchenwald."

"Buchenwald! The bastards! They have the nerve to put you in our room with your germs, your typhus, and God know what else. I'm getting out of here quick."

"Good idea," says the brunette. "Why don't you leave now?"

The redhead turns to me again: "No wonder they have to use foreigners to work in those filthy camps. No honest American girl would work there."

This is too much for me. I pick up the nearest thing, which happens to be one of my boots, and throw it at her with my good arm. It catches her right in her middle. She lets out a shriek and accuses me of crippling her. Snarling over her shoulder that she isn't through with me yet, she leaves, slamming the door behind her.

The next morning, feeling much better, I am released from the hospital. Captain Ball comes to pick me up in his jeep. "Tonight we're celebrating May 8. Everybody was hoping you'd be back."

"Why May 8?" I ask. "I don't even know what day it is."

"The 10th. We came to the hospital to tell you the big news, but you were sleeping like a log."

"And what is this big news?"

"The surrender! VE Day! The Germans signed an unconditional surrender in Berlin on May 8. It's a date for the history books. The war is over!"

I don't know what to say. After a long silence, I finally speak: "It's strange. I should be over the moon with happiness, but I don't feel anything. Maybe the drugs have made me numb."

"No, it's not just the drugs," answers Captain Ball. "To tell the truth, we all reacted the same way. It's a messy end. And for us, the war isn't really over. Things are going badly in the Pacific. It might take years and enormous losses before we defeat the Japanese."

Back at the chalet, I rush to look at the *Stars and Stripes*, the American Army newspaper. I learn that Marshal de Lattre de Tassigny represented both France and de Gaulle at the signing of the surrender and that Germany will be divided into four zones: American, British, French, and Russian. It's an enormous victory for de Gaulle. He, at least, should be happy about VE Day. When I read the articles describing the joyous crowds celebrating in Paris, New York, and London, I feel as if I'm on another planet.

We don't leave Buchenwald until June 4, but from mid-May on, the prisoners who remain are all from Eastern Europe. All the "Westerners" have been repatriated, and the children have also been evacuated, we don't know where. Aside from hosting visitors and doing guided tours, there is not a whole lot left for us to do. Routine sets in. Some of the internees even begin to complain about the food; others, specifically the Czechs, grumble that the Germans showed better movies than the ones they are getting now! Buchenwald is over for us. The

First Army is leaving for the USA. We go to the Elefant Haus in Weimar to say goodbye to the D3F1 detachment and to Colonel Lewis. Emotions run high during the numerous toasts; we have worked together for over a year through the best and the worst, and we know we'll probably never see each other again.

Epilogue
In Germany after VE Day

June–October 1945

The war is over, but not the flow of miseries. While the winners live comfortably in buildings abandoned by German military and dignitaries, millions of DPs, mostly women and children, have to endure life in the camps. For those from Western Europe, things don't go too badly; they are repatriated fairly quickly. But for the DPs from Eastern Europe, it's a different story. Whether they want to or not, they are sent back to their home countries. In Stalin's Russia, this means deportation to Siberia. The UNRRA has taken over the administration and evacuation of the camps. Our MMLA teams are put under its authority but continue to work with US Army units.

At the beginning of June, I end up at the HQ of the Ninth US Army in Braunschweig. From there I go out to supervise twenty or so teams spread out over the vast area occupied by the Ninth and Seventh US Armies. My sector stretches from Leipzig and Dessau in the east, to Augsburg in the south, and Kassel in the west.

Exchange of DPs (East–West)

In Dessau, my team and their American military unit are responsible for the exchange of Russian DPs for Western POWs. The team works in the transit camp near the Dessau train station and also at the Mulde Bridge where the grim East–West exchange takes place. The "bridge" is in reality a sort of raft that the Russians beach every night. When the DPs get to the Soviet side of the river, they pass under a kind of triumphal arch made of tree branches with a banner displaying writing in Cyrillic and a hammer and sickle. The Russian soldiers insist on taking our pictures, but, apparently not knowing much about cameras, they often hold them the wrong way around. Many of them wear several watches on their wrist. Colossal female soldiers keep order.

The transit camp on the Soviet side is limited to the strict minimum, consisting of a fenced area in a field without any shelters. It often rains hard, and if there are DPs there, they have to wait—seated or even lying down—in the mud.

On the American side of the river, the trucks carrying the Russian DPs are often held up for hours. Depending on the day, the Soviets decide to take 150, 200, or 300 DPs, and they insist on the exact number. As a result, families are often separated and young children left behind. When that happens, the children are integrated into the next contingent and, in all likelihood, will never find their mothers again. The DPs are mostly apathetic, but some hang desperately onto the GIs or the trucks. Russian soldiers come to drag them off. I can hardly stand to witness these scenes, but the American officer who is with me reminds me: "These are our orders, and it's the only way to get our POWs back."

Disgusted by this trade in humans, I hurry back to the HQ at Braunschweig and ask to see the colonel in charge. But it turns out he's no Colonel Lewis. He tells me I'm making a big deal over nothing. The exchange is the result of an agreement between governments, and that's the end of it. I request a new assignment for my team. He responds that, in any case, we will be leaving soon since the American Army will have to vacate the Russian Zone.

At our grade level, we don't know what the exact borders of the Russian Zone will be or the date of the transfer of power. That information is a military secret meant to prevent panic in the German population, who fear the arrival of the Russians. We think that we'll probably be here for several months. In fact, it turns out to be only several days.

Transfer of Power

On June 20, our entire unit receives orders to go to Heidelberg to be redeployed. I have learned to be wary, so I decide to go to Heidelberg first myself to find out what is going on even though it is four hundred kilometers from Weimar, where I have temporarily returned. In Heidelberg, I learn that our group of sixty people is not expected on the day we have been told to arrive, and that no provisions have been made to house us. With difficulty, I succeed in obtaining in advance the assignments for each team so that they will be able to travel directly to their new locations without having to go through Heidelberg, where there is total confusion.

I am able to communicate with several teams by telephone, but the lines are so busy that I end up setting out for Dessau and Leipzig where six teams are located so that I can give them their new orders in person. Short on gas, I stop at the American HQ in Leipzig, where I'm lucky enough to run into Major Gardiner, an officer of the 7th Corps, whom I have known since Normandy. I spend a nervous night in the city; the Americans and Russians are already quarreling, seemingly enjoying exchanging fire. The danger is such that, day or night, it is impossible to leave the HQ without an armed escort. At night, from the hotel windows, we witness a veritable street war between American and Soviet tanks.

My efforts to obtain fuel become critical. Since I can't get gas through official channels, I ask Major Gardiner for help. At daybreak, we make our way to a military storehouse protected by a nine-foot-high wall. Standing on his jeep, the major gives me a leg up. We manage to get into the storehouse and succeed in liberating three cans of gasoline, enough to get me back to Weimar.

On the road, there is almost no military traffic since almost all of the Americans have already departed the area, but the road is filled with thousands of civilians fleeing to the West in an effort to escape Soviet occupation. This dreadful exodus reminds me of the worst days of June 1940, when the roads were choked with people fleeing Paris and the German occupation. By the time I finally arrive in Weimar, my car is stuffed with women and children, including one clinging to each running board. Plus, I have another car in tow, equally full. The American troops have left, and my command has already moved out. It is July 1.

I continue on to Erfurt, twenty-five kilometers to the west of Weimar. There I find one of my teams and manage to dig up a truck for them. I also give them my car because I have decided to stay on in Erfurt to try and find a decent vehicle. Thanks to the help of a young lieutenant, I become the happy owner of an almost new, four-door Super Opel with a radio. It's a little large, but since it is in impeccable condition, I gladly take it.

The Russians arrive during the night. We watch the long cavalcade of jeeps and trucks filled with soldiers coming into town. Even though the jeeps are made in the USA, they don't look at all like the US Army jeeps: they are painted bright green, and the seats are covered with multicolored rugs and silk and satin cushions.

In contrast to Leipzig, the occupation of Erfurt takes place peacefully. The occupants stay hunkered down in their houses, and the streets are deserted. On the second night, the electricity goes off, and, in the candlelight, we wonder if the Russkis, as we call them, haven't made the mistake of "removing" the German on duty. Meanwhile, Russian officers come to our office, and we drink vodka toasts to everyone's health. Unfortunately, our exchange is limited to a few grunts and smiles since neither side knows the language of the other.

I set out for Bad Homburg, near Frankfurt, in my new car. I'm looking for my uncle, Colonel Allen, who is stationed there in the command headquarters of the US Air Force. In this impressive HQ, housed in a beautiful villa, everything is calm, efficient, orderly, and clean. Staffed with superior officers and impeccably got up WACs, it presents a marked, almost eerie, contrast to the confusion and uncertainties I have witnessed in the past weeks.

I award myself a two-day leave at Bad Homburg (well deserved in my opinion) before reporting to the HQ of the 12th Army Group at Wiesbaden, only thirty kilometers away. I don't know for sure what army I'm assigned to or where I'm supposed to go. It turns out that, in fact, they have been impatiently waiting for me. They tell me that I have been appointed the head of all the MMLA teams in the American Zone and that I will be attached to the G5 of the Army Group with a large office, two secretaries, and a car with a driver. A letter from

Captain Rothschild informs me that she has come down with jaundice and will be out of action for several weeks. She assigns me the responsibility of negotiating with the UNRRA to try to establish the status of the MMLA teams.

This is bad news, not only because of the invaliding out of my colleague but also because I just requested my recall to Paris prior to being demobilized. My letter and Captain Rothschild's must have crossed in the mail. So here I am, stuck at the 12th Army group HQ. It is beginning to seem that it is as hard to get out of the army as it was to get in.

During the negotiations with the UNRRA, I spend most of my time trying to untangle administrative problems with its officers. What time I have left is spent visiting my teams, thirty in all. They are spread out over the entire American Zone. From my HQ in Wiesbaden I go to Kassel, Munich, Bamberg, Nuremberg, and then complete the circuit going through Augsburg, Karlsruhe, Heidelberg, and Mannheim.

Paradoxically, these months spent in Germany after the end of hostilities are the most difficult and painful of my time in the military. The sense of mission that energized us evaporated with the silencing of the guns and, everywhere, the longed-for victory seems to have brought only confusion and chaos. The peace—rife with discord, envy, hatred, vengeance, and pettiness of all kinds—seems extraordinarily precarious. The camps, with their masses of uprooted DPs, have become unbearable to me, and even my hours on the road have lost their zest.

During these months, the world has changed: the first atomic bomb was dropped on Hiroshima on August 6, killing eighty thousand; the second on Nagasaki three days later has ended the war with the surrender of Japan.

My own war ends with the last beautiful days of summer. In October, I leave Wiesbaden and Germany for Paris. I'm twenty-three years old and I feel very old and very wise.

My two years of military life, which coincided with the passage from youth to adulthood, taught me much: above all to distinguish between what is important and what is not. The best and the worst memories have stayed with me. The best memories include having contributed, however modestly, to a great cause—the liberation of my country and the final victory over Nazism. They also include the camaraderie and team spirit, the efforts we made together, the successes, even the failures, and always the shared laughter. Also, the friendship and trust of men as different as Pastor Lewis, Jim Litton, Peter Ball, Konstantin, and many others. And the brief encounters with the great generals—Bradley, Hodges, Patton. Finally, the rare and fleeting sense of having, in exceptional circumstances, had an effect on the lives of thousands of people.

The worst memories include the heavy cost of Yalta: the abandonment of Central Europe and a part of Germany to the Russians, and the dreadful trade of Russian DPs for our POWs. And, most of all, the degradation and extermination of man by fellow man, of which Buchenwald remains one of the eternal symbols.

All of this is what I think about when I reread the striking phrase of General de Gaulle that is engraved on his memorial at Colombey-les-Deux-Églises: The only battle worth fighting is for the future of mankind.

Appendix 1
Acronyms

AFAT	Auxiliaires Féminines de l'Armée de Terre
AMGOT	Allied Military Government Occupied Territories
ASCZ	Advanced Section Communications Zone
ATS	Auxiliary Territorial Service (women's section of British infantry)
CAB	Citizen's Advice Bureau
CIC	Counter-Intelligence Corps (US Army)
CNR	Comité National de la Résistance
DCA	Department of Civil Aviation
DP	Displaced person
FFI	Forces Françaises de l'Intérieur
FFL	Forces Françaises Libres
FUSA	First US Army
LCI	Landing Craft Infantry
MG	Military Government
MMLA	Mission Militaire de Liaison Administrative
NKVD	Narodnyy Komissariat Vnutrennikh Del (People's Commissariat for Internal Affairs)
OR	Other Ranks
PDR	Prisoners, Displaced Persons, and Refugees
POW	Prisoner of war
SHAEF	Supreme Headquarters of Allied Expeditionary Forces
STO	Service du Travail Obligatoire
UNRRA	United Nations Relief and Rehabilitation Administration
V1	Vergeltung drones
VF	Volontaires Françaises (women's section of the FFL)
WAC	Women's Army Corps

Appendix 2
People

Allen, Julian (1900–1967)

Brother of Vagliano Eloy's mother. During World War II served first in the British Army and then in the US Army Air Force under General Spaatz, first in London and then in the Pacific.

Aubrac, Lucie (1912–2007)

Taught History in Strasbourg. Worked simultaneously for a Quaker group and the Communist Party. With her husband, edited the Resistance newspaper *Libération-Sud* in Lyon beginning in 1941 and participated in many actions. Known for her bravery, with a group of comrades, helped her husband and thirteen other prisoners escape the Gestapo by attacking a police vehicle. Escaped to London in 1944. After the war, returned to teaching. Published her memoirs in 1984. Légion d'Honneur, Croix de Guerre. Palmes académiques.

Ball, Peter (1913–2006)

Born in St. Louis, Missouri. Graduated from Williams College. Captain in the First Army, temporary commander of Buchenwald concentration camp after its liberation in April 1945. Awarded the Legion of Merit for his work with DPs. Worked for United Nations relief and Rehabilitation Administration. Owned a magazine publishing company in Fairfield, Connecticut, where he died.

Blum, Léon (1872–1950)

Three times Prime Minister of France. After brilliant university studies, followed a political career, becoming leader of the left-wing Front Populaire. Head of government in 1936. After resigning in 1939, refused to back Pétain. Arrested in 1940 and indicted for treason in 1942, turned over to the Nazis in 1943. Deported to Buchenwald. After the liberation, became officer of UNESCO. Led the provisional government before the institution of the Fourth Republic. Retired in 1947. Légion d'Honneur.

Boislambert, Claude Hettier de (1906–1986)

Degrees in law and political science. Traveled widely. Mobilized as lieutenant in the cavalry in 1939. Joined de Gaulle in 1940. Imprisoned by Vichy agents in France in 1941 and condemned to death. Escaped and arrived back in London in 1943. Head of the MMLA. Postwar, served as delegate in the Rhineland, elected to the National Assembly, and served as member of de Gaulle's government. Ordre de la Libération.

Boncenne, Monique (1918–2011)

Fled to England with her family in 1940. Along with her father and brothers, worked for the FFL. Second lieutenant in MMLA. Légion d'Honneur.

Bradley, Omar (1893–1981)

The last general to hold five-star rank in the US Armed Forces. Born into a poor family in Missouri. Studied at West Point, then taught there 1920–1924. Following various assignments, promoted to major general in 1942. Served in North Africa and commanded the 11th Corps in the invasion of Sicily. Commander of American ground forces in Normandy. Commanded the 12th Army Group of 900,000 men. Captured the Remagen Bridge over the Rhine and met the Russian Army before

VE Day. Postwar, headed the VA. Served as chairman of the Joint Chiefs of Staff. Left active duty in 1953. Bronze Star, Distinguished Service Medal, Croix de Guerre, Honorary Knight Commander Order of the Bath, and many more.

Burdet, Gioia (1908–?)

English national. First officer to join the VF. Served with the AFAT in London as adjutant to Hélène Terré. Rose to the rank of commander.

Chandon, Claude (1894–1944)

Fought in World War I. In World War II, rallied Guyana to the FFL. Military commander of Gabon in 1942. Named to MMLA in 1943. Killed in Brittany by German fire while protecting his MMLA group. Ordre de la Libération, Légion d'Honneur, British Military Cross.

Coulet, François (1906–1984)

Diplomat, joined the FFL and carried out several missions for de Gaulle. Commanded French air troops at Camberley. Transferred to Corsica in 1943. Landed in Normandy in June 1944 to direct liaison activities. Appointed FFL commissioner in Normandy. Postwar diplomatic career. Part of French air command during Algerian war.

Curie, Eve (1904–2007)

Daughter of Marie and Pierre Curie. An accomplished pianist. Author of her mother's biography, *Madame Curie* (1937). Wrote music and theater reviews for Paris newspapers. Joined the FFL in 1940 and spent most of the war years in England. Married American diplomat, Henry Richardson Labouisse in 1954 and moved to New York City. Became an American citizen and worked for UNICEF. Died in her Sutton Place apartment at the age of 102. Légion d'Honneur, Croix de Guerre, Ordre de Polonia Restituta.

Deloche de Noyelle, Francis (1919–2017)

Served in the Resistance in Isère before joining the FFL. Mountain climber. Member of the support team for the French group who climbed Annapurna in the Himalayas in 1950. Ambassador to Nepal in 1980. Légion d'Honneur, Croix de Guerre.

Diethelm, André (1896–1954)

Fought in World War I in Alsace and Greece. Inspector of Finance 1938–1940. Commissioner in the FFL and Minister of War 1944–1945. Deputy in the National Assembly until his death.

Frenay, Henri (1905–1988)

Officer in the French Army. Escaped from German prisoner-of-war camp. Formed a Resistance unit and helped found the newspaper *Combat*. Met de Gaulle in London in 1942 and became Minister of Prisoners, Deportees, and Refugees. Active anti-Communist and pro-European in the 1950s. Retired from political life and became a businessman. Légion d'Honneur, Croix de la Libération, Ordre National du Mérite, Croix de Guerre, and others.

Haas-Picard, Raymond (1906–1971)

Militant Socialist, represented the Socialist Resistance in London and was a lieutenant in the FFL. Businessman and author, served as prefect of the Seine region from 1963–1967.

Hall, Marian Wells (1896–1972)

American director of Red Cross Club operations in Europe during World War II. After the war, returned to New York and became well-known interior decorator.

Keitel, Wilhelm (1882–1946)

Chief of the Supreme High Command of the German Armed Forces. In 1901, officer cadet in the Prussian Army. In World War I, served on the Western Front. Promoted to general in 1937. War Minister and member of Hitler's cabinet. Signer for Germany of the May 8 surrender. Tried and sentenced to death at Nuremberg. Hanged as a war criminal in 1946. Knight's Cross, Prussian Iron Cross, and many others.

Koch, Ilse (1906–1967)

Wife of the first commandant of Buchenwald. Known for her cruelty, was called the "Bitch of Buchenwald." Most notorious for her collection of articles made from tattooed human skin of camp prisoners. Arrested in 1945 and tried at Dachau in 1947. Sentenced to life imprisonment. Pardoned by General Lucius Clay in 1948. Retried in 1950, sentenced again to life in prison. Hanged herself in Aichach prison in 1967.

Koch, Karl Otto (1897–1945)

Born into a worker's family. In the German Army in World War I, was wounded three times. POW in France. In 1932, member of the SS in Cassel. Commandant of various camps beginning in 1934 including Sachsenshausen. Married to Ilse Köhler in 1937. Named commandant of Buchenwald camp the same year. Known for his cruelty and sadism and for his corruption. Arrested by the Germans for embezzlement, violation of military regulations, incompetence, and mistreatment of prisoners. Sentenced to death in 1944. Imprisoned briefly at Buchenwald. After being executed by firing squad in 1945, his body burned in the camp ovens.

Koenig, Marie Pierre (1898–1970)

Born and educated in Caen. Served in World War I. Joined the FFL in 1940. Became its commander in Normandy. Renowned for defending the fortress at Bir Hakeim, Libya, against the forces of General Rommel (May–June 1942). In April 1945, tasked with arresting Marshal Pétain and escorting him to prison. From 1945–1949, governor of the French Zone in Germany. Made marshal of France. Served in the National Assembly. Minister of Defence 1954–1955. Légion d'Honneur, Croix de Guerre, Compagnon de la Libération, Legion of Merit, Order of the Bath, and many others.

Lattre de Tassigny, Jean de (1889–1952)

Graduated from St Cyr military academy in 1911. Served in the infantry in World War I, surviving five wounds. In 1939, became the youngest general in the French Army. After serving with Vichy, joined the FFL. Participated in the invasion of southern France with the US Seventh Army. Witnessed the May 8 surrender for France. After World War II, was NATO chief of staff, then led the French forces in Indochina. Given a state funeral in Paris. Légion d'Honneur, Croix de Guerre, Compagnon de la Libération, Distinguished Service Medal, Legion of Merit, and many others.

Mandel, Georges (1885–1944)

Born into a modest French Jewish family. Became a journalist and then deputy for the Gironde. Minister in the prewar government, opposed the armistice agreement. Imprisoned by the Vichy government and turned over to the Nazis in 1942. Sent to Buchenwald, where he remained for two years before being returned to France. During a prison transfer, captured by the French Militia, who assassinated him in the Forest of Fontainebleau.

Manziarly, Alexandre de (1898–1973)

Veteran of World War I. Worked at League of Nations 1930–1937. Officer at headquarters of FFL in New York. French consul in Los Angeles (1946–1950) and then in Geneva (1953–1962). Died in Paris in 1973. Légion d'Honneur, Croix de Guerre.

Parodi, Alexandre (1901–1979)

Member of the Conseil d'Etat in 1926. Assistant Secretary General of the National Economic Council. Important role in the Resistance. Participated in the insurrection of Paris. Served as delegate to the French Committee of National Liberation. After the war served as a diplomat at the UN, OTAN and was ambassador to Morocco. Légion d'Honneur, Compagnon de la Libération, Ordre National du Mérite.

Patton, George S. (1885–1945)

Four-star general in the US Army, known for his daring strategic command and his plain-speaking, hard-driving personality. Graduate of West Point, saw action in World War I. Commander of the 2nd Armored Division at the US entry into World War II. Commanded the Seventh Army at the invasion of Sicily. Commander of the Third Army following the Normandy invasion. Critical in winning the Battle of the Bulge. Liberated Ohrdruf and Buchenwald concentration camps. At the end of the war, became military governor of Bavaria. Died in a car accident in Bavaria. Distinguished Service Cross, Legion of Merit, Bronze Star, Purple Heart, Croix de Guerre, Légion d'Honneur, and many others.

Pister, Hermann (1885–1948)

Born in Lübeck, joined the Imperial Navy at the age of seventeen. Joined the Nazi party in 1931. In 1939, head of reeducation camps and, in 1941, followed Otto Koch as commandant of Buchenwald. Tried by the American military tribunal at Dachau in 1947. Condemned to death, died in his cell of a heart attack in 1948.

Renouard, Louis Noël (1885–?)

Fought in World War I. Colonel in the FFL and commanded their Land Forces in Great Britain.

Rothschild, Claude de, Baroness (1905–1964)

Née Claude Dupont. A social worker, married Baron Henri de Rothschild in 1923. Escaped from occupied France in 1942 and served in London as captain in the MMLA. Cited for her service in the battle of Caen. After the war, active in the Compiègne region, where her husband was mayor. Founded a Red Cross hospital and a youth library. Légion d'Honneur.

Rundstedt, Gerd von (1875–1953)

From a military family, served in World War I. Commander of Germany's invasion of Poland. Dismissed after the defeat in Normandy, but recalled as commander of the west for the Ardennes campaign. After the war, was charged with war crimes, but did not face trial because of ill health. Released in 1949. Died penniless in Hannover in 1953.

Schmuhl, Lorenzo C. (1898–1988)

Born and lived in Indiana. Served in World War I. After the war, served as deputy warden in the Indiana state prison at Michigan City. Interim Third Army commander at Buchenwald between liberation of the camp and arrival of the First Army. After the war, returned to his post at Michigan City.

Schumann, Maurice (1911–1998)

Journalist in Paris, first joined the British army as an interpreter, then became the spokesman for de Gaulle's FFL. Participated in the Normandy invasion and the liberation of Paris. Founding member of the MRP (Mouvement Républicain Populaire), first elected to the French National Assembly and then to the Senate. Cabinet minister in several administrations, finally Minister for Foreign Affairs for Georges Pompidou. Member of the French Academy. Légion d'Honneur, Croix de Guerre, Compagnon de la Libération, Ordre de Léopold.

Segard, Dorothée (1921–2018)

Called Lally. Sister of Sonia Vagliano. First marriage to the Vicomte de Saint-Sauveur. Second marriage to Patrick Segard. Golf champion holding fourteen titles. One of first woman members of the Royal and Ancient Club of Saint Andrews. National Order of Sporting Merit.

Spaatz, Carl Andrew (1891–1974)

Graduated from West Point in 1914. Served with the Expeditionary Forces in France in 1917. During World War II, commander of the Eighth Army Air Corps, then of the Twelfth in North Africa. Promoted to general in 1945, witnessed the surrender of May 8 for the United States. First chief of staff of the newly formed Air Force, 1947–1948. After the war, worked for *Newsweek*. Legion of Merit, Distinguished Service Medal, Bronze Star, Légion d'Honneur, Croix de Guerre, and many others.

Tedder, Arthur (1890–1967)

Born in Glasgow and educated at Oxford. Served in World War I in the Royal Flying Corps. In World War II, commander of the Mediterranean Force under Eisenhower. Helped plan and execute the invasion of Italy. Deputy Supreme Commander at SHAEF, signed the surrender document for the English. After the war, was chancellor of the University of Cambridge. Order of the Bath, Legion of Merit, Order of Polonia Restituta, Distinguished Service Medal.

Terré, Hélène (1903–1993)

Edited first edition of the poet Paul Valéry's complete works. Joined French army as an ambulance driver in 1939. Joined the FFL in

London in 1940. Became head of Volontaires Françaises in 1941, which soon became known as "les demoiselles de Gaulle." Commander of the Auxiliaires Féminines de l'Armée de Terre (AFAT) in 1943. In 1947, involved in academic exchanges between France and the United States. Gave numerous lectures in the US and published *L'Enseignement aux Etats-Unis* (1963). Died in Paris at the age of ninety. Légion d'Honneur, Croix de Guerre, Legion of Merit.

Vagliano, André Marino (1896–1971)

Born in Marseille. Father of Sonia Vagliano. Married to Barbara Allen of New York. Served in World War I, then studied at Merton College, Oxford. Worked in the engineering field. During World War II, active in providing support to the Jewish community and provided a safe house for Jews. At the end of the war, received the OBE.

Vagliano, Barbara Gallatin Allen (1897–1951)

From the prominent New York Gallatin-Allen family. Mother of Sonia Vagliano. Volunteer ambulance driver in World War I. First American woman to receive the French Croix de Guerre.

Van Zeeland, Paul (1893–1973)

Professor of Law, became Prime Minister of Belgium in 1935. In 1939, became president of the Committee on Refugees established in London, and in 1944 was made high commissioner for the repatriation of displaced Belgians. Postwar, served as Minister of Foreign Affairs and economic adviser to NATO.

Zhukov, Georgy (1896–1974)

The most decorated general officer in the history of the Soviet Union. Born into a peasant family, conscripted into the Russian Imperial Army in 1915. In World War II, commander of the Leningrad front.

Decisive role in the drive to Berlin. Commander of the Soviet Occupation Zone in Germany. In 1955, became Defense Minister in the Bulganin government. Died of a stroke in 1974. Cross of St. George, Hero of the Soviet Union, Order of Lenin, Legion of Merit, Order of the Bath, and many others.

Acknowledgments

It has been a privilege to work on this translation. Many people contributed generously to its preparation. First, grateful thanks to Sara Vagliano, the sister-in-law of the author, who first handed me the French version of the book many years ago. She encouraged me to do the translation and not only reviewed drafts but also provided much background and family information. I wish she were here to see the final publication. Then to the librarians who were very helpful in guiding me to needed information, especially at the Musée Jean Moulin in Paris and at the National Memorial Holocaust Museum in Washington, DC. And finally, an enormous debt of gratitude to Marina Eloy Jacquillat, the author's daughter, for providing unique information about the Vagliano family, especially her mother; for sharing the original prospectus for the book in her mother's first English version; for reviewing this English translation; and finally, for her unending patience and support throughout the years. *Lieutenant Sonia Vagliano: A Memoir of the World War II Refugee Crisis* would not exist without her generous and sustaining help.

Bibliography

Abzug, Robert H. *Inside the Vicious Heart: Americans and the Liberation of the Nazi Concentration Camps.* New York: Oxford University Press, 1985.

Borowski, Tadeusz. *This Way for the Gas, Ladies and Gentlemen.* New York: Penguin, 1976.

Bradley, Omar Nelson. *A Soldier's Life.* New York: Henry Holt, 1951.

Coles, Harry L., and Albert K. Weinberg. *Civil Affairs: Soldiers Become Governors.* United States Army in World War II. Special Studies. Washington, DC: Center of Military History, US Army, 1964.

Davidson, Bill. *Cut Off; Behind Enemy Lines in the Battle of the Bulge.* New York: Stein and Day, 1972.

Davis, George W. "Handling of Refugees and Displaced Persons by the French MMLA (Section Féminine)." *Social Service Review* 22, no. 1 (March 1948): 34–39.

D'Este, Carlo. *Patton: A Genius for War.* New York: Harper Collins, 1995.

Dominé, Jean-François. *Les femmes au combat: l'arme féminine de la France pendant la Seconde Guerre mondiale.* Paris: Service Historique de la Défense, 2008.

Frank, Mary E. *The Forgotten POW: Second Lieutenant Reba Z. Whittle, AN.* Delhi, India: Gyan Books, 1990.

Gardner, Clinton C., ed. *World War II Remembered by Residents of Kendal at Hanover.* Hanover, NH: Kendal Residents Association, 2012.

Gilbert, Martin. *The Second World War: A Complete History.* New York: Henry Holt, 1989.

Guidez, Guylaine. *Femmes dans la guerre (1939–1945).* Paris: Terre des Femmes/Perrier, 1989.

Hackett, David A., trans. *The Buchenwald Report.* Boulder, CO: Westview, 1995.

Helm, Sarah. *A Life in Secrets: Vera Atkins and the Missing Agents of World War II.* New York: Nan Talese, Doubleday, 2005.

Herz, Bertrand. *Le pull-over de Buchenwald.* Paris: Tallandier, 2015.

Jackson, Julian. *France: The Dark Years, 1940–44.* New York: Oxford University Press, 2001.

Jauneau, Elodie. "Des Femmes dans la France combattante pendant la Deuxième Guerre Mondiale: le corps de Volontaires Françaises et le groupe Rochambeau." *La revue de l'Association Mnémosyne,* no. 3 (automne 2008).

Kogon, Eugen. *L'état SS.* Paris: La Jeune Parque, 1947.

Ledwidge, Bernard. *De Gaulle.* New York: St. Martin's, 1982.

Lowe, Keith. *Savage Continent: Europe in the Aftermath of World War II.* New York: St. Martin's, 2012.

Mann, Carol. *Femmes dans la guerre 1914–1945*. Paris: Pygmalion, 2010.
McManus, John C. *Hell before Their Very Eyes: American Soldiers Liberate Concentration Camps in Germany, April 1945*. Baltimore: Johns Hopkins University Press, 2015.
Miller, F. M. S. "Letter to my Family," *Schmuhl Archives* (RG-10.137). Washington, DC: National Holocaust Memorial Museum.
Monahan, Evelyn, and Rosemary Neidel-Greenlee. *And If I Perish: Frontline US Army Nurses in World War II*. New York: Knopf, 2003.
Monteil, Claudine. *Eve Curie: L'autre fille de Pierre et Marie Curie*. Paris: Odile Jacob, 2016.
Morin-Rotureau, Evelyne, ed. *1939–1945: Combats de femmes françaises et allemandes: les oubliées de la guerre*. Collection Mémoires. Paris: Autrement, 2001.
Nasaw, David. *The Last Million: Europe's Displaced Persons from World War to Cold War*. New York: Penguin Random House, 2020.
Oriol-Maloire, Albert. *Les femmes en guerre 1939–1945: les oubliées de l'histoire*. Amiens, France: Martelle, nd.
Orlowski, Dominique. *Buchenwald par ses témoins: Histoire et dictionnaire du camp et de ses Kommandos (1937–1945)*. Paris: Belin, 2014.
Patton, George S. *War as I Knew It*. New York: Houghton Mifflin, 1947.
Poller, Walter. *Butchers of Buchenwald*. New York: Kensington, 1977.
Roberts, Andrew. *The Storm of War: A New History of the Second World War*. New York: Harper Collins, 2011.
Schmuhl, L. C. *Schmuhl Archives* (RG-10.137). Washington, DC: National Holocaust Memorial Museum.
Skaer, Kenneth. "History of the Civil Government Support Provided to the 12th Army Group's Refugee and Displaced Persons Operation by the Allied Nations of France, Belgium, and Luxembourg from 6 June 1944 through 15 January 1945." Unpublished Master's thesis, General Staff College, Ft. Leavenworth, KS, 1965.
Stein, Sabine, and Harry Stein. *Buchenwald: A Tour of the Memorial Site*. Weimar-Buchenwald, 1993.
Torrès, Tereska. *Une Française libre*. Paris: France Loisirs, 2000.
Tyrer, Nicola. *Sisters in Arms: British Army Nurses Tell Their Story*. London: Weidenfield and Nicholson, 2008.
Vagliano-Eloy, Sonia. Lecture, Smith College, Northampton, MA, May 1983.
———. "Les demoiselles de Gaulle." Lecture, Bayeux, France, May 1994. (Reprinted in *Espoir*, no. 100 [January 1995]).
Weitz, Margaret Collins. *Sisters in the Resistance: How Women Fought to Free France, 1940–1945*. New York: Wiley and Sons, 1995.